AF361444

THE HISTORY OF AL-ṬABARĪ

AN ANNOTATED TRANSLATION

VOLUME XXIV

The Empire in Transition
THE CALIPHATES OF SULAYMĀN, ʿUMAR, AND YAZĪD
A.D. 715–724/A.H. 97–105

The History of al-Ṭabarī

Editorial Board

Ihsan Abbas, University of Jordan, Amman

C. E. Bosworth, The University of Manchester

Jacob Lassner, Wayne State University, Detroit

Franz Rosenthal, Yale University

Ehsan Yar-Shater, Columbia University (*General Editor*)

The preparation of this volume was made possible in part by a grant from the National Endowment for the Humanities, an independent federal agency.

Bibliotheca Persica
Edited by Ehsan Yar-Shater

The History of al-Ṭabarī
(Ta'rīkh al-rusul wa'l mulūk)

VOLUME XXIV

The Empire in Transition

translated and annotated
by

David Stephan Powers

Cornell University

State University of New York Press

Published by
State University of New York Press, Albany
© 1989 State University of New York
All rights reserved
Printed in the United States of America

No part of this book may be used or reproduced
in any manner whatsoever without written permission
except in the case of brief quotations embodied in
critical articles and reviews.

For information, address State University of New York
Press, State University Plaza, Albany, N.Y., 12246

Library of Congress Cataloging-in-Publication Data

Ṭabarī, 838?-923.
  [Ta'rīkh al-rusul wa-al-mulūk. English. Selections]
  The Empire in transition / translated and annotated by David
Stephan Powers.
    p.   cm. — (The history of al-Ṭabarī = Ta'rīkh al-rusul wa'l
mulūk ; v. 24)   (SUNY series in Near Eastern studies) (Bibliotheca
Persica)
  Translation of extracts from: Ta'rīkh al-rusul wa-al-mulūk.
  Bibliography: p.
  Includes index.
  ISBN 0-7914-0072-7. ISBN 0-7914-0073-5 (pbk.)
  1. Islamic Empire—History—661-750. I. Powers, David Stephan.
II. Title. III. Series. IV. Series: Ṭabarī, 838?-923. Ta'rīkh al
-rusul wa-al-mulūk. English ; v. 24. V. Series: Bibliotheca
Persica (Albany, N.Y.)
DS38.2.T313   1985   vol. 24
[DS38.5]
909'.1 s—dc19
[909'.097671'01]   88-39752
                                                              CIP

10 9 8 7 6 5 4 3 2 1

Preface

The History of Prophets and Kings (*Ta'rīkh al-rusul wa'l-muluk*) by Abū Ja'far Muḥammad b. Jarīr al-Ṭabarī (839–923), here rendered as the *History of al-Ṭabarī*, is by common consent the most important universal history produced in the world of Islam. It has been translated here in its entirety for the first time for the benefit of non-Arabists, with historical and philological notes for those interested in the particulars of the text.

Ṭabarī's monumental work explores the history of the ancient nations, with special emphasis on biblical peoples and prophets, the legendary and factual history of ancient Iran, and, in great detail, the rise of Islam, the life of the Prophet Muḥammad, and the history of the Islamic world down to the year 915. The first volume of this translation will contain a biography of al-Ṭabarī and a discussion of the method, scope, and value of his work. It will also provide information on some of the technical considerations that have guided the work of the translators.

The *History* has been divided here into 38 volumes, each of which covers about two hundred pages of the original Arabic text in the Leiden edition. An attempt has been made to draw the dividing lines between the individual volumes in such a way that each is to some degree independent and can be read as such. The page numbers of the original in the Leiden edition appear on the margins of the translated volumes.

Al-Ṭabarī very often quotes his sources verbatim and traces the chain of transmission (*isnād*) to an original source. The chains of transmitters are, for the sake of brevity, rendered by only a dash

(—) between the individual links in the chain. Thus, "According to Ibn Ḥumayd—Salamah—Ibn Isḥāq" means that al-Ṭabarī received the report from Ibn Ḥumayd, who said that he was told by Salamah, who said that he was told by Ibn Isḥāq, and so on. The numerous subtle and important differences in the original Arabic wording have been disregarded.

The table of contents at the beginning of each volume gives a brief survey of the topics dealt with in that particular volume. It also includes the headings and subheadings as they appear in al-Ṭabarī's text, as well as those occasionally introduced by the translator.

Well-known place names, such as, for instance, Mecca, Baghdad, Jerusalem, Damascus, and the Yemen, are given in their English spellings. Less common place names, which are the vast majority, are transliterated. Biblical figures appear in the accepted English spelling. Iranian names are usually transcribed according to their Arabic forms, and the presumed Iranian forms are often discussed in the footnotes.

Technical terms have been translated wherever possible, but some, such as dirham and imām, have been retained in Arabic forms. Others that cannot be translated with sufficient precision have been retained and italicized as well as footnoted.

The annotation aims chiefly at clarifying difficult passages, identifying individuals and place names, and discussing textual difficulties. Much leeway has been left to the translators to include in the footnotes whatever they consider necessary and helpful.

The bibliographies list all the sources mentioned in the annotation.

The index in each volume contains all the names of persons and places referred to in the text, as well as those mentioned in the notes as far as they refer to the medieval period. It does not include the names of modern scholars. A general index, it is hoped, will appear after all the volumes have been published.

For further details concerning the series and acknowledgments, see Preface to Volume 1.

Ehsan Yar-Shater

Contents

The Caliphate of ʿUmar b. ʿAbd al-ʿAzīz

The Caliphate of Yazīd b. ʿAbd al-Malik b. Marwān

Abbreviations

EI: *The Encyclopaedia of Islām*, first edition
EI²: *The Encyclopaedia of Islam*, second edition
GAS: F. Sezgin, *Geschichte des arabischen Schrifttums*. Leiden, 1967–

Translator's Foreword

During the ten-year period covered in this volume, the reins of Umayyad power were held by three caliphs bearing distinctive personalities: Sulaymān b. ʿAbd al-Malik (r. 96–99/715–717), a man with a reputation for luxurious living who is nevertheless favorably remembered for reversing the policies of al-Ḥajjāj and appointing ʿUmar b. ʿAbd al-ʿAzīz as his successor; the pious ʿUmar (r. 99–101/717–720), a quasi-messianic figure whose accession to the caliphate, engineered by Rajāʾ b. Ḥaywah, constituted a virtual coup d'état; and Yazīd b. ʿAbd al-Malik (r. 101–105/720–724), a profligate whose own demise was caused by his inconsolable grief for his singing slave girl, Ḥabābah.

By the year 96/714–715, the Arab conquests had reached what ultimately would become their farthest limits in both the East and the West. With the exception of the disastrous third and final campaign against Constantinople, Sulayman adopted a cautious policy that favored the consolidation of previous conquests over further expansion. This policy was taken to its logical extension by ʿUmar II, who recalled Maslamah from the campaign against Constantinople, ordered a complete stop to every expedition on the eastern front, and called for a general withdrawal of the Arab soldiers from Transoxiana. Initially, this same cautious policy was continued by Yazīd II, whose governor over Khurāsān, Saʿīd b. ʿAbd al-ʿAzīz, did not pass beyond Samarqand. On the two occasions on which he crossed over the Oxus River, he punished his own raiding parties, and was dubbed "Khudhaynah," "the little princess," by his own soldiers because of his perceived weakness. But the governorship of Khudhaynah's successor, Saʿīd al-Ḥarashī, marked a return to a more aggressive policy that resulted in the brutal pacification of Soghdia and the subjugation of Kiss and Rabinjān.

Internally, the unity of the Umayyad Empire was threatened by several phenomena, the most important being the rise of tribal factionalism. Although scholars disagree over whether the terms "Qays" and "Yaman" refer to tribal confederations, political parties, or interest groups, it is generally accepted that the Qays stood for the expansion of the empire and the exclusion of non-Arab clients, while the Yaman criticized the policy of expansion and advocated equal status for Arab Muslims and non-Arab converts to Islam. The accession of Sulaymān, who had allied himself with the Yamanīs while serving as governor of Palestine, signaled a shift in the balance of power away from the Qaysīs, as the new Caliph proceeded to dismiss the Qaysī governors appointed by his predecessors, replacing them with men from the Yaman. In distant Farghānah, the Qaysī commander, Qutaybah b. Muslim al-Bāhilī, realizing that his political usefulness had come to an end, tried to raise a revolt against the new Caliph, but his supporters, both Arab and non-Arab, turned against him, slew him, and returned to their homes. An effort to mollify tribal factionalism was made by 'Umar II, who chose governors over whom he had control and whom he believed to be competent, irrespective of their tribal affiliations. This policy was short-lived, however, as 'Umar reigned for only two years. Under his successor, Yazīd II, who sought to reestablish the old order, the Qaysīs returned to power, embittered by the humiliations they had suffered since the accession of Sulaymān; they were determined to take revenge. It was during the caliphate of Yazīd II, in the year 101/719–720, that Yazīd b. al-Muhallab al-Azdī staged his revolt, an episode to which Ṭabarī devotes considerable attention. Although this was not, strictly speaking, a tribal conflict—Ibn al-Muhallab's own tribe of the Azd sided against him—it nevertheless contributed to the intensification of the factional schism as Qaysīs were installed in Iraq and the East in its aftermath. More than any other factor, these tribal rivalries, which spanned the entire empire, contributed to the downfall of the Umayyads.

The administrative boundaries of Iraq and the eastern provinces shifted several times during the short span of ten years covered in this volume. Previously, Khurāsān had been governed from the usual seat of the governor in Iraq, but Yazīd b. al-Muhallab persuaded Sulaymān to let him govern from Khurāsān itself, which became the base of his campaigns against Jurjān and Ṭabaristān. Under ʿUmar II, who supervised the actions of his governors to an unprecedented degree, the vast eastern governorate was broken up into different units, each responsible to the Caliph. Under Yazīd II, Maslamah was given joint control over al-Kūfah, al-Basrah, and Khurāsān, appointing his own governors over each locality. These shifts in administrative policy point to the fact that by the turn of the century the Umayyad government had effectively lost control of the administration of Khurāsan and the East.

In addition to the conduct of the Holy War, another major concern of the provincial governors was the collection and distribution of tribute money. The governors, the Arab tribesmen, and the Caliph were divided over the issue of whether the income from the yearly tribute should be disposed of in its entirety in the provinces or conveyed to the central government. In the year 97/715–716, Sulaymān, sensitive to the complaints of his subjects in Iraq, who had suffered under the fiscal policy of al-Ḥajjāj, sought to keep the fiscal affairs of that province under his own control by appointing his own personal representative there with special responsibility for taxation. Yazīd b. al-Muhallab was arrested by ʿUmar II in the year 100/718–719 because of his failure to convey to the treasury the fifth of the booty that he had collected during the conquest of Jurjān and Ṭabaristān, a sum of six million dīnārs about which he had vainly boasted in a letter to Sulaymān. Similarly, Maslamah was dismissed by his half brother Yazīd in the year 102/720–721 when he failed to send surplus revenue to the Caliph in Damascus. His replacement, ʿUmar b. Hubayrah, introduced a plan according to which the right of the Arab tribesmen to the yearly tribute was limited to the amount of their stipends, while the surplus belonged to the central treasury. These struggles further reflect the breakdown of central control.

Another major source of discontent was the non-Arabs who expected to be relieved of certain taxes upon converting to Islam. This expectation posed a dilemma for the central government which, in an effort to prevent a decline in revenues, either tried to prevent conversion to Islam or took no note of it when collecting taxes. The issue seems to have reached a climax during the caliphate of ʿUmar II, who instituted his famous fiscal rescript designed to address the problems related to conversion. According to the rescript, non-Arab clients were to be freed from the *kharāj* tax and stipends were to be paid to every Muslim who accepted his military obligation, regardless of whether he was an Arab or a convert. These reforms, however, were allowed to lapse upon ʿUmar's death.

Religious opposition also posed a threat to the Umayyad regime. A Khārijite revolt in the year 100/718–719, led by Shawdhab, was initially handled in a diplomatic manner by ʿUmar II, "the righteous man," who summoned representatives of the rebels to enter into negotiations. After ʿUmar's untimely death, the revolt was brutally suppressed by Yazīd II. Religious opposition was a factor in the revolt of Yazīd b. al-Muhallab, who summoned his followers to "the Book and the *Sunnah*," and received support from both the Khārijites and the Murjiʾites. But the main source of religious opposition was the clandestine ʿAbbāsid movement that would eventually topple the dynasty. Ṭabarī reports that ʿAbbāsid propaganda began in earnest in the year 100/718–719, when three emissaries who were sent to Khurāsān by Muḥammad b. ʿAlī b. ʿAbdallāh b. ʿAbbās succeeded in enlisting seventy recruits for the movement. Even if the suspicions of Western scholars regarding the chronological accuracy of this report are justified, it is nevertheless the case that the ʿAbbāsid propaganda was in place by the year 104/722–23.

Ṭabarī presents the events of the years 96–105/715–724 in considerable detail and with great vividness. We listen to the stirring speeches of Qutaybah b. Muslim in which he urges his followers to renounce their allegiance to Sulaymān; are present at the disastrous third and final attempt to take Constantinople; watch from behind the scenes as Rajāʾ b. Ḥaywah skillfully engineers the accession of ʿUmar II; and follow the remarkable career of Yazīd b. al-Muhallab, first as a governor and conqueror, then as a prisoner, and finally as a rebel. Throughout this volume we observe the struggle of the Umayyad regime to maintain control over a rapidly expanding but increasingly dissatisfied subject population. Governors are appointed and dismissed with dizzying rapidity, administrative boundaries are drawn and redrawn, Arab tribesmen express dissatisfaction with the diminishing rewards of military conquest, non-Arab converts chafe at the differential treatment they receive, and religious opponents revolt in the name of "the Book and the *Sunnah.*" Important in their own respect, the events of this period also constitute an essential key to understanding the ʿAbbāsid revolution that was about to unfold.

There remains the pleasant duty of acknowledging the indispensable assistance of friends and colleagues who contributed to the making of this translation. My colleague, Samia Mehrez, read through much of the Arabic text with me and helped to clarify the meaning of many difficult expressions. Richard Jacquemond offered valuable comments on an early draft of the manuscript. Three members of the Ṭabarī editorial board who read parts or all of the manuscript with great care, Franz Rosenthal, Jacob Lassner, and Ihsan Abbas, were especially helpful with difficult sections of the Arabic text and poetry. Finally, I am grateful to Judith Ginsburg for assistance with the Latin glosses of the Leiden text, to Penny Beebe for help with matters of style, and to Raihana Zaman for her patience and fortitude when called upon to type seemingly endless drafts of the translation. Needless to say, the responsibility for any mistakes that remain are mine and mine alone.

David Stephan Powers

The Caliphate of Sulaymān
b. ʿAbd al-Malik

The
Events of the Year

96 (cont'd)
(SEPTEMBER 16, 714–SEPTEMBER 4, 715)[1]

Abū Jaʿfar (al-Ṭabarī) said: In this year, the oath of allegiance was rendered to Sulaymān b. ʿAbd al-Malik as Caliph.[2] This took place in al-Ramlah on the day on which al-Walīd b. ʿAbd al-Malik died.[3]

In this year, Sulaymān b. ʿAbd al-Malik dismissed the governor of Medina, ʿUthmān b. Ḥayyān.[4] Muḥammad b. ʿUmar mentioned that Sulaymān removed ʿUthmān from Medina on the twenty-fourth of Ramaḍān in the year 96 (June 3, 715). Abū Jaʿfar continued: He served as governor of Medina for three years. It is also said: His term of office was two years, less seven nights.

According to al-Wāqidī: ʿUthmān b. Ḥayyān consented to a

---

1. For other sources on the caliphate of Sulaymān b. ʿAbd al-Malik, see Ibn Qutaybah, *Maʿārif*, 360–61; Yaʿqūbī, *Taʾrīkh*, III, 38–45; Kūfī, *Futūḥ*, VII, 252–306; *FHA*, 16–37; Masʿūdī, *Murūj* (Beirut), III, 173–81; Ibn Kathīr, *Bidāyah*, IX, 166–84; Wellhausen, *Arab Kingdom*, 257ff.

2. See Ibn Khayyāṭ, *Taʾrīkh*, I, 314; Ibn Kathīr, *Bidāyah*, IX, 166.

3. Al-Walīd died on a Saturday in the middle of Jumādā II in the year 96 (February 23, 715). See text above, II/1269–70.

4. That is, ʿUthmān b. Ḥayyān al-Murrī, who al-Walīd had appointed in Shaʿbān of the year 93 (May 13—June 10, 712) or Shawwāl of 94 (June 30—July 28, 713). See text above, II/1255, 1258ff.; Yaʿqūbī, *Taʾrīkh*, III, 39.

request from Abū Bakr b. Muḥammad b. ʿAmr b. Ḥazm[5] for permission to sleep (late) the following morning and not to grant an audience to the people, so that he might observe the twenty-first night of Ramaḍān.[6] Ayyūb b. Salamah al-Makhzūmī, who was on bad terms with Abū Bakr b. ʿAmr b. Ḥazm, was with ʿUthmān at that time, and he said to him, "Have you not considered what that one is saying? He is merely making a show of piety." ʿUthmān answered, "I thought of that, but, if I do not find him holding court tomorrow morning when I send for him, then as surely as I am my father's son, I shall flog him one hundred lashes and shave his head and his beard." Ayyūb said, "Pleasantly surprised by his statement, I hastened at dawn to his house, through which I found my way by candlelight. I said (to myself), 'al-Murrī (that is, ʿUthmān) has also come in haste (to fulfill his oath).' " But lo and behold, Sulaymān's messenger had already arrived, carrying orders to appoint Abū Bakr as governor and to have ʿUthmān dismissed and flogged.[7] Ayyūb continued, "I entered the governor's residence, and there was Ibn Ḥayyān sitting on the floor, while Abū Bakr was sitting on a chair saying to the blacksmith, 'Put the chains on this man's feet.' ʿUthmān looked at me and recited:

They turned their backs and fled
　　But things are not forever the same."

In this year, Sulaymān removed Yazīd b. Abī Muslim from Iraq, replacing him with Yazīd b. al-Muhallab.[8] He put Ṣāliḥ b. ʿAbd al-Raḥmān in charge of the fiscal administration and ordered him to torture and kill the family of Abū ʿAqīl.[9]

---

5. Abū Bakr b. Muḥammad b. ʿAmr b. Ḥazm was chief qāḍī of Medina, apparently from the year 88 (706–07). See text above, II/1191, 1255.

6. It is particularly meritorious to undertake the *iʿtikāf*—a period of retreat in a mosque during which the believer fasts, prays, and recites the Qurʾān. It occurs during the last ten days of the month of Ramaḍān, when the *laylat al-qadr* (night on which the Qurʾān was first revealed) is presumed to have taken place. See *EI*, s.v. Ramaḍān; *EI²*, s.v. Iʿtikāf.

7. ʿUthmān was reportedly flogged twice, once for drinking wine, and a second time in retaliation for an accusation he had leveled against ʿAbdallāh b. ʿAmr b. ʿUthmān b. ʿAffān. See Yaʿqūbī, *Taʾrīkh*, III, 39.

8. See Yaʿqūbī, *Taʾrīkh*, III, 40.

9. That is, the family of al-Ḥajjāj b. Yūsuf, who had slain Ṣāliḥ's brother, Ādam. See Crone, *Slaves*, 43; *EI²*, s.v. al-Ḥadjdjādj b. Yūsuf; Balādhurī, *Futūḥ* (Cairo), III, 540.

According to 'Umar b. Shabbah—'Alī b. Muḥammad: Ṣāliḥ reached Iraq, where he took charge of the fiscal administration, while Yazīd was in charge of military affairs. Yazīd then sent Ziyād b. al-Muhallab to serve as governor of 'Umān,[10] saying to him, "Correspond with Ṣāliḥ, and, when you write to him, mention his name first." (Upon reaching Iraq) Ṣāliḥ seized the family of Abū 'Aqīl and tortured them; 'Abd al-Malik b. al-Muhallab administered the torture.

[1283]

In this year, Qutaybah b. Muslim[11] was slain in Khurāsān.[12]

The Slaying of Qutaybah b. Muslim

The circumstances surrounding this: Al-Walīd b. 'Abd al-Malik wanted to designate his son, 'Abd al-'Azīz b. al-Walīd, as the heir apparent, and he secretly conveyed his intent to the generals and the poets.[13] Jarīr[14] said with regard to this:

When they ask, "Which man would be the best Caliph?"
    the fingers point to 'Abd al-'Azīz.
They consider him the most deserving of all the people,
    and they were not mistaken when they hurried and swore
    the oath of allegiance to him.[15]

Jarīr also recited, urging al-Walīd to nominate 'Abd al-'Azīz:

Toward 'Abd al-'Azīz the eyes of the people turned,
    when the rulers were at a loss about whom to choose.
To him his merits call attention, when
    the pillars of state and the heavens fall down.
And the leaders of Quraysh say,

---

10. See *EI*, s.v. 'Oman.

11. Qutaybah is Abū Ḥafṣ Qutaybah b. Abī Ṣāliḥ Muslim b. 'Amr al-Bāhilī. He was an Arab commander who extended Arab power over the boundaries of Khurāsān. See *EI²*, s.v. Ḳutayba b. Muslim; Wellhausen, *Arab Kingdom*, 434–35; Ibn Khallikān, *Wafayāt*, IV, 86–91.

12. See Ibn Khayyāṭ, *Ta'rīkh*, I, 318; Balādhurī, *Futūḥ* (Cairo), III, 519–22; Ya'-qūbī, *Ta'rīkh*, III, 40–41; Kūfī, *Futūḥ*, VII, 253–80, *FHA*, 17–19; Ibn Kathīr, *Bidāyah*, IX, 167–69; Wellhausen, *Arab Kingdom*, 439ff.

13. 'Abd al-Malik had stipulated in his succession covenant that Sulaymān was to succeed al-Walīd as Caliph. See text above, II/1170.

14. Jarīr b. 'Aṭiyyah b. al-Khaṭafah (Ḥudhayfah) b. Badr (d. 110/728–29) was one of the most famous poets of the Umayyad period. See *EI²*, s.v. Djarīr.

15. *Fa-bāyi'ūhu wa-sāri'ū*; read *fa-bāya'ūhu wa-sāra'ū*, following Band P. See *Naḳā'iḍ Jarīr wa-l-Farazdaq*, I, 351.

"We must swear the oath of allegiance now that the race
     has reached its end."
They consider ʿAbd al-ʿAzīz to be the heir apparent,
     and they have not made a mistake or done wrong.
What do you wait for, when you are the ones that bear
     onerous deeds and rise to glory?
So pass it (that is, the caliphate) on to him wholly,
     O Commander of the Faithful, if you so desire.
[1284] For the people have already extended their hands to him,
     and the matter has become generally known.
And had they given the oath of allegiance to you as heir
     apparent,
     the balance would have been even and the building would
     have been straight.[16]

Al-Ḥajjāj b. Yūsuf and Qutaybah concurred in the renunciation
of Sulaymān. Then al-Walīd died, and Sulaymān b. ʿAbd al-Malik
assumed power. This was why Qutaybah feared him.

According to ʿAlī b. Muḥammad—Bishr b. ʿĪsā, al-Ḥasan b. Rushayd and Kulayb b. Khalaf—Ṭufayl b. Mirdās and Jabalah b.
Farrūkh—Muḥammad b. ʿUzayz al-Kindī, Jabalah b. Abī Rawwād,[17] and Maslamah b. Muḥārib—al-Sakin b. Qatādah: When
Qutaybah learned of the death of al-Walīd b. ʿAbd al-Malik and
the accession of Sulaymān, he feared Sulaymān because, together
with al-Ḥajjāj, he had worked for the nomination of ʿAbd al-ʿAzīz
b. al-Walīd. Thus, he feared that Sulaymān would appoint Yazīd
b. al-Muhallab as governor of Khurāsān.[18]

Qutaybah wrote a letter to Sulaymān in which he congratu-
lated him on becoming Caliph, consoled him about al-Walīd, and
informed him of his achievements and of his obedience to ʿAbd al-
Malik and al-Walīd. He also indicated that Sulaymān could count
on the same measure of obedience and sincere advice as had the
former two, provided he did not remove him from Khurāsān. He
(also) wrote him another letter in which he informed him of his
conquests and his ferocity against the enemy, of his exalted

16. Ibid., I, 350–51.
17. Text: Dāwūd; read Rawwād, following the Cairo ed.
18. Ten years earlier, in 86/705, al-Ḥajjāj had dismissed Yazīd b. al-Muhallab as
governor of Khurāsān and appointed Qutaybah in his place. See text above,
II/1178ff., sub anno 86.

standing among the non-Arab rulers, of the awe he inspired in their hearts, and of his great renown among them. He also disparaged al-Muhallab and his family and swore by God that if Yazīd b. al-Muhallab were appointed governor of Khurāsān, he (that is, Qutaybah) would throw off his allegiance to Sulaymān. And (finally) he wrote a third letter in which he renounced his allegiance to him.

Qutaybah sent the three letters with a man from the tribe of Bāhilah, saying: "Give the first letter to the Caliph. If Yazīd b. al-Muhallab is present and the Caliph reads it and then hands it to him, give him the second letter. If the Caliph reads it and gives it to Yazīd, give him the third letter. But if he reads the first letter and does not give it to Yazīd, hold on to the other two."

Qutaybah's messenger arrived and presented himself to Sulaymān, who was with Yazīd b. al-Muhallab. The messenger gave the letter to the Caliph, who read it and then showed it to Yazīd. The messenger gave the Caliph another letter, which he read and threw at Yazīd. Then he gave him the third letter. The Caliph read it, and the color of his face changed. He called for some clay, sealed the letter, and kept it in his possession.

According to Abū 'Ubaydah Ma'mar b. al-Muthannā: The first letter contained slanderous remarks about Yazīd b. al-Muhallab, noting his perfidy, infidelity, and ingratitude. The second letter contained praise of Yazīd. The third letter contained the following statement: "If you do not confirm me in my present position and if you do not grant me a writ of safe conduct, I will renounce my allegiance to you as quickly as one removes a shoe, and I will fill the earth around you with horsemen and foot soldiers."

He also said: When Sulaymān read the third letter, he put it between two mattresses under him and made no comment.

Returning to the account of 'Alī b. Muḥammad: Then he—that is, Sulaymān—ordered that Qutaybah's messenger be provided with accommodations, whereupon the latter was transferred to the guest house. That evening, Sulaymān called for him. He gave him a purse containing some dīnārs and said, "Here is your reward, and here is your master's document of appointment as governor of Khurāsān. Be on your way in the company of my messenger, who is carrying Qutaybah's document of appointment."

The Bāhilī tribesman set out, and Sulaymān sent with him a

[1285]

[1286]

man from the tribe of ʿAbd al-Qays, one of the Banū Layth by the name of Ṣaʿṣaʿah or Muṣʿab. When they reached Ḥulwān,[19] the people informed them that Qutaybah had renounced the Caliph. The ʿAbdī tribesman turned back, having given the document of appointment to Qutaybah's messenger, although Qutaybah had already renounced the Caliph. There was considerable confusion.[20] The messenger gave the document of appointment to Qutaybah, who then sought the counsel of his brothers. They said, "Sulaymān will not trust you, after this."

According to ʿAlī—one of the ʿAnbarīs—some of their shaykhs—Tawbah b. Abī Asīd al-ʿAnbarī: Ṣāliḥ[21] arrived in Iraq and sent me to Qutaybah in order to find out about the latter's situation. I was accompanied by a man from the Banū Asad, who asked me about the nature of my journey, but I concealed it from him. While we were traveling, a bird passed from our left to our right, causing my companion to look at me and say, "I think that you are on an important mission and that you are hiding it from me." I continued on my way. When I reached Ḥulwān, the people informed me that Qutaybah had been slain.

According to ʿAlī—Abū al-Dhayyāl, Kulayb b. Khalaf and Abū ʿAlī al-Jūzjānī—Ṭufayl b. Mirdās, Abū al-Ḥasan al-Jashamī, and Muṣʿab b. Ḥayyān[22]—his brother, Muqātil b. Ḥayyān, Abū Mikhnaf, and others: When Qutaybah was contemplating renouncing his allegiance to the Caliph, he sought the counsel of his brothers. ʿAbd al-Raḥmān said to him, "Dispatch an army and include in it all those whom you fear: Send one contingent to Marw;[23] then you set out, until you reach Samarqand.[24] Then say to those who are with you, 'Whoever wants to stay will receive his share of the booty; whoever wants to leave will not be compelled to stay, and no evil will befall him.' In this way, only those

[1287]

---

19. An ancient town situated near the entrance to the Paytak Pass through the Zagros range, on the Khurāsān highway. See *EI*[2], s.v. Ḥulwān.

20. According to Kūfī, *Futūḥ*, VII, 258–59, the Caliph's messenger returned to Syria, taking the document of appointment with him, thereby causing Qutaybah to regret his actions.

21. That is, Ṣāliḥ b. ʿAbd al-Raḥmān.

22. Text: Ḥabbān; read Ḥayyān, following the Cairo ed.

23. Marw was the capital and most famous city in Khurāsān. See *EI, Supplement*, s.v. Merw al-Shāhidjān; Le Strange, *Lands*, 397ff.

24. Samarqand and Bukhārā were the principle towns of Transoxiana. See *EI*, s.v. Samarḳand; Le Strange, *Lands*, 463ff.

who are loyal will remain with you."[25] 'Abdallāh said to him, "Repudiate the Caliph right here, and call on the soldiers to repudiate him, for no one will oppose you."

Qutaybah accepted 'Abdallāh's advice: He renounced his allegiance to Sulaymān and called on the troops to repudiate him, saying:

> I have brought you together from 'Ayn al-Tamr[26] and Fayḍ al-Baḥr.[27] I have united brother with brother and son with father. I have distributed your booty among you, and I have paid you your stipends in full and without delay. You have had experience with the governors who preceded me: Umayyah[28] came to you and wrote to the Commander of the Faithful, saying, 'The tribute of Khurāsān does not support[29] the expenses of my kitchen.' Then Abū Saʿīd[30] came to you and he spun you around for three years, during which time you did not know whether you were in obedience or in disobedience. He did not collect any levies or hurt an enemy. Then his son, Yazīd,[31] came to you, after him, a stallion for whom women compete.[32] Your Caliph is (as foolish as) Yazīd b. Tharwān Habbanaqat al-Qaysī.[33]

25. Kūfī, *Futūḥ*, VII, 260, adds: "Then renounce your allegiance to Sulaymān."

26. 'Ayn al-Tamr was a small town in Iraq on the borders of the desert, between Anbār and al-Kūfah, that commanded the military approaches to Iraq. See *EI²*, s.v. 'Ayn al-Tamr.

27. Fayḍ al-Baḥr was a well-known canal in al-Baṣrah. See Yāqūt, *Muʿjam*, IV, 285.

28. Umayyah b. 'Abdallāh was the governor of Khurāsān under 'Abd al-Malik until 78/697–98. See text above, II/1032ff.; Crone, *Slaves*, 232, n. 289.

29. Text: *lā yuqīmu*. The Cairo ed. has *lā yaqūmu*.

30. Abū Saʿīd al-Muhallab b. Abī Ṣufrah, deputy governor of Khurāsān under al-Ḥajjāj, reopened the campaigns towards Central Asia. He died in 82/701–02 and was succeeded by his son, Yazīd. See text above, II/1033ff., sub anno 78; *EI²*, s.v. 'Abd al-Malik b. Marwān.

31. Yazīd b. al-Muhallab was appointed governor of Khurāsān by al-Ḥajjāj in the year 82/701–02, upon the death of his father, al-Muhallab. See text above, II/1085ff.

32. Text: *faḥlun tabārā ilayhi al-nisā'*. If one were to read *tabāzā* instead of *tabārā* the sense would be, "a stud to whom women raise their hips." Jāḥiẓ, *Bayān*, II, 134, has *thumma atākum banūhu baʿdahu mithla aṭbā'i-l-kalbah minhum Ibn al-Daḥmah*, "Then their sons came to you, after him, like bitch's teats, among them Ibn al-Daḥmah (that is, Yazīd b. al-Muhallab)."

33. Yazīd b. Tharwān (his nickname was Dhū al-Wadaʿāt) would give his fat camels much fodder and pasture, to the neglect of his thin ones. Likewise, Sulaymān would confer favors on the wealthy and prosperous and neglect others. See Balādhurī, *Futūḥ* (Cairo), III, 519–20.

Our source continued: But no one responded, so Qutaybah became angry and said:

> May God never give strength to whomever you support. By God, were you to unite in order to attack a goat, you would not break its horn. O people of lowly places—I do not say people of elevated places[34]—O rabble of the alms tax, I have gathered you, just as the camels of the alms tax are brought together from all directions. O tribe of Bakr b. Wāʾil, O people of pretense, lying, and stinginess, during which of your two days do you boast? The day you go out to war or the day you make peace? By God, I am more powerful than you, O followers of Musaylimah,[35] O blameworthy ones—I do not call you upright ones[36]—O people of weakness and perfidy. You used to call "perfidy," during the pre-Islamic era (jāhiliyyah), "Kaysān."[37] O followers of Sajāḥ,[38] O tribe of ʿAbd al-Qays, the farters,[39] you have taken up the pollination of palm trees in exchange for horses' reins. O tribe of Azd, you have taken ships' cables in exchange for the reins of fleet[40] stallions. This is innovation in Islam! And the Bedouins? What are the Bedouins? May the curse of God be on the Bedouins. O refuse of al-Kūfah and al-Baṣrah, I have brought you together from the places where wormwood, southernwood, and wild senna[41] are grown.[42] You were riding

[1288]

---

34. Text: yā ahl al-sāfilah wa-lā aqūlu ahl al-ʿāliyah. It is a pun.

35. Musaylimah was a prophet of the Banū Ḥanīfah in al-Yamāmah; he was contemporary with Muḥammad. See EI, s.v. Musailimah.

36. Text: yā banī dhamīm wa-lā aqūlu tamīm. This is a pun on the tribe of Tamīm, who are being addressed here.

37. Kaysān is a name for perfidy. It is not related to Kaysān, the companion of al-Mukhtār. See Lisān, s.v. k-y-s.

38. Sajāḥ, Umm Ṣādir bt. Aws b. Ḥikk b. Usāmah, or Bint al-Ḥārith b. Suwayd b. ʿUqfān, was a prophetess and soothsayer who appeared in Arabia during the riddah wars. See EI, s.v. Sadjāḥ.

39. Text: quṣāt, "the cruel ones"; read fusāt. I owe this point to Professor Ihsan Abbas.

40. Text: al-ḥuṣun, "horses." This should be amended to read al-ḥuḍur. I owe this point to Professor Abbas.

41. Text: al-filfil, "pepper." Read: al-qilqil, as in Jāḥiẓ, Bayān, II, 133. There are no pepper trees in Arabia.

42. These three plants grow in the desert.

cows and donkeys on the island of Ibn Kāwān,[43] and, when I gathered you, just as the scattered portions of clouds[44] are brought together at the beginning of winter, you started saying such and such! By God, I am the son of his father and the brother of his brother. By God, I will draw you together and beat you as one does the *salamah* tree.[45] Verily, around the *ṣilliyān* plant is neighing.[46] O army of Khurāsān, do you know who your leader is? Your leader is Yazīd b. Tharwān. It is as if I am confronted by a commander from the Ḥā' and the Ḥakam[47] who came to you and displaced you from your homes and your abodes.[48] There is a fire over there. Shoot at it, and I will shoot with you. Aim for your farthest mark! Abū Nāfiʿ, Dhū al-Wadaʿāt, has been put in charge of you.[49] Syria is a father who is treated with filial respect, while Iraq is a father who is treated with ingratitude. How long will the Syrian army[50] continue to lie in your courtyards and under the roofs of your homes? O army of Khurāsān, if you investigate my ancestry, you will find that I have an Iraqi mother, an Iraqi father, an Iraqi birthplace, and Iraqi inclinations, opinions, and religion. Today, as you know,

---

43. The largest island in the Persian Gulf, situated off the southern coast of Persia between ʿUmān and al-Baḥrayn; it takes its name from a certain al-Ḥārith b. Imru 'l-Qays. See *EI²*, s.v. Kishm; Yāqūt, *Muʿjam*, II, 139, s.v. Jazīrat Kāwān.

44. Text: *qaraʿ*; read *qazaʿ*, following the Cairo ed.

45. A *salamah* tree has thorns and leaves; the latter are used to tan hides. The leaves are removed by drawing the branches of the tree together, binding them tightly with a rope, and beating them with a staff. See Lane, *Lexicon*, pt. 4, p. 1414.

46. The *ṣilliyān* is a plant known as "the bread of the camels." The phrase *ḥawl al-ṣilliyān al-zamzamah* is a proverbial expression applied to a man who hovers round a thing without making apparent his desire. See Lane, *Lexicon*, pt. 3, p. 1248.

47. The Ḥā' are a tribe from the Madhḥij, and the Ḥakam are a tribe from the Yemen. See Jāḥiẓ, *Bayān*, II, 132, n. 7.

48. Text: *ka-annī bi-amīr mizjāʾ wa-ḥakam qad jāʾakum fa-ghalabakum ʿalā fayʾikum wa-aẓlālikum*. My translation follows Jāḥiẓ, *Bayān*, II, 132–33: *ka-annī bi-amīr min ḥāʾ wa-ḥakam qad atākum*. Ibn al-Athīr, *Kāmil*, V, 14, has *ka-annī bi-amīr jāʾakum fa-ghalabakum ʿalā fayʾikum wa-ẓilālikum*.

49. That is, Yazīd b. Tharwān.

50. Text: *ahl al-Shām*. The Imperial Army were composed of warriors from Syria unequivocally loyal to the Umayyad rulers; they were stationed in fortified cities and sensitive areas where disturbances were expected to break out. See Sharon, *Black Banners*, 61–2.

you enjoy a state of safety and well-being. God has laid open countries to you and made your roads secure, so that a woman can travel in a litter from Marw to Balkh[51] without an escort. So praise God for the blessing He has bestowed on you and ask Him for forgiveness and increase.

[1289]

Then Qutaybah stepped down and entered his house. The members of his household came to him and said: "We have never seen a day like today.[52] By God, you did not limit yourself to the Ahl-ʿĀliyah, who are your close friends, but you even included the Bakr, your followers. Not satisfied with that, you included the Tamīm, your brothers. Still not satisfied, you included the Azd, your supporters."

Qutaybah said: "When I spoke, and not a single person responded, I became angry, and I did not know what I was saying. The Ahl al-ʿĀliyah are like the camels of the alms tax that have been gathered from every direction;[53] the Bakr are like a slave girl who does not ward off a sexual advance; the Tamīm are like mangy camels; the ʿAbd al-Qays are that part of the wild ass that he hits with his tail; and the Azd are wild asses—the worst that God created. Were I their master, I would brand them."[54]

The troops were angry and unwilling to throw off allegiance to Sulaymān, and the tribes were also angry, because of the abusive terms that Qutaybah had cast at them. They all agreed to oppose and denounce Qutaybah. The first to speak in this matter were the Azd, who approached Ḥuḍayn b. al-Mundhir[55] and said, "That one has called for what he has called for, namely, throwing off allegiance to the Caliph; however, that way will lead to corruption in matters of both religion and the temporal world. Not

---

51. An important city in Khurāsān situated at the meeting place of the trade routes; the city was subdued by Qutaybah b. Muslim. See *EI*[2], s.v. Balkh; Le Strange, *Lands*, 420ff.

52. Text: *mā raʾaynā ka-l-yawmi qaṭṭ*. Ibn al-Athīr, *Kāmil*, V, 14, has *mā raʾaynāka ka-l-yawmi qaṭṭ*: "We have never seen you behave as you did today."

53. The Ahl al-ʿĀliyah were a heterogeneous group made up of sundry tribes.

54. This statement may be an allusion to al-Ḥajjāj, who branded peoples' hands. For parallel versions of Qutaybah's speeches, see al-Jāḥiẓ, *Bayān*, II, 132–35; Kūfī, *Futūḥ*, VII, 261–65.

55. Ḥuḍayn b. al-Mundhir was a notable and poet of al-Baṣrah, who was head of the Bakr b. Wāʾil; he died ca. 100/718–19. See *EI*[2], s.v. al-Ḥuḍayn b. al-Mundhir; Crone, *Slaves*, 113.

satisfied with this, he has humiliated and reviled us. What do you recommend, O Abū Ḥafṣ?" His nom de guerre was Abū Sāsān; it is also said that his patronymic is Abū Muḥammad. Ḥudayn said to them, "The Muḍar in Khurāsān are equal to the other three tribal groups (khums), and within the Muḍar the Tamīm form the majority. They are the heroes of Khurāsān who will never agree that the ruling power pass from the Muḍar. Thus, if you exclude them from power, they will support Qutaybah."[56] The Azd said, "Qutaybah wronged the Banū Tamīm by the slaying of Ibn al-Ahtam."[57] Ḥudayn said, "Do not pay any attention to that, for the Banū Tamīm are partisans of the Muḍar confederation." The Azd left, rejecting Ḥudayn's advice. They wanted to put ʿAbdallāh b. Ḥawdhān al-Jahḍamī[58] in charge, but he refused. After arguing among themselves, with each refusing to be the leader, they went back to Ḥudayn and said, "We have debated the question of leadership and decided to put you in charge of us, for the Rabīʿah will not oppose you." He said, "I will have nothing to do with this matter." They said, "What do you suggest?" He said, "If you give the leadership to the Tamīm, you will be powerful." They said, "Whom do you recommend from the Tamīm?" He said, "Only Wakīʿ."[59]

[1290]

Ḥayyān, a client of the Banū Shaybān, said: "Only that Bedouin, Wakīʿ, will take charge of this affair, enduring its heat, shedding his blood, and exposing himself to death, and, if a governor comes, he will punish him for what he has done though the credit goes to somebody else, for he is a brave man who neither cares what he mounts nor what the consequences will be. He has many loyal kinsmen and a score to settle; he has a claim against Qutaybah because of the leadership that the latter took from him and gave to Ḍirār b. Ḥuṣayn b. Zayd al-Fawāris b. Ḥuṣayn b. Ḍirār

---

56. See Sharon, *Black Banners*, 60.

57. During the campaign against Bukhārā in the year 91 (709–10), Qutaybah had appointed ʿAbdallāh b. al-Ahtam as his deputy governor in Marw. ʿAbdallāh had taken the opportunity to intrigue with al-Ḥajjāj against Qutaybah, but fared badly and was forced to flee to Syria. Qutaybah made ʿAbdallāh's brothers pay the penalty in his stead—he slew some of them and cut off the arms and legs of the others, thereby calling down upon himself the revenge of Tamīm. See text above, II/1218; Yaʿqūbī, *Taʾrīkh*, III, 40; Balādhurī, *Futūḥ* (Cairo), III, 522–23; Wellhausen, *Arab Kingdom*, 441–42.

58. ʿAbdallāh b. Ḥawdhān al-Jahḍamī was one of the chiefs of the Azd. See Kūfī, *Futūḥ*, VII, 266.

59. Abū Muṭarrif al-Ghudānī, Waqīʿ b. Ḥassān b. Qays b. Abī Sūd al-Tamīmī.

al-Ḍabbī."[60] The troops then began to consult with one another in secret.

Someone said to Qutaybah, "No one creates dissension among the troops except Ḥayyān." Qutaybah therefore wanted to murder him; however, Ḥayyān had ingratiated himself with the servants of the governors,[61] who would not conceal anything from him. Qutaybah summoned a man and ordered him to kill Ḥayyān. But one of the servants heard him, came to Ḥayyān and told him of the order. Thus, when Qutaybah sent a message to Ḥayyān, summoning him, the latter was on his guard and feigned illness. Meanwhile, Wakīʿ accepted the soldiers' request that he serve as their leader.

(Wakīʿ) cited the verse of al-Ashhab b. Rumaylah:

I will reap what I have sown. Verily, my power
    rests on a solid foundation.

[1291] In Khurāsān there were at that time nine thousand warriors from the Baṣran army representing the Ahl al-ʿĀliyah; seven thousand from the Bakr, headed by al-Ḥuḍayn b. al-Mundhir; ten thousand from the Tamīm, led by Ḍirār b. Ḥuṣayn al-Ḍabbī; four thousand from the ʿAbd al-Qays, led by ʿAbdallāh b. ʿAlwān al-ʿAwdhī;[62] and ten thousand from the Azd, headed by ʿAbdallāh b. Ḥawdhān. There were seven thousand from the Kūfan army, led by Jahm b. Zaḥr or ʿUbaydallāh b. ʿAlī, and seven thousand of the clients (mawālī),[63] led by Ḥayyān. Some say that Ḥayyān is from al-Daylam,[64] while others say that he is from Khurāsān. He is called "Nabaṭī" (the Nabataean) because of his mispronunciation of Arabic.[65]

---

60. Wakīʿ had sworn to take vengeance on Qutaybah because the latter had removed him from his position as head of the Banū Tamīm in Khurāsān, replacing him with al-Ḍabbī. See Balādhurī, *Futūḥ* (Cairo), III, 523; *EI²*, s.v. Ḍabba.

61. Text: *ḥasham al-wulāt*. Ibn al-Athīr, *Kāmil*, V, 15, has *khadam al-wulāt*, which means the same thing.

62. Text: ʿAwdhī; read al-ʿAwdhī, following the Cairo ed.

63. A *mawlā* (pl. *mawālī*) was a non-Arab convert to Islam who attached himself to an Arab tribe. See Crone, *Slaves*, 49ff.

64. A region encompassing the entire southern coast of the Caspian and the lands forming a belt to the south of the Alburz range. See *EI²*, s.v. Daylam.

65. Text: *li-luknatihi*. Ḥayyān apparently had difficulty pronouncing the guttural consonants of the Arabic language, such as *ḥā* and *ʿayin*. See *FHA*, 68–69, where examples of his speech are quoted.

Ḥayyān sent to Wakīʿ, saying, "If I leave you alone and lend you my support, will you assign me the land tax of one side of the Balkh River for as long as I am alive and you are governor?" When Wakīʿ agreed, Ḥayyān said to the non-Arabs, "Those (Arabs) are fighting over something other than religion, so let them kill one another." They agreed and swore allegiance to Wakīʿ in secret.

Ḍirār b. Ḥuṣayn approached Qutaybah, saying, "The troops are going back and forth to Wakīʿ, swearing allegiance to him." Now Wakīʿ was in the habit of visiting ʿAbdallāh b. Muslim al-Faqīr at his house, where the two of them would drink together. ʿAbdallāh said, "That one (that is, Ḍirār) is envious of Wakīʿ, and this claim is false. Wakīʿ is in my house, drinking, becoming intoxicated, and shitting in his clothes, yet Ḍirār claims that they are swearing allegiance to him."

Wakīʿ then came to Qutaybah and said, "Beware of Ḍirār, for I do not trust him with you." Qutaybah therefore attributed what they said to their mutual envy. Wakīʿ pretended to be sick, whereupon Qutaybah sent Ḍirār b. Sinān al-Ḍabbī to Wakīʿ as a spy. Ḍirār swore allegiance to Wakīʿ secretly. In this manner, Qutaybah learned that the soldiers were, in fact, swearing allegiance to Wakīʿ, and Qutaybah now said to Ḍirār (b. Ḥuṣayn), "You spoke the truth." He replied, "I reported to you nothing but what I knew, but you attributed what I said to my envy. I have   [1292] fulfilled my obligation." "You were right," said Qutaybah.

Now Qutaybah sent a message to Wakīʿ, summoning him, but Qutaybah's messenger found him with a sticky substance smeared on his foot and beads and shells placed on his leg.[66] He was attended by two men from the Zahrān, who were uttering incantations over his foot. When the messenger said to Wakīʿ, "Answer the governor," the latter replied, "You see the problem with my foot." The messenger then returned to Qutaybah, who sent him back to Wakīʿ, saying, "Qutaybah says to you, ' Come to me carried on a litter.'" Wakīʿ answered, "I cannot." Qutaybah said to Sharīk b. al-Ṣāmit al-Bāhilī, one of the Banū Wāʾil—the commander of his guard—and to a man from the Ghanī, "Go to Wakīʿ and bring him to me. If he refuses, cut off his head." He sent

---

66. Text: *wa-ʿalā sāqihi kharazan wa-wadaʿan.* See Ibn al-Athīr, *Kāmil*, V, 16: *wa-ʿallaqa ʿalā raʾsihi ḥirzan,* "He tied an amulet on his head."

horsemen with them—some say that Warqāʾ b. Naṣr al-Bāhilī was the commander of the guard in Khurāsān.

According to ʿAlī—Abū al-Dhayyāl—Thumāmah b. Nājidh al-ʿAdawī: Qutaybah sent someone to fetch Wakīʿ, and I said, "I will bring him to you, may God cause you to prosper." Qutaybah said, "Bring him to me." So I went to Wakīʿ, who had already been informed that the horsemen were on their way. When he saw me, he said, "O Thumāmah, summon the troops." I called out, and the first one to arrive was Huraym b. Abī Ṭaḥmah, with eight men.

Al-Ḥasan b. Rushayd al-Jūzjānī related: Qutaybah sent for Wakīʿ, and Huraym said, "I will bring him to you," whereupon Qutaybah replied, "Go." Huraym reported: "I mounted my horse, fearing that he would recall me, and I went to Wakīʿ. But he had already set out."

Kulayb b. Khalaf said: Qutaybah sent Shuʿbah b. Ẓahīr,[67] one of the Banū Ṣakhr b. Nahshal, to Wakīʿ. When he arrived, Wakīʿ exclaimed, "O Ibn Ẓahīr, wait a while until the cavalry catch up." Then Wakīʿ called for a knife and cut off the beads that were on his legs. Next, he put on his armor and quoted the verse:

[1293]

Tightly tie my navel so that it will not burst.
   One day for the Hamdān and one day for the Ṣadif.[68]

Wakīʿ set out by himself, and some women who noticed him said, "Abū Muṭarrif[69] is alone." It was at this moment that Huraym b. Abī Ṭaḥmah arrived with eight men, including ʿAmīrat al-Barīd[70] b. Rabīʿah al-ʿUjayfī.

According to Ḥamzah b. Ibrāhīm and others: Wakīʿ set out and was met by a man who asked, "What is your tribe?" He answered, "The Banū Asad." The man then asked, "What is your name?" He replied, "Ḍirghāmah." He asked, "The son of whom?" He answered, "Ibn Layth." The man said, "Take this banner."

According to al-Mufaḍḍal b. Muḥammad al-Ḍabbī: Wakīʿ gave his banner to ʿUqbah b. Shihāb al-Māzinī.

Then returning to our original chain of transmission, our

---

67. Ibn al-Athīr, Kāmil, V, 16: Ẓuhayr; cf. below, pp. 150–53, 159.
68. See Kūfī, Futūḥ, VII, 270.
69. Wakīʿ's patronymic was Abū Muṭarrif. See note 59 above.
70. Text: ʿAmīrah b. al-Barīd; read ʿAmīrat al-Barīd, following the Cairo ed.

source said: When Wakī' set out, he ordered his servants, saying, "Take my baggage to (my) paternal cousins." They replied, "We do not know where their camp is." He said, "Look for two spears that have been tied together, one on top of the other, with a nosebag on top of them. They are my paternal cousins." There were five hundred of them in the army.

Wakī' called out to the troops, who approached him, one company after the other, from every direction. He set out, leading the troops, saying:

A brave man who, when he is required to carry out an onerous
　　task,
　　keeps his ribs and his bosom tightly drawn.[71]

Some people said that when Wakī' set out he recited:

Do we face Luqmān b. 'Ād[72] and his type?
　　Bring me my sword. They shall not carry off an unarmed
　　man.

Qutaybah was joined by the members of his household and the　　[1294]
chiefs from among his companions and trusted supporters, including: Iyās b. Bayhas b. 'Amr, Qutaybah's paternal cousin, who was closely related, and 'Abdallāh b. Wa'lān al-'Adawī, with men from his tribe, the Banū Wā'il. Ḥayyān b. Iyās al-'Adawī came to him with ten men, including 'Abd al-'Azīz b. al-Ḥārith.

Maysarah al-Jadalī, who was a brave man, came to him, saying, "If you want, I will bring you Wakī''s head." He said, "Stay where you are." Qutaybah ordered one of his men, saying, "Call out among the soldiers, 'Where are the Banū 'Āmir?'"[73] He called out, "Where are the Banū 'Āmir?" Mihfan b. Jaz' al-Kilābī[74] said, "Where you placed them"—Qutaybah had treated them roughly. Qutaybah then said, "Call out, 'I remind you of God and our kinship.'" But Mihfan called out, "You severed the ties of rela-

---

71. This saying means that a brave man gets himself fully ready for the task. See text below, II/1298, where the verse is repeated with a slight variant; see also Kūfī, *Futūḥ*, VII, 271.

72. Luqmān b. 'Ād was a legendary hero of pre-Islamic Arabia, famous for his wisdom and longevity. See *EI²*, s.v. Luḳmān.

73. The Banū 'Āmir b. Ṣa'ṣa'ah, of the Qays. See Caskel, *Ğamharah*, I, 92.

74. Ibn al-Athīr (*Kāmil*, V, 16) gives his name as Muḥaqqir b. Jaz' al-'Alā'ī. Both men were from the Qays.

tionship." Qutaybah said, "Call out, 'Accept our conciliation.'" But Miḥfan, or someone else, called out, "No, may God never forgive us if we do." Qutaybah then recited:

O my soul, endure the pain with patience,
  since I have not found equals to the tribe's eminent ones.

Then Qutaybah called for a turban that his mother had sent him, put it on—it was his custom to wear it in times of difficulty—and called for one of his well-trained horses that he considered lucky in war.[75] The horse was brought close to him so that he might mount it, but it started to jump about until it exhausted him. When Qutaybah saw this, he returned to his couch, lay down, and said, "Let it be, for this is God's will."[76]

Ḥayyān al-Nabaṭī approached, leading the non-Arabs, and made his stand, even though Qutaybah was angry with him, and ʿAbdallāh b. Muslim[77] made his stand next to him. ʿAbdallāh said to Ḥayyān, "Attack both wings." When he answered, "It is not time for that," ʿAbdallāh became angry and said, "Give me my bow." Ḥayyān said, "This is not a day for the bow." Wakīʿ then sent a message to Ḥayyān that said, "I am waiting for you to fulfill your promise." Ḥayyān said to his son, "When you see me turn my cap around and move in the direction of Wakīʿ's troops, bring to me the non-Arabs who are with you." Ibn Ḥayyān stood with the non-Arabs and, when Ḥayyān turned his cap around, they moved in the direction of Wakīʿ's troops, whereupon his followers exclaimed, "God is great."

[1295]

Qutaybah sent his brother, Ṣāliḥ, to the soldiers, but he was wounded in the head by a man from the Banū Ḍabbah known as Sulaymān al-Zanjirj, that is, the Carob[78]—some say that he was shot by one of (Wakīʿ's) paternal cousins.[79] Ṣāliḥ was carried to Qutaybah, his head leaning to the side, and placed in his prayer room. Qutaybah shifted his position and sat with Ṣāliḥ for a while. Then he went back to his couch.

---

75. Text: *kāna yataṭayyir ilayhi fi-l-zuḥūf.*
76. Text: *fa-inna hādha amrun yurād.* Compare text below, II/1295, where a parallel passage specifies *inna lahu la-sha'n.*
77. That is, Qutaybah's brother.
78. Text: al-Khurnūb. Kūfī (*Futūḥ*, VII, 273) gives his nickname as Barīḥ Atranj.
79. Text: *Balʿamm,* an abbreviated form of *banū-l-ʿamm,* "the paternal cousins."

Abū al-Sarī al-Azdī said: Ṣāliḥ was shot and felled by a man from the Banū Ḍabbah; he was then stabbed by Ziyād b. ʿAbd al-Raḥmān al-Azdī, one of the Banū Sharīk b. Mālik.

Abū Mikhnaf said: A man from the Ghanī attacked the troops and saw a man who was wearing a coat of mail.[80] He mistook him for Jahm b. Zaḥr b. Qays and stabbed him, saying:

The Ghanī are mighty and trustworthy
> when they go to war, even if the other soldiers quarrel
> among themselves.

But the man who was stabbed was a non-Arab, and the troops were aroused. ʿAbd al-Raḥmān b. Muslim advanced toward them, but he was stoned to death by the market people and the rabble. The soldiers set fire to an enclosure containing Qutaybah's camels and riding animals; they closed in on him. Fighting for him was a man from the Bāhilah, from the Banū Wāʾil, and Qutaybah said to him, "Save yourself." But he replied, "How miserable a repayment, in that case, for you gave me bread to eat and soft clothes to wear."[81]

Qutaybah now called for a riding animal. A horse was brought to him, but it would not stand still long enough for him to mount it. He said, "There is something the matter with it."[82] So he did not mount the horse but sat, and the troops advanced toward the tent. When the troops reached the tent, Iyās b. Bayhas and ʿAbdal-lāh b. Waʾlān fled, abandoning Qutaybah. ʿAbd al-ʿAzīz b. al-Ḥārith went out looking for his son, ʿAmr—or ʿUmar; al-Ṭāʾī met him but was wary of engaging him, so that ʿAbd al-ʿAzīz found his son, who mounted the horse behind his father.

[1296]

Qutaybah observed al-Haytham b. al-Munakhkhal, who was one of those who had plotted against him, and said:

I used to teach him to shoot every day.
> However, when his arm became well-trained with the
> bow,[83] he shot at me.

---

80. Text: *mujaffaf*, from *tijfāf*, which Lane defines as "a kind of armor with which a horse is clad in war, in the manner of a coat of mail." See *Lexicon*, pt. 2, p. 432.

81. Kūfī, who identifies the man as a certain Junādah, adds: "So he fought and was slain." See *Futūḥ*, VII, 275.

82. Text: *inna lahu la-shaʾn*. See note 76, above.

83. Text: *istadda*; the Cairo ed. has *ishtadda*, "when he became powerful."

Slain along with Qutaybah were his brothers, ʿAbd al-Raḥmān, ʿAbdallāh, Ṣāliḥ, Ḥusayn, and ʿAbd al-Karīm, the sons of Muslim. His son, Kathīr b. Qutaybah, was also slain, as were several members of his household. But his brother, Ḍirār, escaped, having been saved by his maternal uncles—the latter's mother was Gharrāʾ bt. Ḍirār b. al-Qaʿqāʿ b. Maʿbad b. Zurārah.

Some people said: ʿAbd al-Karīm b. Muslim was killed in Qazwīn.[84]

According to Abū ʿUbaydah—Abū Mālik: They slew Qutaybah in the year 96/715. Eleven of Muslim's descendants were slain—Wakīʿ crucified them. Seven of them were the sons of Muslim, and four were grandsons: Qutaybah, ʿAbd al-Raḥmān, ʿAbdallāh al-Faqīr, ʿUbaydallāh, Ṣāliḥ, Bashshār, and Muḥammad, the sons of Muslim; and Kathīr b. Qutaybah and Mughallis b. ʿAbd al-Raḥmān (and two others, the grandsons).[85] None of Muslim's sons escaped, except for ʿAmr, who was the governor of al-Jūz-[1297] jān,[86] and Ḍirār, whose mother was al-Gharrāʾ bt. Ḍirār b. al-Qaʿqāʿ b. Maʿbad b. Zurārah; his maternal uncles came and removed him (from his position), thereby saving him.[87]

Al-Farazdaq recited about this:

The evening that Ibn Gharrāʾ did not wish—when he called
    out—that he had parents from a tribe other than us.[88]

Iyās b. ʿAmr, the nephew of Muslim b. ʿAmr, was wounded in the collarbone, but he lived.

The source continued: When the tribe overran the great tent, they cut its ropes.

According to Zuhayr: Jahm b. Zaḥr said to Saʿd,[89] "Dismount and cut off his head, for he has been weakened by the wounds."

---

84. A famous city 102 km. from al-Rayy and 72 km. from Abhar. See Yāqūt, *Muʿjam*, IV, 342–44; *EI²*, s.v. Ḳazwīn; Le Strange, *Lands*, 218–20.

85. Compare Kūfī, *Futūḥ*, VII, 274–75; Ibn al-Athīr, *Kāmil*, V, 17.

86. Al-Jūzjān was one of the districts of Balkh, in Khurāsān. See Yāqūt, *Muʿjam*, II, 182–83.

87. Text: *najjawhu*; read *naḥḥawhu*, following the Cairo ed. Compare Ibn al-Athīr, *Kāmil*, V, 17–18, where it is ʿUmar [*sic*] b. Muslim, who is saved by his maternal uncles.

88. See *Dīwān*, II, 332. "Ibn Gharrāʾ" refers to Ḍirār b. Muslim, Qutaybah's brother, who was dismissed as governor of Khurāsān by Sulaymān b. ʿAbd al-Malik. Compare text below, II/1301.

89. This man was probably Saʿd b. Najd al-Azdī. See Kūfī, *Futūḥ*, VII, 275.

Sa'd replied, "I fear that the horses will bolt." Jahm exclaimed, "You are afraid, though I am next to you!" Sa'd dismounted, split the top of the tent, and cut off his head. Ḥuḍayn b. al-Mundhir recited:

Verily, Ibn Sa'd and Ibn Zaḥr took turns
　　with their swords on the head of the crowned hero.
The evening that we brought Ibn Zaḥr and you brought
　　a black-nosed (man) with brands on his arms, blackish,
Deaf, from the Ghudānah, as if his forehead
　　were a blot of ink on a skin that had been scrawled over.[90]

When Maslamah slew Yazīd b. al-Muhallab, he appointed Sa'īd Khudhaynah b. 'Abd al-'Azīz b. al-Ḥārith b. al-Ḥakam b. Abī al-'Āṣ governor of Khurāsān, and Yazīd's subgovernors were imprisoned.[91] Among those imprisoned was Jahm b. Zaḥr al-Ju'fī, who was tortured by a man from the Bāhilah. Someone said to the Bāhilī tribesman, "This is Qutaybah's murderer," whereupon he tortured him to death. Sa'īd criticized him for this, but the man retorted, "You ordered me to extract money from him; I tortured him, and it was his time to die."

On the day that Qutaybah was slain, one of his Khwārazmian slave girls was with him; when he was slain, she fled. Subsequently, Yazīd b. al-Muhallab captured her. She is Umm Khulaydah. [1298]

According to 'Alī—Ḥamzah b. Ibrāhīm and Abū al-Yaqẓān: When Qutaybah was slain, 'Umārah b. Junayyah[92] al-Riyāḥī ascended the pulpit and spoke at length. Wakī' said to him, "Spare us your filth and gossip." Then Wakī' began to speak, saying, "The likes of me and the likes of Qutaybah are as the first one said:

He who fucks an ass fucks a catamite.[93]

Qutaybah sought to slay me, but I am deadly.

---

90. Text: *ka-anna jabīnahu luṭakhat niqs fī adīm mumajmaj*. See *Naḳā'iḍ Jarīr wa-l-Farazdaq*, I, 362.

91. See text below, II/1417, sub anno 102.

92. The vocalization of Junayyah is conjectural.

93. See text above, I/901.

They tried me once; then they tried me again,
>   from a distance of two bow shots and from a distance of a
>   hundred bow shots.
Until, when I grew old and they gave me white hair,
>   they gave up on my rein and avoided me.

I am Abū Muṭarrif!"
     According to Abū Mu'āwiyah—Ṭalḥah b. Iyās: Wakī' recited on
the day that Qutaybah was slain:

I am the son of Khindif.[94] Her tribes ascribe
>   good deeds to me. And my paternal uncle is Qays 'Aylān.[95]

Then he grabbed his beard and recited:

A shaykh who, when he is required to carry out an onerous
>   task,
>   keeps his ribs and his bosom tightly drawn.[96]

"By God, I will slay, indeed I will slay, and I will crucify, indeed I
will crucify. I want to taste blood. This Marzubān[97] of yours, the
son of the adulteress, has inflated the prices of your goods. By
God, if he does not set the price of one qafīz[98] in the market
tomorrow at four (dirhams), I will crucify him. Remember the
Prophet in your prayers." Then he stepped down from the pulpit.
     According to 'Alī—al-Mufaḍḍal b. Muḥammad and a shaykh
[1299] from the Banū Tamīm, and Maslamah b. Muḥārib: Wakī' de-
manded Qutaybah's head and his signet ring but was told, "The
Azd have taken it." Wakī' emerged, saying, "You have added
falsehood to falsehood, O Sa'd the blacksmith."[99]

---

94. The Khindif was a major division of the Muḍar that included the Hudhayl,
the Tamīm, and the Kinānah. See EI², s.v. Djazīrat al-'Arab.

95. Qays 'Aylān was one of the two subdivisions of Muḍar. See EI², s.v. Ḳays
'Aylān.

96. Compare text above, II/1293.

97. By referring to Qutaybah as a Marzubān, the Arabic form of the title of
provincial governors in the Sasanian Empire, Wakī' likened him to an alien gran-
dee after the Iranian fashion. See EI, s.v. Marzuban.

98. A qafīz is a measure of dry goods equivalent to eight makākīk or twelve ṣā'.
See Kazimirski, Dictionnaire, II, 788; Hinz, Islamische Masse und Gewichte, 48–
50.

99. Text: Dūh durrayni Sa'd alqayni, a proverbial expression. See Lane,
Lexicon, pt. 3, pp. 922–23, s.v. dahdara.

On which of my two days will I escape[100] from death,
    a day that has not been ordained or a day that has been?
There is no good in a broad-breasted horse, the fleet
    ones that run in the races,
    Is there a day on which I will neither frighten (others)
    nor be frightened (myself)?

"By God—than Whom there is no other God—I will not leave until either Qutaybah's head is brought to me, or my head is added to his." Then he brought some wooden stakes and said, "These horses must have riders"—thereby alluding to the threat of crucifixion. Ḥuḍayn said to him, "O Abū Muṭarrif, it will be brought to you, so calm down."

Ḥuḍayn came to the Azd and said, "Are you fools? We swore allegiance to Wakīʿ and accepted his leadership. He exposed himself to danger, and then you take Qutaybah's head! Give it up," that is, the head, "may God curse it." They brought out the head, saying, "O Abū Muṭarrif, this person is the one who cut it off, so reward him." He agreed and gave him three thousand dirhams. He sent the head (to Sulaymān) with Salīṭ b. ʿAbd al-Karīm al-Ḥanafī and men from the various tribes—who were led by Salīṭ—but he did not send anyone from the Banū Tamīm.

According to Abū al-Dhayyāl: Among those who accompanied the head was Unayf b. Ḥassān, one of the Banū ʿAdī.

According to Abū Mikhnaf: Wakīʿ paid Ḥayyān al-Nabaṭī in return for what the latter had given him.[101]   [1300]

According to Khuraym b. Abī Yaḥyā—shaykhs from the Qays: Sulaymān asked al-Hudhayl b. Zufar, when Qutaybah's head and the heads of the members of his household were put in front of him, "Does this distress you, Hudhayl?"[102] He replied, "If it distresses me, it distresses many others as well." Then Khuraym b. ʿAmr[103] and al-Qaʿqāʿ b. Khulayd[104] spoke to Sulaymān saying,

---

100. Text: *afir*; read *afirru*, following the Cairo ed.

101. See text above, II/1291.

102. Zufar's family were considered to be the very incarnation of *Qaysiyyah*. See Crone, *Slaves*, 108.

103. Khuraym b. ʿAmr al-Murrī seems to have been implicated in Qutaybah's revolt. See text below, II/1312, sub anno 97; Crone, *Slaves*, 98, no. 6.

104. Al-Qaʿqāʿ appears to have supported al-Walīd's efforts to deprive Sulaymān of the succession. See text below, II/1312, sub anno 97; Crone, *Slaves*, 105–6, n. 15.

"Grant permission to bury their heads." He said, "Certainly, for I did not want any of this."

According to ʿAlī—Abū ʿAbdallāh al-Sulamī—Yazīd b. Suwayd: A Persian from the army of Khurāsān said: "O ye Arabs, you have slain Qutaybah. By God, had Qutaybah been one of us and had he died among us, we would have put him in a coffin that would have served as a mascot for us in our raids. Nobody ever accomplished in Khurāsān what Qutaybah did. Nevertheless, he betrayed (us). This is because al-Ḥajjāj wrote to him, saying, 'Lay a trap for them and slay them, for the sake of God.' "

According to al-Ḥasan b. Rushayd: The *iṣbahbadh*[105] said to a man, "O ye Arabs, you have slain Qutaybah and Yazīd,[106] the two lords of the Arabs." The man asked, "Which of the two, in your opinion, was more awesome and commanded more respect?" The *iṣbahbadh* replied, "If Qutaybah were in the Maghrib, in the deepest hole in the earth, tied up in chains, and Yazīd was with us, in our country, serving as our governor, Qutaybah would still be more awesome and more highly respected than Yazīd."

According to ʿAlī—al-Mufaḍḍal b. Muḥammad al-Ḍabbī: A man approached Qutaybah on the day he died, while he was holding court, and said, "Today the King of the Arabs will be slain"— they considered Qutaybah to be the King of the Arabs. Qutaybah said to him, "Sit down!"

According to Kulayb b. Khalaf—a man from among those who were with Wakīʿ when Qutaybah was slain: On Wakīʿ's order, a man called out, "No spoils are to be taken from any corpse." But Ibn ʿAbīd al-Hajarī passed by Abū al-Ḥujr al-Bāhilī and stripped him. When Wakīʿ was informed of this, he cut off the man's head.

According to Abū ʿUbaydah—ʿAbdallāh b. ʿUmar from the Taym Allāt: Wakīʿ mounted his horse one day, and they brought him a man who was drunk. On his order, the man was killed. Someone said to Wakīʿ, "He deserved to be flogged,[107] not killed." He replied, "I punish with the sword, not the whip."

[1301]

---

105. *Iṣbahbadh* in Persian means "army chief"; it is the Islamic form of a military title used in the pre-Islamic Persian Empires. See *EI²*, s.v. Ispahbadh.

106. Yazīd b. al-Muhallab was slain in the year 102/720–21. See text below, II/1405, sub anno 102.

107. Text: *ḥadd*, a term that refers to certain acts, namely, unlawful intercourse, false accusation of unlawful intercourse, drinking wine, theft, and highway robbery, which have been forbidden or sanctioned by punishments in the Qur'ān. The punishment for drinking wine is eighty lashes. See *EI²*, s.v. Ḥadd.

Nahār b. Tawsi'ah[108] recited:

We used to cry because of al-Bāhilī,
    but this Ghudānī is much more evil.[109]

He also recited:

When we saw al-Bāhilī, Ibn Muslim,
    acting tyrannically, we struck him on the head with a
    sharp sword.

Al-Farazdaq recited, recalling the battle of Wakī':

To us belongs the one who drew swords and sheathed them,
    the evening of the battle of the Gate of al-Qaṣr, from
    Farghānah.[110]
The evening that no tribe could defend its sons
    by invoking an Iraqi or Yemenite glory.
The evening that Ibn Gharrā' did not wish—when he called
    out—that he had parents from a tribe other than us.
The evening that the Hawāzin of 'Āmir and Ghaṭafān
    did not cover the nakedness of Ibn Dukhān.[111]
The evening that the people wished to be our slaves,
    when the two armies were fighting.
They saw one mountain towering over the others,[112] when the
    heads of their two leaders met, butting together.
Men for Islam who, as soon as they fought   [1302]
    for religion, caused it to spread in every place.
Until a herald called out from the walls of every city,
    issuing the call to prayer.
But Wakī' will be rewarded in the name of the community,
    since he realized
    its solidarity with a cutting sword and spearhead.
A reward for the deeds of men, just as a reward was given
    at Badr and al-Yarmūk from the shades of Paradise.[113]

---

108. See Ibn Qutaybah, *Shi'r*, I, 448–49, no. 95.
109. "Al-Bāhilī" refers to Qutaybah, and "Ghudānī" to Wakī'.
110. See *EI²*, s.v. Farghāna.
111. Ibn Dukhān is the nickname of Bāhilah, Qutaybah's tribe.
112. The text is *ya'lū-l-jibāl. Dīwān*, II, 332, has *daqqa-l-jibāl*, "They saw one
mountain crushing the others."
113. See *Dīwān*, II, 331–32.

Al-Farazdaq also recited about this:

I received the news, when my saddlebags were in Medina,
    about a battle waged by the family of Tamīm; it was
    satisfying and comforting.[114]

According to ʿAlī—Khuraym b. Abī Yaḥyā—one of his paternal
uncles—shaykhs from the Ghassān: We were in the gap of
al-ʿUqāb[115] when suddenly we encountered a man carrying a stick
and a leather bag who looked like one of the Caliph's messengers.
We asked, "Where have you come from?" He replied, "From
Khurāsān." We asked, "Is there any news?" He replied, "Yes,
Qutaybah b. Muslim was slain yesterday." We were amazed at his
statement, and, seeing that we did not believe him, he asked,
"How far shall I be from Ifrīqiyah tonight, do you think?" He set
off and we followed him on our horses, but he was so fast that he
disappeared at the blink of an eye.

Al-Ṭirimmāḥ[116] recited:

Had it not been for the horsemen of Madhḥij, the daughter of
    Madhḥij, and (the horsemen of) Azd, the army would have
    been discomfited and plundered
And dispersed in the lands, and nobody bringing news
    about them would have returned to the army of Iraq.
The bonds of the community would have been loosened, scorn
    heaped on the authority of the Caliph, and illicit doings
    would have become permissible.
People who slew Qutaybah by violence,
    while the horses were racing inclined to the ground,
    covered with dust.
In the meadow, the meadow of al-Ṣīn, where
    the Muḍar of Iraq understood who was the noblest and
    greatest.
[1303] When all of Rabīʿah gave themselves up to despair,

---

114. Text: *aqʿadat kulla qāʾim*, literally, "It caused every standing person to sit
down." See ibid., II, 310, l.4.

115. A gap in the mountains overlooking the oasis of Damascus. See Yāqūt,
Muʿjam, IV, 133.

116. Al-Ṭirimmāḥ b. Ḥakīm al-Ṭāʾī was a celebrated poet of the first century of
Islam. See *EI*, s.v. al-Ṭirimmāḥ; Ibn Qutaybah, *Shiʿr*, II, 585–90, no. 160.

and the Muḍar and those who claimed to belong to the
   Muḍar were scattered abroad.
And the Azd of Iraq and the Madhḥij advanced
   toward death, one common ancestor uniting them both.
The Qaḥṭān were smiting the head of every full-armed warrior;
   they protect their eyes, but they do not see.[117]
And the Azd know that under their standard is either a
   glorious sovereignty or bloody death.
For by our strength the Prophet Muḥammad triumphed,
   and through us it has come to pass that the pulpit is firmly
   established in Damascus.[118]

   ʿAbd al-Raḥmān b. Jumānah al-Bāhilī recited:

It is as if Abū Ḥafṣ Qutaybah never led
   one army to the other, and never ascended a pulpit.
And the flags did not flutter when the tribe was standing
   around him, and the people never witnessed an army under
   his command.
The Fates called him, so he answered his Lord
   and went to Paradise, chaste and pure.
Islam did not suffer a loss—after Muḥammad—
   like that of Abū Ḥafṣ. So mourn him, ʿAbhar.[119]

"ʿAbhar" refers to an *umm walad*[120] belonging to Qutaybah.
   Al-Aṣamm b. al-Ḥajjāj recited, elegizing Qutaybah:

Is it not time for the living to recognize (our distinction) for us?
   Surely we are the people most deserving of praise and
   glory.
We lead the Tamīm, the clients, and the Madhḥij,
   the Azd, ʿAbd al-Qays, and the tribe from Bakr.
We massacre whomever we wish by the power of our   [1304]
   sovereignty,

---

117. Text: *taḥmī baṣāʾirahunna idh lā tubṣiru*. See *Dīwān al-Ṭirimmāḥ*, p. 251,
where the text is *wa-ʿalā baṣāʾirihā wa-idh lā tubṣiru* "(smiting the head of every
full-armed warrior) and their eyes, and so they become unable to see."
   118. See *The Dīwāns of aṭ-Ṭufail and aṭ-Ṭirimmāḥ*, 147 (Arabic text), and 62
(translation).
   119. See *Naḳāʾiḍ Jarīr wa-l-Farazdaq*, I, 363.
   120. An *umm walad* is a slave girl who has borne her master a child; she
becomes free on the death of her master. See *EI*, s.v. Umm al-Walad.

and force whomever we wish to succumb to disgrace and
    subjugation.
Sulaymān—Many are the soldiers that we rounded up for you
    by our spears while our horses were riding at full speed.
Many are the impregnable fortresses that we ravaged.
    And many are the lowlands and the rocky mountains.
And towns which no soldiers had raided before us,
    we raided, driving the horses month after month.
Our horses became used to protracted raids, and to be quiet at
    the sight of charging warriors so that they were no longer
    frightened by them.
Even if the fire is kindled, and they are forced
    toward the fire, they rush into the brunt of fire in war.
With their breasts they toy with spearheads and lances,
    while death is surging with black waves.
With these horses we have ravaged many a city
    of unbelievers, until they passed beyond the place where
    the dawn breaks.
And if Fate had not hurried us, they would have carried
    us beyond Dhū al-Qarnayn's wall of rock and molten
    brass.[121]
But the good Banū ʿAmr met their preordained fate
    when their life-span came to an end.

[1305]   In this year, Sulaymān b. ʿAbd al-Mālik dismissed Khālid b.
ʿAbdallāh al-Qasrī as governor of Mecca, replacing him with Ṭalḥah b. Dāwūd al-Ḥaḍramī.

In this year, Maslamah b. ʿAbd al-Mālik raided Byzantium in a
summer expedition and conquered a fortress (ḥiṣn) known as
"Ḥiṣn ʿAwf."[122]

In this year, Qurrah b. Sharīk al-ʿAbsī, the governor of Egypt,
died, in the month of Ṣafar (October 16–November 13), according
to some of the biographers. Others said: Qurrah died during the

---

121. Text: *wa-l-qaṭri*, "and rain"; read *wa-l-qiṭri*, which means molten brass.
Dhū al-Qarnayn ("the two-horned one") refers to Alexander the Great who, according to Qurʾān 18:82–98, was given power on earth. In response to an appeal
from oppressed people, he built a rampart of iron and brass against the incursions
of Gog and Magog. See *EI²*, s.v. al-Iskandar.

122. I have not been able to identify Ḥiṣn ʿAwf.

lifetime of al-Walīd (b. ʿAbd al-Malik), in the year 95/714, in the month in which al-Ḥajjāj died.[123]

In this year, the pilgrimage was led by Abū Bakr b. Muḥammad b. ʿAmr b. Ḥazm al-Anṣārī—as I was told by Aḥmad b. Thābit, on the authority of the one he mentioned—on the authority of Isḥāq b. ʿĪsā—on the authority of Abū Maʿshar; and the same was related by al-Wāqidī and others.

The governor of Medina in this year was Abū Bakr b. Muḥammad b. ʿAmr b. Ḥazm, and the governor of Mecca was ʿAbd al-ʿAzīz b. ʿAbdallāh b. Khālid b. Asīd.[124]

In Iraq, Yazīd b. al-Muhallab was in charge of military and religious affairs, and Ṣāliḥ b. ʿAbd al-Raḥmān was in charge of the fiscal administration. Sufyān b. ʿAbdallāh al-Kindī, serving on behalf of Yazīd b. al-Muhallab, was governor of al-Baṣrah. ʿAbd al-Raḥmān b. Udhaynah was in charge of the judiciary there. In charge of the judiciary in al-Kūfah was Abū Bakr b. Abī Mūsā. Wakīʿ b. Abī Sūd was responsible for military affairs in Khurāsān.[125]

---

123. Al-Ḥajjāj died in Ramaḍān. See *EI2*, s.v. al-Ḥadjdjādj b. Yūsuf.

124. The identification of ʿAbd al-ʿAzīz as the governor of Mecca may be a mistake. See text below, II/1314, sub anno 97, where Ṭabarī indicates that Ṭalḥah b. Dāwūd continued to serve as governor of Mecca until the year 97/715–16, at which time he was replaced by ʿAbd al-ʿAzīz b. ʿAbdallāh b. Khālid b. Asīd.

125. See Yaʿqūbī, *Taʾrīkh*, III, 41; Wellhausen, *Arab Kingdom*, 444–45.

The
Events of the Year

97
(SEPTEMBER 5, 715—AUGUST 24, 716)

[1306] Among the events taking place in this year: Sulaymān b. ʿAbd al-Malik equipped the armies and dispatched them to Constantinople. He put his son, Dāwūd b. Sulaymān, in charge of the summer campaign, which resulted in the capture of Ḥiṣn al-Marʾah.[126]

According to al-Wāqidī, in this year Maslamah b. ʿAbd al-Malik raided Byzantium and conquered the fortress that had previously been taken by al-Waḍḍāḥ, the leader of the Waḍḍāḥiyyah.[127]

In this year, ʿUmar[128] b. Hubayrah al-Fazārī undertook a naval expedition against Byzantium, where he spent the winter.

In this year, ʿAbd al-ʿAzīz b. Mūsā b. Nuṣayr was killed in al-Andalus and Ḥabīb b. Abī ʿUbayd al-Fihrī brought his head to Sulaymān.

In this year, Sulaymān b. ʿAbd al-Malik appointed Yazīd b. al-Muhallab as governor of Khurāsān.[129]

---

126. "The Woman's Fortress" was in the region of Malaṭyah. See text below, II/1335, sub anno 98.

127. The Waḍḍāḥiyyah were a separate military regiment of non-Arabs, named after their commander, a Berber freedman of ʿAbd al-Malik. See Crone, *Slaves*, 38.

128. Text: ʿAmr; read ʿUmar, following the Cairo ed.

129. See Ibn Khayyāṭ, *Taʾrīkh*, I, 319; Yaʿqūbī, *Taʾrīkh*, III, 41; Kūfī, *Futūḥ*, VII, 278–85; Ibn Kathīr, *Bidāyah*, IX, 170.

The Appointment of Yazīd b. al-Muhallab as Governor of Khurāsān

The circumstances: When Sulaymān b. ʿAbd al-Malik became Caliph, he put Yazīd b. al-Muhallab in charge of military, religious, and fiscal affairs in Iraq.

According to Hishām b. Muḥammad—Abū Mikhnaf: Upon being given these responsibilities in Iraq, Yazīd reflected as follows: "Iraq has been ruined by al-Ḥajjāj. Today I am the hope of the people of Iraq. But if I go there and force the people to pay the tribute and punish them for nonpayment, I will have become just like al-Ḥajjāj, throwing the people into conflict and returning them to those prisons from which God had released them. On the other hand, if I do not send Sulaymān an amount equal to what was collected by al-Ḥajjāj, he will not be pleased with me." Therefore, Yazīd approached Sulaymān, saying, "I should like to bring to your attention a man who is very skillful in collecting the tribute, and whom you may want to put in charge of that function, so that you will receive it from him: Ṣāliḥ b. ʿAbd al-Raḥmān, a client of the Banū Tamīm." Sulaymān said to him, "We accept your suggestion." Whereupon Yazīd set off for Iraq. [1307]

According to ʿUmar b. Shabbah—ʿAlī: Ṣāliḥ preceded Yazīd to Iraq, where he established himself in Wāsiṭ.[130]

According to ʿAlī—ʿAbbād b. Ayyūb: Yazīd approached, and the troops went out to meet him. Someone said to Ṣāliḥ, "Yazīd is here, and the troops have gone out to meet him." However, he did not go out until Yazīd drew near to the city. Then Ṣāliḥ went out, wearing a tunic (*durrāʿah*)[131] and (carrying) a small, yellow mace. He was leading four hundred men from the Syrian army. He met Yazīd and traveled along with him. When Yazīd entered the city, Ṣāliḥ pointed to a house, saying, "I have emptied this house for you." Yazīd dismounted and Ṣāliḥ went to his residence.

Ṣāliḥ placed severe restraints upon Yazīd, refusing to transfer any money to him. Yazīd prepared one thousand tables to feed his

---

130. Wāsiṭ was built by al-Ḥajjāj b. Yūsuf in 83–84/702–3 and served as the capital of Iraq for most of the Umayyad period; the city was called "Wāsiṭ" (middle) because it was equidistant between al-Kūfah and al-Baṣrah. See *EI*, s.v. Wāsiṭ.

131. See Dozy, *Vêtements*, 177–81.

men, but Ṣāliḥ seized them. Yazīd said to him, "Charge the cost of the tables to me." Yazīd purchased many goods and wrote checks[132] to Ṣāliḥ for the benefit of the vendors; however, Ṣāliḥ would not accept the checks, and they referred to Yazīd. Yazīd became angry and said, "I have brought this upon myself." Soon thereafter, Ṣāliḥ came, and Yazīd set aside a place for him. He sat down and said to Yazīd, "What are these checks? The levies are not to be used for those purposes. Several days ago I cashed a check for one hundred thousand dirhams, and I have paid your (soldiers') stipends promptly, and when you asked for money for the army, I gave it to you. But this expense cannot be covered.[133]

[1308] The Commander of the Faithful will not be pleased, and you will be questioned about it." Yazīd said to him, "O Abū al-Walīd, accept these checks, just this once." And he joked with him. Ṣāliḥ asked, "If I allow them, will you not ask me again?" Yazīd replied, "No, I will not."

According to ʿAlī b. Muḥammad—Maslamah b. Muḥārib, Abū al-ʿAlāʾ al-Taymī, al-Ṭufayl b. Mirdās al-ʿAmmī, and Abū Ḥafṣ al-Azdī—his source—Jahm b. Zaḥr b. Qays and al-Ḥasan b. Rushayd—Sulaymān b. Kathīr and Abū al-Ḥasan al-Khurāsānī—al-Kirmānī, ʿĀmir b. Ḥafṣ, and Abū Mikhnaf—ʿUthmān b. ʿAmr b. Miḥṣan al-Azdī, Zuhayr b. Hunayd, and others—the reports of some of these men contain details not contained in the reports of others, and I (that is, Ṭabarī) have collated them: Sulaymān b. ʿAbd al-Malik appointed Yazīd b. al-Muhallab as governor of Iraq, not of Khurāsān. Sulaymān b. ʿAbd al-Malik asked ʿAbd al-Malik b. al-Muhallab, when the latter was in Syria and Yazīd was in Iraq, "What would you think, O ʿAbd al-Malik, if I appointed you as governor of Khurāsān?" He replied, "The Commander of the Faithful will find me wherever he wants." Subsequently, however, Sulaymān's attention was diverted from that.

Our source continued: ʿAbd al-Malik b. al-Muhallab wrote to Jarīr b. Yazīd al-Jahḍamī and to some of his close associates, saying, "The Commander of the Faithful has offered me the governorship of Khurāsān." The news reached Yazīd b. al-Muhallab in

---

132. On the use of checks and other instruments of credit, see *Dictionary of the Middle Ages*, s.v. Banking, Islamic.
133. Ṣāliḥ is referring to the expense for the one thousand tables.

Iraq, where he was greatly vexed because Ṣāliḥ b. ʿAbd al-Raḥmān was placing severe constraints upon him in such a way that Yazīd could not attain anything he wanted. Yazīd summoned ʿAbdallāh b. al-Ahtam, saying, "I need your assistance in a matter that has been troubling me and I want you to resolve it for me." He said, "I am at your command." He said, "As you see, I am in straitened circumstances, and this has made me uneasy. At the same time, Khurāsān has no governor, and I have learned that the Commander of the Faithful has offered this position to ʿAbd al-Malik b. al-Muhallab. Is there any stratagem we might employ (to get it)?" He said, "Yes. Send me to the Commander of the Faithful, and I hope to bring you your document of appointment as governor of Khurāsān." Yazīd said, "Don't tell anyone about our conversation." Yazīd wrote two letters to Sulaymān: In the first, he mentioned the condition of Iraq and spoke highly of Ibn al-Ahtam, stressing the latter's knowledge of the country. He dispatched Ibn al-Ahtam on a post-horse, giving him thirty thousand dirhams. He traveled for seven nights bringing Yazīd's letter to Sulaymān. When he reached Sulaymān, the Caliph was dining, so he sat off to the side and ate two hens that were brought to him.

Ibn al-Ahtam entered, and Sulaymān said to him, "I will receive you on another occasion." Then Sulaymān summoned him three nights later and said to him, "Yazīd b. al-Muhallab wrote to me, praising you and mentioning your expertise with regard to Iraq and Khurāsān. What is the extent of your knowledge about these countries?" Ibn al-Ahtam replied, "I know more about them than anyone, for I was born and raised there, and I have knowledge and information about them and their people." Sulaymān said, "The Commander of the Faithful needs someone like you to advise him about Iraq and Khurāsān. Whom do you recommend that I appoint as governor of Khurāsān?" Ibn al-Ahtam answered, "The Commander of the Faithful knows best whom he wants to appoint as governor, but if he mentions the name of a candidate, I will tell him whether or not I think he is qualified for the appointment."

Sulaymān mentioned the name of a man from the Quraysh, and Ibn al-Ahtam said, "O Commander of the Faithful, he is not the real man for Khurāsān." Sulaymān then said, "Then ʿAbd al-Malik b. al-Muhallab." He said, "No." The Caliph enumerated

[1309]

the names of many men, the last one being that of Wakīʿ b. Abī Sūd. Ibn al-Ahtam said, "O Commander of the Faithful, although Wakīʿ is bold, fearless, courageous, and brave, he is not right for the job, for he has neither led three hundred men nor acknowledged that he owes submission to anyone."[134] The Caliph responded, "You are right, woe unto you, so whom?" Ibn al-Ahtam said, "There is one man whom I know and whose name you have not mentioned." He asked, "Who is he?" Ibn al-Ahtam replied, "I will not disclose his name unless the Commander of the Faithful assures me that he will keep this matter secret, and that he will protect me from the person in question should the latter learn of it." The Caliph said, "Agreed. Name him. Who is he?" He said, "Yazīd b. al-Muhallab." [The Caliph] said, "But he is in Iraq, which he prefers to Khurāsān." He said, "That is true, O Commander of the Faithful, but if you compelled him to transfer, he would appoint a deputy governor over Iraq and go." At that, the Caliph said, "That is a good idea." Sulaymān then wrote a document in which he appointed Yazīd as governor of Khurāsān. He also wrote him a letter, saying: "I found Ibn al-Ahtam to be as intelligent, pious, virtuous, and as wise as you mentioned." He gave the letter to Ibn al-Ahtam, together with Yazīd's document of appointment. Seven nights after setting out, Ibn al-Ahtam reached Yazīd, who asked him, "What news have you brought me?"

Ibn al-Ahtam gave him the letter, causing Yazīd to exclaim, "Woe is you! Don't you have anything better than this?" Then he gave him the document of appointment, whereupon Yazīd ordered that provisions be made for setting out immediately; he summoned his son, Makhlad,[135] sending him ahead to Khurāsān.

Makhlad set out that very day, and Yazīd set out soon thereafter, having designated al-Jarrāḥ b. ʿAbdallāh al-Ḥakamī as his representative in Wāsiṭ, and ʿAbdallāh b. Hilāl al-Kilābī as his deputy in al-Baṣrah. He assigned to Marwān b. al-Muhallab,

---

134. Text: *fa-raʾā li-aḥad ʿalayhi ṭāʿatan*. See Kūfī, *Futūḥ*, VII, 279: *wathiqa bi-thalāthimiʾah rajul min aṣḥābihi lā yarā li-aḥad ʿalayhi ṭāʿah*, "If he trusts three hundred of his soldiers, he will not obey anyone who is over him."

135. The text gives Makhlad, here, but Mukhallad below, II/1312. I vocalize this name as Makhlad throughout the translation.

whom he considered the most trustworthy of his brothers, the responsibility for his personal wealth and affairs in al-Baṣrah.

Abū al-Bahā' al-Iyādī recited to Marwān:

I found Abū Qabīṣah every day
    to be the most noble among them under all circumstances.
When they refused to undertake
    the heavy part of the affair, he took on what he could.
And if they are overwhelmed by something,
    you excel them in magnanimity and generosity.

[1311]

As for Abū 'Ubaydah Ma'mar b. al-Muthannā—Abū Mālik: When Wakī' b. Abī Sūd sent an expression of his obedience, together with Qutaybah's head, to Sulaymān, that made a great impression on the Caliph. But Yazīd b. al-Muhallab promised 'Abdallāh b. al-Ahtam one hundred thousand dirhams on the condition that he denounce Wakī' in the presence of Sulaymān. Therefore, Ibn al-Ahtam said to the Caliph: "May God cause the Commander of the Faithful to prosper! By God, there is no one who is more deserving of my gratitude and no one who has rendered me greater services than Wakī'. He took blood revenge on my behalf and dealt with my enemy to my contentment. Nevertheless, my duty to the Commander of the Faithful is greater and more compelling, and the obligation to provide good counsel requires me to inform the Commander of the Faithful that Wakī' never assembled one hundred horsemen without thinking of an act of perfidy. He is nobody where the collective good is concerned, but remarkable in mischief." Sulaymān said, "He is not, therefore, one of those upon whom we can call for help."

Now the Qays were claiming that Qutaybah had not thrown off allegiance to the Caliph. When Sulaymān put Yazīd b. al-Muhallab in charge of military affairs in Iraq, he gave him the following order: "If the Qays can prove that Qutaybah did not throw off allegiance and did not withdraw obedience, then retaliate against Wakī' for him." But Yazīd acted treacherously. He did not give 'Abdallāh b. al-Ahtam what he had promised him and he sent his son, Makhlad b. Yazīd, against Wakī'.

The transmission of the account returns to 'Alī. According to 'Alī—Abū Mikhnaf—'Uthmān b. 'Amr b. Miḥṣan and Abū al-

Ḥasan al-Khurāsānī—al-Kirmānī: Yazīd sent his son, Makhlad, to Khurāsān. When Makhlad approached Marw, he sent ahead ʿAmr b. ʿAbdallāh b. Sinān al-ʿAtakī (also, al-Ṣunābihī). Upon his arrival in Marw, ʿAmr sent a message to Wakīʿ, saying, "Meet me." But he refused, and ʿAmr sent to him, saying, "You stupid, foolish, crude Bedouin, come out to meet your commander." The leading men from the army of Marw went out to meet Makhlad, but Wakīʿ held back from going out until ʿAmr al-Azdī forced him to go out. When they reached Makhlad, all of the soldiers dismounted, except for Wakīʿ, Muḥammad b. Ḥumrān al-Saʿdī, and ʿAbbād b. Laqīṭ, one of the Banū Qays b. Thaʿlabah. Eventually, however, they were forced to dismount. When Makhlad reached Marw he put Wakīʿ in prison and tortured him, and he seized his followers and tortured them. This took place prior to the arrival of his father.

According to ʿAlī—Kulayb b. Khalaf—Idrīs b. Ḥanẓalah: When Makhlad reached Khurāsān, he put me in prison, whereupon Ibn al-Ahtam came to me, saying, "Do you want to save yourself?" I said, "Yes." He said, "Take out the letters that al-Qaʿqāʿ b. Khulayd al-ʿAbsī and Khuraym b. ʿAmr al-Murrī wrote to Qutaybah about throwing off allegiance to Sulaymān." I asked him, "O Ibn al-Ahtam, are you tricking me out of my religion?" Then Ibn al-Ahtam called for some papyrus and said, "You are a fool." He wrote letters to Qutaybah in the name of al-Qaʿqāʿ and certain men from the Qays, saying, "Al-Walīd b. ʿAbd al-Malik has just died, and Sulaymān will send this Mazūnī[136] to Khurāsān. So renounce your allegiance to Sulaymān." I said, "O Ibn al-Ahtam, by God, you are destroying yourself. By God, if I enter into his presence, I will surely tell him that the letters were written by you."

In this year, Yazīd b. al-Muhallab went to Khurāsān as its governor.

According to ʿAlī b. Muḥammad—Abū al-Sarī al-Azdī—his paternal uncle: After Qutaybah was slain, Wakīʿ served as governor of Khurāsān for nine or ten months. Yazīd b. al-Muhallab arrived

---

136. Mazūnī refers to an ʿUmānī or southern Arab; Mazūn is one of the names of ʿUmān. See Yāqūt, *Muʿjam*, V, 122. The allusion is to Yazīd b. al-Muhallab.

in the year 97/715–16. According to ʿAlī—al-Mufaḍḍal b. Muḥammad—his father: Yazīd drew near to himself the army of Syria[137] and a group from the army of Khurāsān. (With respect to this,) Nahār b. Tawsiʿah recited:

> We never expected from any governor
>   what we expected from Yazīd.
> But we were wrong about him and it has been our custom
>   to abstain from dealing with the unworthy.
> If a governor did not give us justice,
>   we set out toward him like lions.
> So gently, O Yazīd, come back to us,
>   and let aside the company of slaves.
> We come, but you turn away from us,
>   although we send greetings from afar.
> And we return disappointed, without any gifts.
>   What is the reason for the sour face and aversion?

According to ʿAlī—Ziyād b. al-Rabīʿ—Ghālib al-Qaṭṭān: I saw ʿUmar b. ʿAbd al-ʿAzīz standing at ʿArafāt[138] during the Caliphate of Sulaymān—Sulaymān had performed the pilgrimage that year—saying to ʿAbd al-ʿAzīz b. ʿAbdallāh b. Khālid b. Asīd, "How strange that the Commander of the Faithful appointed (such) a man as governor of the Muslims' best frontier post! I have learned from one of the merchants coming from that direction that that governor gives one of his slave girls a stipend equal to that of a thousand soldiers. By God, the Caliph's appointment of him as governor was not done for the sake of God!" Knowing that ʿUmar was referring to Yazīd and the Juhanī woman,[139] I said to him, "He is rewarding them for their tribulations during the war against the Azāriqah."[140]

---

137. The Syrian government troops had been kept away from Khurāsān by al-Ḥajjāj, who employed them exclusively in India. See Wellhausen, *Arab Kingdom*, 446.

138. ʿArafāt is a plain about twenty-one km. east of Mecca; it is the site of the central ceremonies of the annual Pilgrimage. See *EI²*, s.v. ʿArafa.

139. The Juhanī woman was Yazīd b. al-Muhallab's concubine.

140. The Azāriqah were a Khārijite sect named after their leader, Nāfiʿ b. al-Azraq, who maintained that all adversaries should be put to death with their wives and children. The Azāriqah were defeated by Yazīd's father, al-Muhallab b. Abī Ṣufrah, in 78/692, after several years of fighting. See *EI²*, s.v. Azāriḳa; Dixon, *The Umayyad Caliphate*, 181.

Our source continued: Yazīd bestowed a gift upon ʿAbd al-Malik b. Sallām al-Salūlī, whereupon the latter recited:

Your copious rain, O Yazīd, kept falling on my need[141]
    until my thirst was quenched, and your generosity cannot
    be denied.
You are the spring by means of which, when starvation
    prevails,
    the sick and the destitute live.
[1314] The cloud of spring has spread over all your lands,
    so they drank their fill; and rain-bearing clouds yielded
    copious rain.
May God send you, wherever you are, a cloud full
    of rain, every evening and every morning.[142]

In this year, Sulaymān b. ʿAbd al-Malik led the pilgrimage. I was told that by Aḥmad b. Thābit—his source—Isḥāq b. ʿĪsā—Abū Maʿshar.

In this year, Sulaymān dismissed Ṭalḥah b. Dāwūd al-Haḍramī as governor of Mecca.[143]

According to al-Wāqidī—Ibrāhīm b. Nāfiʿ—Ibn Abī Mulaykah: When Sulaymān b. ʿAbd al-Malik returned from the pilgrimage, he dismissed Ṭalḥah b. Dāwūd al-Haḍramī as governor of Mecca after the latter had served in office for six months, and he appointed in his place ʿAbd al-ʿAzīz b. ʿAbdallāh b. Khālid b. Asīd b. Abī al-ʿĪṣ b. Umayyah b. ʿAbd Shams b. ʿAbd Manāf.

The governors of the garrison towns in this year were the same as they had been in the previous year, with the exception of Khurāsān, where Yazīd b. al-Muhallab was responsible for military, fiscal, and religious affairs. His representative in al-Kūfah—according to some—was Ḥarmalah b. ʿUmayr al-Lakhmī, who served for a few months, after which he was dismissed; he was replaced by Bashīr b. Ḥassān al-Nahdī.

---

141. Text: ḥawbah, which means the same as ḥājah.
142. See Kūfī, Futūḥ, VII, 285.
143. But see text above, II/1305, sub anno 96.

The
Events of the Year

98
(August 25, 716—August 13, 717)

Maslamah b. ʿAbd al-Malik Besieges Constantinople

Among the events which took place that year: Sulaymān b. ʿAbd al-Malik sent his brother, Maslamah b. ʿAbd al-Malik, to Constantinople, and ordered him to stay there until he either conquered the city or received Sulaymān's order to return. So he spent the winter and the summer there.[144]

According to Muḥammad b. ʿUmar—Thawr b. Yazīd—Sulaymān b. Mūsā: When Maslamah approached Constantinople, he ordered every horseman to load two *mudds*[145] of food on the back of his horse so that he might bring it to Constantinople. Upon his command, the food was heaped as high as certain mountains. Then Maslamah said to the Muslims, "Do not eat any of this food; rather, attack their lands and sow for yourselves." He built houses made of wood and passed the winter in them. The soldiers

[1315]

---

144. See Yaʿqūbī, *Taʾrīkh*, III, 44; Kūfī, *Futūḥ*, VII, 298–306; *FHA*, 25ff.; Ibn Kathīr, *Bidāyah*, IX, 174–75; Maqdisī, *Badʾ*, VI, 43–44.

145. Text: *muddayn*. The Cairo ed. has *mudyayn*. A *mudd* is a dry measure for grain, used in Syria and Egypt. See Ṭabarī, *Glossary*, CDLXXXII; Hinz, *Islamische Masse*, 45–47.

cultivated the land, while the aforementioned food remained in the desert, totally exposed; the soldiers ate what they obtained from raiding and, later, from what they had sown. Maslamah remained, besieging Constantinople and oppressing its inhabitants; he was accompanied by the most illustrious commanders of the Syrian army: Khālid b. Maʿdān, ʿAbdallāh b. Abī Zakariyyāʾ al-Khuzāʿī, and Mujāhid b. Jabr. He remained there until he learned of Sulaymān's death. A poet recited:

> It carries her two *mudd*s and the two *mudd*s of Maslamah.

According to Aḥmad b. Zuhayr—ʿAlī b. Muḥammad: When Sulaymān became Caliph he raided the Byzantines, setting up camp in Dābiq[146] and sending Maslamah ahead. The Byzantines feared him. Leo[147] came up from Armenia[148] and said to Maslamah, "Send someone to negotiate with me." Maslamah sent Ibn Hubayrah, who asked Leo, "What do you consider to be the height of stupidity?" He replied, "The man who fills his stomach with everything that he finds."[149] Ibn Hubayrah said to him, "We are men of religion, and our religion calls for obedience to our leaders." Leo said, "You are right. In the past, we used to fight one another and get angry for the sake of religion. Today, however, we fight for the sake of conquest and sovereignty. (But, if you withdraw) we will give you one dīnār for the head of every (soldier who leaves)." Ibn Hubayrah returned to the Byzantines the next day and said, "Maslamah does not accept your terms. I approached him after he had eaten the morning meal, filled his stomach, and taken a nap. When he woke up, he was groggy[150] and did not understand what I said."

The Byzantine commanders said to Leo, "If you rid us of Maslamah, we will make you emperor." And they bound themselves to him by the oath. Then Leo came to Maslamah and said, "The

[1316]

---

146. A village in the ʿAzāz district north of Aleppo, situated on the edge of a plain where the Umayyad armies prepared for their annual summer raids into Byzantine Anatolia. See *EI²*, s.v. Dābiḳ.

147. Leo III, the Isaurian.

148. See *EI²*, s.v. Armīniya.

149. This saying is an allusion to Sulaymān, who reportedly consumed one hundred *raṭl* of food daily. See Masʿūdī, *Murūj* (Beirut), III, 175; *FHA*, 34; Ibn Kathīr, *Bidāyah*, IX, 180.

150. Literally, this means, "The phlegm had overcome him."

people (of Constantinople) know that you will not advance against them in a bold attack and that you intend to prolong the siege as long as you have food. But if you were to burn the food, they would submit." So Maslamah burned it. Then the enemy became strong, while the Muslims entered into dire straits until they were on the point of death. This was their situation until Sulaymān died.

When Sulaymān b. ʿAbd al-Malik set up camp in Dābiq, he swore to God that he would not leave until the army that he had sent against the Byzantines entered Constantinople.

When the Byzantine emperor died, Leo came to (Sulaymān), gave him the news, and assured him that he would deliver the land of the Byzantines (to the Caliph). So the latter sent Maslamah with Leo, and Maslamah set up camp there, collected all the food around Constantinople, and laid siege to the city. But Leo went to the inhabitants of the city, who made him emperor. He then wrote to Maslamah informing him of what had taken place and asking him to allow enough food to enter the city to feed the people; in this way, the people would believe that his word and Maslamah's word were one and that they were safe from being captured and expelled from their lands; he also asked Maslamah to give them permission to gather food one night. Meanwhile, Leo had prepared ships and men. Maslamah agreed to his request, and the inhabitants of the city carried away large quantities of food from those enclosures in a single night. At this point, Leo began to act in a hostile manner, having deceived Maslamah by means of a trick that would shame even a woman. The Muslim army suffered what no army had suffered previously, to the extent that a soldier was afraid to leave camp by himself. They ate animals, skins, tree roots, leaves—indeed, everything [1317] except dirt. Meanwhile, Sulaymān, who was residing in Dābiq, was unable to send reinforcements due to the arrival of winter. This was the situation until Sulaymān died.[151]

In this year, Sulaymān b. ʿAbd al-Malik had the oath of allegiance taken to his son, Ayyūb b. Sulaymān, making him his heir apparent.[152]

According to ʿUmar b. Shabbah—ʿAlī b. Muḥammad: ʿAbd al-

---

151. For the Byzantine perspective, see *The Chronicle of Theophanes*, 82–90.
152. See Yaʿqūbī, *Taʾrīkh*, III, 43; Ibn Kathīr, *Bidāyah*, IX, 175.

Malik had charged al-Walīd and Sulaymān to take the oath of allegiance on behalf of Ibn ʿĀtikah,[153] and to Marwān b. ʿAbd al-Malik after him.

According to Ṭāriq b. al-Mubārak: Marwān b. ʿAbd al-Malik died during the Caliphate of Sulaymān, on his way out of Mecca, whereupon Sulaymān took the oath of allegiance on behalf of Ayyūb. He withheld (the nomination) from Yazīd, waiting for something bad to happen to him and hoping that he would die. But (it was) Ayyūb (who) died while he was heir apparent.

In this year, the city of the Slavs[154] was conquered.

According to Muḥammad b. ʿUmar: In the year 98/716–717, Burjān[155] attacked Maslamah b. ʿAbd al-Malik when he was short of men. Sulaymān b. ʿAbd al-Malik dispatched either Masʿadah or ʿAmr b. Qays with reinforcements, but the Slavs tricked them. Then God put them to flight after they had slain Sharāḥīl (b. ʿAbd) b. ʿAbdah.[156]

According to what has been claimed by al-Wāqidī, in this year al-Walīd b. Hishām and ʿAmr b. Qays carried out a raid in which some soldiers from the army of Antioch were killed. Al-Walīd killed people living on the outskirts of Byzantium, taking many of them captive.

[The Conquest of Jurjān and Ṭabaristān][157]

In this year, Yazīd b. al-Muhallab raided Jurjān[158] and Ṭabaristān.[159]

---

153. Ibn ʿĀtikah is Yazīd b. ʿAbd al-Malik, whose mother was ʿAtikah bt. Yazīd b. Muʿāwiyah b. Abī Sufyān.

154. The city of the Slavs was a city immediately beyond the Byzantine border. See *EI²*, s.v. Slavs.

155. Burjān is the name of the most important Bulghār state and its inhabitants. See *EI²*, s.v. Bulghār.

156. Sharāḥīl is Abū ʿĀmir al-Shaʿbī. The words within parentheses (b. ʿAbd) are added by the Cairo ed.

157. The text lacks the rubric, which is supplied by the Cairo ed. See Ibn Khayyāṭ, *Taʾrīkh*, I, 319–20; Balādhurī, *Futūḥ* (Cairo), II, 412–17; Yaʿqūbī, *Taʾrīkh*, III, 41; Kūfī, *Futūḥ*, VII, 286–98; Maqdisī, *Badʾ*, VI, 42–43; FHA, 21–24; Ibn Kathīr, *Bidāyah*, IX, 175–76; Wellhausen, *Arab Kingdom*, 446–48.

158. Jurjān is a province situated at the southeastern corner of the Caspian Sea. See *EI²*, s.v. Gurgān; Le Strange, *Lands*, 376–81.

159. Ṭabaristān is a Persian province north of Mount Alburz, called "the land of Ṭabar" because of the thick forests that cover the country. See *EI*, s.v. Ṭabaristān; Le Strange, *Lands*, 368–76.

According to Hishām b. Muḥammad—Abū Mikhnaf: Yazīd b. al-Muhallab reached Khurāsān, where he remained for three or four months; then he advanced toward Dihistān[160] and Jurjān, sending his son, Makhlad, to serve (as deputy governor) over Khurāsān. When he reached Dihistān, which was inhabited by a tribe of Turks, he established himself there and besieged its inhabitants. With him were the armies of al-Kūfah, al-Baṣrah, and Syria, together with the leading men from the armies of Khurāsān and al-Rayy.[161] He had one hundred thousand soldiers, not including clients, slave soldiers, and irregular volunteers.[162] The Muslims attacked the enemy, quickly putting them to flight and causing them to return to their fortress. Later, they would emerge from time to time and fight with intensity. [1318]

Jahm and Jamāl, the two sons of Zaḥr, had a favored position with Yazīd, who honored them. Muḥammad b. ʿAbd al-Raḥmān b. Abī Sabrah al-Juʿfī was an eloquent and courageous man, except for the fact that he used to corrupt himself with drink. However, it was not his custom to visit Yazīd and his household frequently. Perhaps the good influence they had on the two sons of Zaḥr, Jahm and Jamāl, kept him away. Now, when the herald would cry out, "O ye horsemen of God, mount up and rejoice at the good news," Muḥammad b. ʿAbd al-Raḥmān b. Abī Sabrah would be the first horseman from among the troops to hasten to the brunt of battle. One day, the call went out to the soldiers, and Ibn Abī Sabrah preceded all the others. He was standing on a mound when ʿUthmān b. al-Mufaḍḍal passed by him and said, "O Ibn Abī Sabrah, I have never been able to beat you to the muster." He replied, "What good is that to me, when you prefer the boys of the Madhḥij and ignore the worth of the elderly men of experience and prowess?" He said, "Had you wanted what we have, we would not have withheld from you what you deserve." [1319]

Our source continued: The troops went out and fought with

---

160. A rich agricultural region located to the north of the lower Atrek. Its capital, Akhūr, was a four-day journey to the north of Jurjān, on the road to Khwārazm. See *EI²*, s.v. Dihistān; Le Strange, *Lands*, 379–80.

161. The capital of al-Jibāl; its ruins can be seen five miles south-southeast of modern Tehran. See Yāqūt, *Muʿjam*, III, 116–22; *EI*, s.v. Raiy; Le Strange, *Lands*, 214–17.

162. Text: *wa-l-mutaṭawwiʿīn*. On these unpaid and/or irregular volunteers, see Crone, *Slaves*, 53.

intensity. Muḥammad b. Abī Sabrah attacked a Turk, whom the other soldiers had avoided. They exchanged blows, and the Turk's sword became fixed in Ibn Abī Sabrah's helmet. But Ibn Abī Sabrah struck him dead. Then he advanced, bloody sword in hand, with the Turk's sword stuck in his helmet, and the soldiers witnessed the finest spectacle that they had ever seen on the part of a horseman. When Yazīd saw the glitter of the two swords, the helmet, and the armor, he asked, "Who is that?" They answered, "Ibn Abī Sabrah." He said, "How excellent a father who gave birth to such a son![163] What a man he would be, were it not for the fact that he drinks to excess!"

Subsequently, Yazīd went out one day, seeking a place from which he might attack the enemy. Suddenly, a band of Turks attacked him from out of nowhere. With him at the time were the leading soldiers and their horsemen. He had approximately four hundred men, while the enemy had approximately four thousand. After fighting the Turks for a while, Yazīd's men said to him, "O Commander, leave and we will fight for you." But he refused. Yazīd himself engaged in the fighting on that day, like one of his soldiers. Ibn Abī Sabrah, the two sons of Zaḥr, al-Ḥajjāj b. Jāriyah al-Khathʿamī, and his most distinguished followers fought valiantly. Finally, when they wanted to leave, Yazīd put al-Ḥajjāj b. Jāriyah in charge of the rear guard; he fought those who were behind him until the others reached water, for they were thirsty. They drank, and the enemy moved away without gaining anything from them.

Sufyān b. Ṣafwān al-Khathʿamī recited:

[1320]
Were it not for Ibn Jāriyah, the white-faced one,
    you would have been given a bitter cup to drink.
He protected you with his horsemen and his horses
    until you reached water, unafflicted.

Then Yazīd persisted in the siege, stationing the troops on every side of the city,[164] thereby cutting off its supplies. When the Turks tired and were unable to fight the Muslims, for the

---

163. Text: *lillāhi abūhu*, which means, to God alone belongs the power to create the likes of this man from whom has proceeded this wonderful action. See Lane, *Lexicon*, pt. 1, p. 11.
164. Probably the city of Dihistan.

siege and trial weighed heavily on them, Ṣūl, the *dihqān*[165] of
Dihistān, sent to Yazīd, saying, "I will make peace with you on
the condition that you provide safe-conduct for me, for the members of my household, and for my animals, in which case, I will
deliver the city to you, together with its contents and its inhabitants." Yazīd made peace with Ṣūl, who submitted to him; he
carried out the agreement. He entered the city and seized the
animals, treasures, and numberless captives, and put to the sword
fourteen thousand defenseless Turks. He wrote about this to Sulaymān b. ʿAbd al-Malik.

Then he set out, making his way to Jurjān. Now, it had been
customary for the Jurjānīs to pay the army of al-Kūfah one hundred thousand, two hundred thousand, and sometimes even three
hundred thousand (dirhams) in return for peace. These were the
terms upon which they would make peace with them. When
Yazīd came to them, they presented themselves to him with the
peace treaty, for they regarded him with awe, and they offered
him more than they were accustomed to paying. He appointed a
man from the Azd by the name of Asad b. ʿAbdallāh as their
governor.

Yazīd then entered the territory of the *ispahbadh* in Ṭabaristān,
accompanied by laborers who cut down trees and smoothed the
roads. Finally, they reached him, and Yazīd set up camp, besieging the *ispahbadh* and occupying his land. The *ispahbadh* sued
Yazīd for peace, offering him more than it was his custom to pay.
But Yazīd refused, hoping to conquer the land by force. One day,
he sent out his brother, Abū ʿUyaynah, leading the armies of al-
Kūfah and al-Baṣrah; he climbed into the mountains making his
way toward the *ispahbadh*. Meanwhile, the *ispahbadh* had sent
to Daylam, summoning additional military forces. The two armies met in battle, and the Muslims prevailed over them for a   [1321]
while, putting them to flight. When the chief of al-Daylam[166]
came forward, challenging the Muslims, Ibn Abī Sabrah went out
to engage him in combat and he slew him. The rout continued

---

165. The *dihqān* was the village head and a member of the lesser feudal nobility
of Sassanian Persia who, after the Arab conquest, continued to be responsible for
local administration and the collection of tribute. In Transoxiana, the local rulers
were designated by the term *dihqān*. See *EI*², s.v. Dihḳān.

166. The chief of Daylam is identified by Kūfī (*Futūḥ*, VII, 290) as Sulaymān al-
Daylamī.

until the Muslims reached the opening of the mountain pass. As they began their ascent, the enemy soldiers, who were looking down on them, opened fire on them with arrows and stones. The soldiers fled from the opening of the mountain pass without suffering great losses, for the enemy did not have the strength to pursue them and search for them. But the Muslims began to press on one another, to the point that they began to fall over one another into the ravines, and the men rolled from the top of the mountain until they reached Yazīd's army, oblivious to their misfortune.[167]

Yazīd held his ground, unperturbed. Meanwhile, the *iṣpahbadh* wrote to the army of Jurjān, asking them to attack Yazīd's followers and to cut off his supplies and the roads between him and the Arabs, and promising to compensate them for their efforts. Accordingly, they fell upon the Muslims that Yazīd had left behind, slaying those that they could. The survivors assembled and fortified themselves in a secluded spot, where they remained until Yazīd rescued them. Yazīd continued to press against the *iṣpahbadh* in his land until he made peace with him in return for seven hundred thousand dirhams, four hundred thousand in cash,[168] two hundred thousand (garments),[169] four hundred donkeys loaded with saffron, and four hundred slaves; on the head of each slave, he requested a cloak, and on the cloak a scarf, a silver cup, and a piece of fine white silk[170]—previously they had sued for peace in exchange for two hundred thousand dirhams. Then Yazīd and his followers left, looking as if they had been defeated! Had it not been for the actions of the Jurjānīs, he would not have [1322] left Ṭabaristān until he had conquered it by force.

As for sources other than Abū Mikhnaf on the subject of the encounter between Yazīd and the Jurjānīs: According to Aḥmad b. Zuhayr—ʿAlī b. Muḥammad—Kulayb b. Khalaf and others: Saʿīd b. al-ʿĀṣ[171] made peace with the people of Jurjān.[172] Subse-

---

167. Text: *sharr*, which may also mean "danger."
168. Text: *naqdan*. Ibn Kathīr, *Bidāyah*, IX, 176, has *dīnārs*.
169. The text states "two hundred thousand." Ibn Kathīr, *Bidāyah*, IX, 176, adds the word *thawb*, "garments."
170. See Balādhurī, *Futūḥ* (Cairo), II, 414.
171. Saʿīd b. al-ʿĀṣ died in 59/768–9. See *EI*, s.v. Saʿīd b. al-ʿĀṣ.
172. For further details on the initial conquest of Jurjān, see Balādhurī, *Futūḥ* (Cairo), II, 411.

quently, however, they refused to pay and violated their treaty.[173] No Muslim went to Jurjān after Saʿīd, for they blocked that road. Indeed, no one could travel the Khurāsān road from that direction except in fear and dread of the Jurjānīs. This was the road to Khurāsān from Fārs[174] to Kirmān. The first person to traverse the road from Qūmis[175] was Qutaybah b. Muslim, when he became governor of Khurāsān. Then Maṣqalah raided Khurāsān, in the days of Muʿāwiyah, leading ten thousand soldiers. But he was slain when his army was in Rūyān,[176] which is adjacent to Ṭabaristān. They died in one of the wādīs of that region when the enemy attacked them in the mountain passes, killing all of them. Therefore, it is called "Maṣqalah's Wādī." Our source said: He is the one referred to in the proverb, "Until Maṣqalah returns from Ṭabaristān."[177]

According to ʿAlī—Kulayb b. Khalaf al-ʿAmmī—Ṭufayl b. Mirdās al-ʿAmmī and Idrīs b. Ḥanzalah: Saʿīd b. al-ʿĀṣ concluded a peace treaty with the people of Jurjān. Sometimes they would bring one hundred thousand (dirhams) and say, "This is our settlement." And sometimes two hundred thousand, and sometimes three hundred thousand. Sometimes they would pay one of these amounts; at other times they would refuse to pay. Then they refused to pay and violated the treaty.[178] They failed to pay the tribute until Yazīd b. al-Muhallab came to them, for no one opposed him when he reached Jurjān. When he made peace with Ṣūl and conquered al-Buḥayrah and Dihistān, he concluded a peace treaty with the people of Jurjān on the same terms they had received from Saʿīd b. al-ʿĀṣ.

[1323]

According to Aḥmad—ʿAlī—Kulayb b. Khalaf al-ʿAmmī—Ṭu-

---

173. The text specifies *wa-kafarū*, which literally means "and they turned away from Islam." But since the Jurjānīs had not become Muslims upon payment of the poll tax, the word *kafarū* here should be taken in the sense of *naqaḍū-l-ʿahd*, "they violated the treaty." I owe this point to Professor Abbas.

174. A Persian province bounded on the northwest by Khūzistān, on the northeast by Iṣfahān, on the east by Kirmān, and on the west and southwest by the Persian Gulf. See *EI²*, s.v. Fārs; Le Strange, *Lands*, 248–98.

175. A small province lying to the south of the Alburz chain watershed between al-Rayy and Nīshābūr. See *EI²*, s.v. Ḳūmis; Le Strange, *Lands*, 264–68.

176. Rūyān was an independent district attached to Ṭabaristān. See *EI*, s.v. Rūyān; Yāqūt, *Muʿjam*, III, 104–5; Le Strange, *Lands*, 373–74.

177. See Balādhurī, *Futūḥ* (Cairo), II, 411–12.

178. See note 173 above.

fayl b. Mirdās and Bishr b. ʿĪsā—Abū Ṣafwān[179]—ʿAlī said (I was told this also by Abū Ḥafṣ al-Azdī—Sulaymān b. Kathīr, and others): Ṣūl the Turk used to camp at Dihistān and at al-Buḥayrah, an island in the (Caspian) sea five *farsakhs* (30 km.) from Dihistān, both of which were part of Jurjān, on the side of Khwārazm. Ṣūl used to carry out raids against Fayrūz b. Qūl, the Marzubān of Jurjān—they were twenty-five *farsakhs* (150 km.) apart—during which he would kill their noble men and then return to al-Buḥayrah and Dihistān. Now, a dispute broke out between Fayrūz and one of his paternal cousins, who was called, "the Marzubān," as a result of which the Marzubān separated himself from Fayrūz and settled in al-Bayāsān.[180] Fearing that the Turks would carry out raids against him, Fayrūz set out for Yazīd b. al-Muhallab in Khurāsān. Meanwhile, Ṣūl seized Jurjān. When Fayrūz reached Yazīd b. al-Muhallab, the latter asked him, "Why have you come here?" Fayrūz replied, "I was afraid of Ṣūl, so I fled." Yazīd asked him, "Is there any stratagem we might use to fight him?" Fayrūz answered, "Yes, there is one thing which, if you attain it, either you will kill him or he will submit." Yazīd asked, "What is it?" Fayrūz counseled, "If he leaves Jurjān in order to establish camp in al-Buḥayrah, and then you come to him there and lay siege to the island, you will be victorious over him. Therefore, write a letter to the *ispahbadh* in which you ask him to trick Ṣūl by having him remain in Jurjān. Pay him something for this and promise him more. He will then send your letter to Ṣūl, seeking to ingratiate himself with him, because he regards him with great honor. As a result, Ṣūl will leave Jurjān and set up camp in al-Buḥayrah."

[1324]   Yazīd b. al-Muhallab therefore wrote to the leader of Ṭabaristān: "I intend to carry out a raid against Ṣūl while he is in Jurjān, but I fear that if he learns of my intention he will leave for al-Buḥayrah and set up camp there. If he does go there, I will not be able to attack him. Now, he listens to you and considers you to be a faithful adviser. If you were to confine him in Jurjān this year, so that he would not go to al-Buḥayrah, I will convey to you fifty

---

179. Text: Ṣafwān. The Cairo ed. specifies Abū Ṣafwān.
180. A village in Marw al-Shāhijān. See Yāqūt, *Muʿjam*, I, 528.

thousand mithqāls.[181] So devise some stratagem to keep him in
Jurjān, for, if he stays there, he will be mine." When the
ispahbadh saw the letter, he sought to ingratiate himself with Şūl
by sending the letter to him. When the letter arrived, Şūl ordered
the troops to depart for al-Buḥayrah; he loaded foodstuffs so that
he would be secure there.

Yazīd learned that Şūl had traveled from Jurjān to al-Buḥayrah;
he determined to leave for Jurjān. He set out, leading thirty thousand men, accompanied by Fayrūz b. Qūl. He appointed Makhlad
b. Yazīd as his deputy in Khurāsān, designated his son, Muʿāwiyah
b. Yazīd, as his deputy in Samarqand, Kiss,[182] Nasaf,[183] and
Bukhārā, and appointed Ḥātim b. Qabīṣah b. al-Muhallab as his
deputy in Ṭukhāristān.[184] He marched to Jurjān which, at that
time, was not a city, but rather a locality surrounded by mountains, with gates and rugged roads[185]—when a man stood at one of
the gates, no one could advance against him. Yazīd entered Jurjān
without encountering any resistance and he captured great wealth.
The Marzubān fled, and Yazīd set out, with his soldiers, for al-
Buḥayrah, where he laid siege to Şūl.

When he attacked them, he recited:

The sword flashed and his hands trembled;
    By him, himself, souls were saved.

Our source continued: He besieged them. Şūl would come out
toward him during the day and fight, and then return to his fortress. With Yazīd were the armies of al-Kūfah and al-Baṣrah.

Then he mentioned the story of Jahm b. Zaḥr and his brother,
and Muḥammad (b. Abī Sabrah), more or less as was reported by

---

181. A unit of weight for gold, taken over by ʿAbd al-Malik from the Roman
solidus of the Constantinian system, equivalent to 65.6 grains or 4.25 grams.
"Mithqāl" is used as a synonym for "dīnār." See *EI*, s.v. Mithḳāl.

182. A town near Samarqand. See Yāqūt, *Muʿjam*, IV, 460.

183. A town in the district of Bukhārā. See *EI*, s.v. Nakhshab; Yāqūt, *Muʿjam*, V,
285.

184. Ṭukhāristān was the region situated between Balkh and Badakhshān. See
EI², s.v. Badakhshān.

185. See Balādhurī *Futūḥ* (Cairo), II, 413: "Surrounded by a wall of baked bricks
that reached to the sea." See also Kūfī, *Futūḥ*, VII, 286; *FHA*, 21; Ibn al-Athīr,
Kāmil, V, 29.

[1325]   Hishām, except that he said, regarding the Turk's striking of Ibn Abī Sabrah: "The Turk's sword became caught in Ibn Abī Sabrah's shield."[186]

According to ʿAlī b. Muḥammad—ʿAlī b. Mujāhid—ʿAnbasah: Muḥammad b. Abī Sabrah fought the Turks in Jurjān. They surrounded him, taking turns against him with their swords. Three swords broke in his hand.

Then, returning to our original chain of transmission, our source said: They, that is, the Turks, were under siege for six months, during which time they would emerge, fight, and then return to their fortress.[187] Finally, they were reduced to drinking ground water, whereupon they were afflicted with a disease known as *al-suʾād*[188] and began to die. At this point Ṣūl sued for peace, but Yazīd b. al-Muhallab said, "No, not unless he submits to my rule." Ṣūl refused and sent a message to Yazīd, saying: "I will make peace with you on behalf of myself, my belongings, and three hundred members of my household and companions, on the condition that you provide safe passage for me. If you accept these terms, you may occupy al-Buḥayrah." Yazīd agreed to these terms, and Ṣūl emerged with his belongings and three hundred of his favorites and joined Yazīd. Then Yazīd put to the sword fourteen thousand defenseless Turks, letting the others go without killing any of them. The soldiers said to Yazīd, "Give us our stipends," so he summoned Idrīs b. Ḥanẓalah al-ʿAmmī, saying, "O Ibn Ḥanẓalah, give us an account of al-Buḥayrah's wealth so that we may pay the troops." Idrīs entered al-Buḥayrah, but he was unable to estimate the value of its wealth. He said to Yazīd, "I am unable to assess its wealth because it is stored in receptacles. We will have to count the sacks, make a sign indicating the contents of each sack, and say to the soldiers, 'Enter and take.' In this way, when someone takes something, we will announce what he took, that is, wheat, barley, rice, sesame, and honey." At that, Yazīd said, "That is a good idea." They determined the

---

186. See text above, II/1319, where it is stated that the sword became stuck in Ibn Abī Sabrah's helmet.

187. Wellhausen argues that the siege could not have lasted six months. See *Arab Kingdom*, 447, n. 1.

188. A disease that attacks the liver as a result of drinking brackish water. See Lane, *Lexicon*, pt. 4, p. 1462.

number of sacks, put a sign on each sack indicating its contents,   [1326]
and said to the soldiers, "Take." As each man left al-Buḥayrah,
having taken clothing, food, or whatever could be carried away,
the number of sacks he had taken would be recorded in his name.
They took considerable amounts.

According to ʿAlī—Abū Bakr al-Hudhalī: Shahr b. Ḥawshab,[189]
who was in charge of Yazīd b. al-Muhallab's coffers, was accused
of stealing a leather purse.[190] Yazīd asked him about it, and Shahr
brought it to him. Then Yazīd summoned the person who had
made the accusation, rebuked him, and said to Shahr, "It's
yours." Shahr said, "I have no need for it."

The following was recited by al-Quṭāmī al-Kalbī[191]—some say
by Sinān b. Mukammal al-Numayrī:

Shahr sold his religion for a purse of leather.
   Now who will trust the Qur'ān reciters[192] after you, O
   Shahr?
You received for it something insignificant and sold it
   to Ibn Jūnabūdh. Verily, this is perfidy.

Murrah al-Nakhaʿī recited, with regard to Shahr:

O Ibn al-Muhallab, what did you have in mind for a man
   who,[193]
   were it not for you, would have been an upright reciter (of
   the Qur'ān)?

According to ʿAlī—Abū Muḥammad al-Thaqafī: Yazīd b. al-
Muhallab acquired a crown in Jurjān in which there was a pre-
cious stone and he asked, "Do you know anyone who would not
desire this crown?" They replied, "No." Yazīd then summoned
Muḥammad b. Wāsiʿ al-Azdī and said, "Take this crown—it's
yours." He said, "I have no need for it." Yazīd said, "I insist." So
Muḥammad took it and left. Then Yazīd ordered someone to

---

189. Abū Saʿīd Shahr b. Ḥawshab al-Ashʿarī (d. 111 or 112/730 or 731), a Syrian
transmitter of *ḥadīth*. See Ibn Ḥajar al-ʿAsqalānī, *Tahdhīb*, IV, 369–72.
190. Ibn Kathīr, *Bidāyah*, IX, 176, adds: "With one hundred dīnārs in it."
191. Al-Ḥusayn b. Jammāl b. Ḥabīb al-Quṭāmī al-Kalbī, d. 101/720. See Sezgin,
GAS, II, 339; and *EI²*, s.v. al-Ḳuṭāmī.
192. Text: *al-qurrāʾ*, which could also mean "officials." See note 408 below.
193. Text: *mā aradta ilā-mriʾin*.

observe what he would do with the crown. Muḥammad met a beggar and gave it to him. Yazīd's agent took the beggar, brought him to Yazīd, and told him what had happened. Yazīd took the crown and gave the beggar a large sum of money in return.

According to ʿAlī: Every time that Qutaybah made a new conquest, Sulaymān b. ʿAbd al-Malik would say to Yazīd b. al-Muhallab, "Don't you see what God is accomplishing through Qutaybah?" Yazīd would reply, "What about Jurjān, which separated the soldiers from the 'Main Road,'[194] and thus disrupted things in Qūmis and Abrashahr?"[195] Yazīd would also say, "These conquests are nothing. Jurjān is what counts." Thus, when Yazīd b. al-Muhallab became governor, his sole ambition was to conquer Jurjān. It is said: Yazīd b. al-Muhallab had one hundred and twenty thousand fighting men, including sixty thousand soldiers from the Syrian army.

According to ʿAlī—the one who mentioned the Jurjān report—on their authority, supplemented by ʿAlī b. Mujāhid—Khālid b. Ṣubayḥ: After Yazīd b. al-Muhallab made peace with Ṣūl, he had a great desire to conquer Ṭabaristān. Having resolved to travel there, he designated ʿAbdallāh b. al-Muʿammar al-Yashkurī as his governor in al-Bayāsān and Dihistān, leaving him with four thousand men. Then he advanced toward the nearest parts of Jurjān, adjacent to Ṭabaristān. He designated Asad b. ʿAmr—or b. ʿAbdallāh b. al-Rubʿah—as his governor in Andarastān,[196] which is adjacent to Ṭabaristān, leaving him with four thousand men. Then Yazīd entered the lands of the *ispahbadh*, who sent to him, suing for peace and asking him to leave Ṭabaristān. But Yazīd refused, for he hoped to conquer it by force. He then sent his brother, Abū ʿUyaynah, in one direction, his son, Khālid b. Yazīd, in another, and Abū al-Jahm al-Kalbī in a third, saying, "When you join forces, Abū ʿUyaynah is to be in command of the troops." Yazīd said to Abū ʿUyaynah, as the latter set out leading the armies of

---

194. Text: *al-ṭarīq al-aʿẓam.* Kūfī, *Futūḥ,* VII, 287, has "Khurāsān" instead of "the Main Road."

195. Abrashahr, the ancient name of Nīshāpūr, was the capital of one of the four quarters of the province of Khurāsān. See *EI²,* s.v. Abrashahr; also *EI,* s.v. Ṭūs; Le Strange, *Lands,* 383.

196. A village in Khwārazm, about one day's march south of Jurjāniyyah. See Le Strange, *Lands,* 453.

al-Kūfah and al-Baṣrah, accompanied by Huraym b. Abī Ṭaḥmah, "Take counsel with Huraym, for he is a faithful adviser." Yazīd remained in the camp.

The *ispahbadh* sought support from the people of Jīlān and al-Daylam, and they came to him. The two opposing armies met near the foot of a mountain.[197] The polytheists were put to rout, and the Muslims pursued them until they reached the mouth of the mountain pass. But when the Muslims entered the passageway, the polytheists climbed up into the mountains, pursued by the Muslims. The enemy then shot at them with arrows and stones, putting Abū ʿUyaynah and the Muslims to flight. They pressed on one another, falling over one another from the mountain, not stopping until they reached Yazīd's troops. At this point, the enemy gave up the chase.

The *ispahbadh*, fearing the Muslims, wrote to the Marzubān, the paternal cousin of Fayrūz b. Qūl, who was at the farthest reaches of Jurjān, adjacent to al-Bayāsān, saying, "We have slain Yazīd [*sic*] and his followers,[198] so kill the Arabs in al-Bayāsān." The Marzubān and his men joined the army of Bayāsān, having reached a consensus to kill the Muslims, who were (carelessly asleep) in their dwellings. They were all slain during a single night. ʿAbdallāh b. al-Muʿammar was slain, together with four thousand Muslims—not one of them escaped; fifty of the Banū-l-ʿAmm were slain, among them al-Ḥusayn b. ʿAbd al-Raḥmān and Ismāʿīl b. Ibrāhīm b. Shammās. The Marzubān wrote to the *ispahbadh* that he should take control of the mountain passes and the roads.

When Yazīd learned that ʿAbdallāh b. al-Muʿammar and his followers had been slain, his men were distressed and frightened. Yazīd, therefore, sought the assistance of Ḥayyān al-Nabaṭī, saying, "Do not let the misunderstanding between us prevent you from serving the Muslims.[199] We have heard the news from Jurjān, where that one (that is, the *ispahbadh*) has seized control of   [1329]

---

197. Text: *fī sanad jabal*, "near the face of a mountain." The translation follows Ibn al-Athīr, *Kāmil*, V, 31, who specifies *fī safḥ jabal*, "near the foot of a mountain."

198. Text: *Yazīd wa-aṣḥābahu*. Balādhurī, *Futūḥ* (Cairo), II, 413, has *aṣḥāb Yazīd*, "Yazīd's followers," which makes better sense.

199. The misunderstanding will be explained below.

the roads, so make peace." Ḥayyān agreed and approached the *ispahbadh*, saying, "I am one of you, even if religion has separated us.[200] I will give you good advice, for you are dearer to me than Yazīd. He has summoned reinforcements, and his soldiers are nearby. Since the Jurjānīs eliminated only one segment of his army, I am concerned that you will not be able to withstand him. So relieve yourself from him and make peace with him, for, if you make peace with him, he will turn his weapons against the Jurjānīs,[201] who deceived and killed many Muslims." The *ispahbadh* made peace with Yazīd, agreeing to pay seven hundred thousand dirhams.

According to ʿAlī b. Mujāhid: The terms were five hundred thousand dirhams,[202] four hundred loads of saffron or their value in ready money, and four hundred slaves—each slave wearing a cloak and a scarf and carrying a silver vessel, a piece of silk cloth and a suit of clothes.[203]

Then Ḥayyān returned to Yazīd b. al-Muhallab, saying, "Send some people to carry away the terms of the agreement that I have concluded with them." He asked, "Who is paying, we or they?" He replied, "They are." Yazīd, who would have been happy to give them whatever they asked for and return to Jurjān, sent some people to carry away the terms of the agreement that Ḥayyān had worked out with them, and he set out for Jurjān. Previously, Yazīd had penalized Ḥayyān two hundred thousand dirhams. This was why he feared that Ḥayyān would not provide him with good counsel.

The circumstances of his having penalized Ḥayyān in this manner were related to me as follows by ʿAlī b. Mujāhid—Khālid b. Ṣubayḥ: I was serving as a tutor to Ḥayyān's son, when he summoned me, saying, "Write a letter to Makhlad b. Yazīd." Makhlad, at that particular time, was in Balkh, while Yazīd was in Marw. I took up a scroll of papyrus, and he said, "Write: 'From Ḥayyān, the client of Maṣqalah, to Makhlad b. Yazīd.'" But Mu-

[1330]

---

200. It is reported that Ḥayyān was originally from al-Daylam. See text above, II/1291.

201. Text: *ṣayyara ḥaddahu ʿalā ahl Jurjān.* Kufi, *Futūḥ*, VII, 292, has *yakūnu ḥarbuhu wa-saṭwatuhu ʿalayhim*, "His war and attack will be against them."

202. Ibn Khayyāṭ, *Taʾrīkh*, I, 320, mentions seven hundred thousand dirhams.

203. See text above, II/1321, for another version of the agreement.

qātil b. Ḥayyān gestured to me, indicating, "Don't write that."
Then he approached his father and said, "O my father! You write
to Makhlad and yet mention yourself first!" He said, "Yes, my
son, and if he does not like it he will suffer the same fate as
Qutaybah." Then he said to me, "Write." So I wrote. He had
Makhlad bring the letter to his father. This was why Yazīd made
Ḥayyān pay two hundred thousand dirhams.

In this year, Yazīd reconquered Jurjān after the Jurjānīs had
treacherously waylaid his army and broken the agreement.[204]

According to 'Alī—the group that transmitted to him the report
about Jurjān and Ṭabaristān: Then, when Yazīd made peace with
the army of Ṭabaristān, he headed for Jurjān. He swore to God
that if he triumphed over them, he would neither loosen his hold
on them nor raise the sword from them until he mixed blood into
the wheat, made bread out of the mixture, and ate the bread.

When the Marzubān learned that Yazīd had made peace with
the *ispahbadh* and was making his way toward Jurjān, he gathered his supporters and went to al-Wajāh,[205] where he fortified
himself. Whoever controls al-Wajāh needs no reserves of food or
water. Meanwhile, Yazīd arrived and surrounded the place, while
the Marzubān and his men fortified themselves inside. Al-Wajāh
was surrounded by dense thickets, so that only one way in and
out was known. Yazīd maintained the siege for seven months[206]
without making any progress against them, for he did not know of
any way to approach them except from the one side. The Marzubān and his men would emerge during the day, fight, and then
return to their fortress. Now, while matters were like this, it   [1331]
happened that a man—one of the Persians from Khurāsān who
was with Yazīd—went out to hunt, accompanied by members of
his Shākiriyyah corps.[207]

According to Hishām b. Muḥammad—Abū Mikhnaf: One of
his soldiers, from the tribe of Ṭayyi', went out to hunt and spotted
an antelope climbing in the mountains. He followed it, saying to
his companions, "Stay where you are." He climbed the mountain
following the tracks. Suddenly he came upon their army, where-

---

204. See Ibn Khayyāṭ, *Ta'rīkh*, I, 320–21; Ya'qūbī, *Ta'rīkh*, III, 41; *FHA*, 23.
205. Apparently, the name of a fortress in the mountainous region of Jurjān.
206. Kūfī, *Futūḥ*, VII, 293–94, specifies "four months."
207. On this term, see Wellhausen, *Arab Kingdom*, 496.

upon he turned back seeking his companions. Afraid that he would not be able to find his way back, he began to tear up his garment and tie markers on the trees. Finally, he reached his companions and then returned to the army camp. It is said: the man who was hunting was al-Hayyāj b. ʿAbd al-Raḥmān al-Azdī, a resident of Ṭūs[208] and an avid hunter. When he returned to the army camp, he approached ʿĀmir b. Aynam al-Wāshijī, who was the commander of Yazīd's guard. But they would not let him enter, so he cried out, "I have important information."

According to Hishām—Abū Mikhnaf: Finally, he brought the matter to the attention of the two sons of Zaḥr b. Qays, who took him and brought him to Yazīd. Al-Hayyāj gave him the report, and Yazīd gave him an assurance, confirmed by al-Juhaniyyah, a slave girl of his who had borne him a child,[209] to pay him an agreed-upon sum.

According to ʿAlī b. Muḥammad—his companions: Yazīd called for al-Hayyāj and asked, "What information do you have?" He replied, "Do you want to enter Wajāh without a fight?" He said, "Certainly." He said, "What will you give me?" He said, "Name [1332] your price." He said, "Four thousand." He said, "You are entitled to blood payment (diyah)."[210] He said, "Give me four thousand now and whatever you give me later will be a gratuity." Whereupon Yazīd gave an order to pay him four thousand dirhams. Then he called out to his soldiers, fourteen hundred of whom responded. Al-Hayyāj said, "Due to the density of the thickets, the path will not bear such a large group." Yazīd therefore chose three hundred and sent them off under the command of Jahm b. Zaḥr.

Some sources said: He put his son, Khālid b. Yazīd, in command of them, saying, "You may be deprived of life, but you cannot be deprived of death.[211] God help you if I see you in my presence after having been put to flight." He sent Jahm b. Zaḥr along with him. Yazīd asked the man who called out to the sol-

---

208. A district in Khurāsān containing the towns of Nawqān and Ṭābarān. See *EI*, s.v. Ṭūs; Le Strange, *Lands*, 388–90.

209. See text above, II/1313, sub anno 97.

210. A specified amount of money (either one thousand dīnārs or twelve thousand dirhams), or goods, due in cases of homicide or other injuries unjustly committed upon the person of another. See *EI²*, s.v. Diya.

211. Text: *in ghulibta ʿalā-l-ḥayāt fa-lā tughlibanna ʿalā-l-mawt*, that is, "Do not let fear of death dampen your courage."

diers, "When will you reach them?" He replied, "Tomorrow at noon, in the interval between the two prayers."[212] He said, "Go, with the blessing of God, and I will endeavor to engage them tomorrow at the time of the noon prayer." They set out. The next day, shortly before the time of the afternoon prayer, Yazīd ordered his men to set fire to some wood that he had collected and put into piles during the course of the siege. They set fire to the piles of wood, and before the sun had declined from the meridian, his army was surrounded by mountain-like flames of fire. When the enemy saw the fire, they were frightened by the magnitude of what they saw and they came out toward them. When the sun had declined from the meridian, Yazīd ordered his men to pray, and they combined the two prayers. Then they marched off toward them, and the two armies met in battle.

Meanwhile, the other contingent marched for the remainder of that day and the morrow, and attacked the Turk's army shortly before the time of the afternoon prayer. The Jurjānīs, engaged in combat with Yazīd on the one side, and, believing themselves to be secure on the other, did not sense anything until the moment when they heard the takbīr[213] behind them, whereupon they all headed for their fortress, with the Muslims in hot pursuit. They surrendered, submitting to Yazīd's rule. He captured their women and children and slew their soldiers, crucifying them at a distance of two farsakhs (12 km.) to the left and right of the road. He also drove twelve thousand of them to al-Andarhaz,[214] the Wādī of [1333] Jurjān,[215] and said, "Whoever seeks blood revenge from them may slay whomever he wishes." A single Muslim slew as many as four or five men in the wādī, turning the wādī's water into blood. There was a millstone by the wādī, and Yazīd was able to mix blood into the ground wheat, thereby releasing himself from his oath.[216] He ground wheat, made bread, ate, and built the city of Jurjān.

Some sources said: Yazīd killed forty thousand of the people of

---

212. The noon and midday prayers.
213. The takbīr is the formula "God is great." See *EI*, s.v. Takbīr.
214. Ibn Khayyāṭ, *Taʾrīkh*, I, 321, has al-Andar rather than al-Andarhaz.
215. The Wādī of Jurjān is the modern Gurgān river. See *EI²*, s.v. Gurgān; Le Strange, *Lands*, 376–77.
216. See text above, II/1330.

Jurjān. There had been no city there previously. Then he returned to Khurāsān, leaving Jahm b. Zaḥr al-Juʿfī as his governor of Jurjān.

According to Hishām b. Muḥammad–Abū Mikhnaf: Yazīd summoned Jahm b. Zaḥr and sent four hundred men with him. They began with the place to which they had been directed, having been instructed by Yazīd as follows: "When you reach the city, wait until daybreak, then pronounce the *takbīr* and proceed toward the city gate. You will find me there, having already rushed all of the men to the gate." Accordingly, when Ibn Zaḥr entered the city he waited until the hour at which Yazīd had ordered him to attack and then ordered his men to advance. They slew every single one of the guards that they encountered and pronounced the *takbīr*. The inhabitants of the city were filled with terror the likes of which they had never experienced previously. All of a sudden they saw the Muslims with them in their city pronouncing the *takbīr*, which astonished them. God cast terror in their hearts until they didn't know in which direction they were turning. However, one group of men—not a large one—advanced toward Jahm b. Zaḥr, and the two sides fought for a while. Jahm's hand was broken, but he and his men held their positions; it was not long before they killed most of them. When Yazīd b. al-Muhallab heard the *takbīr*, he drove the soldiers toward the gate, where they found that the guards had been drawn away by Jahm b. Zaḥr; thus, there was no one there to keep Yazīd from entering, or to put up serious resistance. He stormed the gate and entered the fortress at that very hour. He brought out the soldiers that were inside and, after erecting palm trunks at a distance of two *farsakh*s (12 km.) to the right and left of the road, he crucified them over the course of four *farsakh*s (24 km.). Yazīd then captured the inhabitants of the fortress and took possession of its contents.

[1334]

According to ʿAlī—his authorities: Yazīd wrote to Sulaymān b. ʿAbd al-Malik: "Now then, God has made a great conquest on behalf of the Commander of the Faithful and He has performed the greatest favor for the Muslims. Praise be to our Lord for His blessings and His kindness, for He has granted us victory, during the caliphate of the Commander of the Faithful, over Jurjān and Ṭabaristān—something which had escaped Sābūr Dhū al-Akṭāf,[217] Kisrā b. Qubādh,[218] and Kisrā b. Hurmuz.[219] Likewise, al-Fārūq 'Umar b. al-Khaṭṭāb, 'Uthmān b. 'Affān, and the Caliphs of God who succeeded them were unable to achieve this, until God made this conquest on behalf of the Commander of the Faithful, in order to bestow His honor upon him, and in order to increase the blessing He has bestowed upon him. Now, I have in my possession the fifth[220] that God has bestowed upon the Muslims, after every man took the share of the booty to which he was entitled, which amounts to six million (dīnārs),[221] and I shall bring this to the Commander of the Faithful, if God wills."

But his scribe, al-Mughīrah b. Abī Qurrah, a client of the Banū Sadūs, said to him, "Do not mention a specific amount of money, for you will be caught between two possible responses: Either he will consider it to be a large sum of money, in which case he will order you to bring it to him; or he will express disdain for it[222] and confer it on you, in which case you will be obligated to make a gift. In the latter case, he will find whatever he receives from you to be insignificant.[223] It seems to me that you would risk all that you have named without impressing him. The amount you name will remain forever in their records as a debit against you. Thus, if someone assumes authority after him, he will claim it from you; furthermore, if the person who assumes authority does not favor you, he will not accept even twice that sum from you. Therefore, do not send your letter; rather, write about your victory and ask him for permission to appear before him so that you can speak to him directly about whatever you desire. But shorten your account, for it is more appropriate to abbreviate the account

[1335]

---

217. Shāpūr II b. Hurmizd (A.D. 310–79) was called Dhū al-Aktāf because he had the shoulders of Arab prisoners dislocated or pierced. See *EI*, s.v. Shāpūr.

218. Khusraw I b. Kawādh (r. 531–79), a Sāsānian King of Persia, known in Persian sources as Anūshirvān (of the immortal soul). See *EI*, s.v. Sāsānians.

219. Khusraw II Parviz (The Victorious) b. Hurmizd (r. 590–628), a Sāsānian King of Persia. See *EI*, s.v. Sāsānians.

220. The *khums* is the share of God and the Prophet that is to be spent on the community as a whole. See *EI²*, s.v. Bayt al-Māl.

221. The translation follows *FHA*, 24, where dīnārs are specifically mentioned. Kūfī, *Futūḥ*, VII, 297, mentions "twenty million dirhams."

222. Text: *sakhat nafsuhu laka bihi*. Ibn al-Athīr, *Kāmil*, V, 35, has *samaḥat nafsuhu laka bihi*, "He will treat you generously regarding it."

223. Text: *istaqallahu*; the Cairo ed. has *istaqbalahu*: "He will accept it."

you wish to make than to exaggerate it." But Yazīd refused and he sent the letter.

Some said: The letter mentioned the figure of four million dirhams.[224]

Abū Jaʿfar (al-Ṭabarī) said: In this year, Ayyūb b. Sulaymān b. ʿAbd al-Malik died.[225] According to ʿAlī b. Muḥammad—ʿAlī b. Mujāhid—a shaykh from al-Rayy who was a contemporary of Yazīd: After finishing with Jurjān, Yazīd b. al-Muhallab went to al-Rayy, where he learned of Ayyūb b. Sulaymān's death while he was walking in the vineyard of Abū Ṣāliḥ, near the gate of al-Rayy. A poet recited some *rajaz* verse[226] in his presence:

Although Ayyūb has died,
    Dāwūd has taken his place,
Restoring whatever power had been lost.[227]

In this year, the city of the Slavs was conquered.[228]

In this year, Dāwūd b. Sulaymān b. ʿAbd al-Malik raided the land of the Byzantines and conquered "Ḥiṣn al-Marʾah,"[229] which is near Malaṭyah.[230]

In this year, the pilgrimage was led by ʿAbd al-ʿAzīz b. ʿAbdallāh b. Khālid b. Asīd who, at that time, was governor of Mecca. I was [1336] informed of this by Aḥmad b. Thābit—on the authority of the one he mentioned—Isḥāq b. ʿĪsā—Abū Maʿshar.

The governors of the garrison towns in this year were the same as in the year 97/715–716, as noted earlier, except that Yazīd b. al-Muhallab's governor over al-Baṣrah in this year was, according to some, Sufyān b. ʿAbdallāh al-Kindī.

---

224. Balādhurī, *Futūḥ* (Cairo), II, 414, mentions the figure of twenty-five million dirhams.

225. Ayyūb was the heir apparent. See text above, II/1317.

226. *Rajaz* verse is the simplest and, according to the tradition, the oldest meter of Arabic poetry. See *EI²*, s.v. ʿArūḍ.

227. See Kūfī, *Futūḥ*, VII, 307.

228. See text above, II/1317, note 154. See also Ibn Khayyāṭ, *Taʾrīkh*, I, 321; Yaʿqūbī, *Taʾrīkh*, III, 44; FHA, 25.

229. See text above, II/1306, sub anno 97, note 126.

230. An old city, not far from the upper Euphrates, that served as headquarters for the summer campaign against Byzantium. See *EI*, s.v. Malaṭya; Yāqūt, *Muʿjam*, V, 192–93.

The
Events of the Year

99
(August 14, 717—August 2, 718)

[The Death of Sulaymān b. ʿAbd al-Malik][231]

Among the events taking place that year was the death of Sulaymān b. ʿAbd al-Malik.[232] I was told on the authority of Hishām—
Abū Mikhnaf, that he died in Dābiq, in the province of Qin-
nasrīn,[233] on Friday the nineteenth of Ṣafar (October 1, 717).
Thus, his term of office was two years and eight months, less five
days.

It is said that he died on the tenth of Ṣafar (September 22,
717).[234] According to some, his caliphate lasted two years and
seven months, while others maintain that it lasted two years,
eight months, and five days.

According to al-Ḥasan b. Ḥammād—Ṭalḥah Abū Muḥam-

---

231. The text lacks the rubric, which is supplied from the Cairo ed.
232. See Ibn Khayyāṭ, *Taʾrīkh*, I, 322; Yaʿqūbī, *Taʾrīkh*, III, 44; Kūfī, *Futūḥ*, VII,
306; Masʿūdī, *Murūj* (Beirut), III, 173; *FHA*, 33–34; Ibn Kathīr, *Bidāyah*, IX, 177–
79.
233. One of the provinces of Syria. See *EI*², s.v. Ḳinnasrīn.
234. The discrepancy in the date is apparently due to confusion as to whether
Sulaymān died ten days into the month of Ṣafar, or ten days before the end of the
month. (Ṣafar has twenty-nine days.)

mad—his shaykhs: Sulaymān b. ʿAbd al-Malik served as caliph after al-Walīd for three years. ʿUmar b. ʿAbd al-ʿAzīz prayed over his body.

According to Aḥmad b. Thābit—his source—Isḥāq b. ʿĪsā—Abū Maʿshar: Sulaymān b. ʿAbd al-Malik died on Friday the nineteenth of Ṣafar in the year 99 (October 1, 717). His caliphate lasted three years, less four months.

[1337]   *Aspects of His Character*

According to ʿAlī b. Muḥammad: The people used to say, "Sulaymān is the key to goodness." When al-Ḥajjāj left them and Sulaymān assumed power he freed the captives, released the prisoners, treated the people well, and designated ʿUmar b. ʿAbd al-ʿAzīz as his successor.[235]

Ibn Bīḍ recited:

Your grandfather and your father both assumed the caliphate,
    amidst the anger of the malcontent, or the obedient one.[236]
Your grandfather and your father, then your brother became the
    third, and on your forehead is the light of the kingship of
    the fourth.

According to ʿAlī—al-Mufaḍḍal b. al-Muhallab: I went in to see Sulaymān at Dābiq on Friday, and he called for some robes. He put them on, but he did not like them, so he called for others—for green Sūsī[237] robes that had been sent by Yazīd b. al-Muhallab. After he put them on and arranged his turban, he asked, "O Ibn al-Muhallab, do you like them?" I replied, "Yes." He uncovered his forearms and said, "I am a king in the prime of his manhood." Then he prayed the Friday prayers for the last time. He wrote his last will and testament and summoned Ibn Abī Nuʿaym, the bearer of the seal, who sealed it.

According to ʿAlī—some of the scholars: One day Sulaymān

---

235. Sulaymān was called "the key to goodness" (*miftāḥ-l-khayr*) because his reign opened and closed with acts of goodness. See *FHA*, 17.

236. This is a conjectural translation. The text gives *min bayna sukhṭati sākhiṭ aw ṭāʾiʿ*.

237. Sūs was a town in Khūzistān famous for its weaving and silk. See *EI*, s.v. al-Sūs; Le Strange, *Lands*, 240.

put on a green robe and a green turban and he looked in the mirror and said, "I am a king in the prime of his manhood." He lived only one week after that.

According to ʿAlī—Suḥaym b. Ḥafṣ: A slave girl belonging to Sulaymān looked at him one day, and he asked, "How do you like what you see?" She recited:

You are the best object of delight—if only you would last.
    But man does not possess immortality.
I do not know of any blemish in you [1338]
    that other people have, except that you will pass away.

He then unwound[238] his turban.

According to ʿAlī: Sulaymān's qāḍī was Sulaymān b. Ḥabīb al-Muḥāribī. Ibn Abī ʿUyaynah used to tell stories in his presence.

According to Abū ʿUbaydah—Ru'bah b. al-ʿAjjāj: Sulaymān b. ʿAbd al-Malik performed the pilgrimage, accompanied by the poets, myself included. When he was in Medina, on the way back, the troops came to meet him with approximately four hundred Byzantine prisoners. Sulaymān sat down and the person sitting closest to him was ʿAbdallāh b. al-Ḥasan b. al-Ḥasan b. ʿAlī b. Abī Ṭālib. The Byzantine commander was brought forward, and Sulaymān said, "O ʿAbdallāh, strike off his neck." ʿAbdallāh stood up, but no one gave him a sword; eventually, one of the guards handed him his sword, and ʿAbdallāh smote the commander, severing his head and cutting off his forearm and part of the chains. Sulaymān exclaimed, "By God, it is not because of the excellence of the sword that the stroke was exquisite, but because of his ancestry." Sulaymān continued to hand over the rest of the prisoners to the commanders and men for execution. Eventually, he gave one of the prisoners to Jarīr, into whose hand the Banū ʿAbs thrust a sword sheathed in a white scabbard, whereupon he smote him and severed his head. Then one of the prisoners was given to al-Farazdaq, but he could not find a sword. Into his hand they thrust a crooked,[239] blunt sword that would not cut, and he smote the prisoner with it several times, but nothing happened. Sulaymān and the people laughed, and the Banū ʿAbs, Sulaymān's

238. Text: *fa-nafaḍa,* "to shake off." This should be amended to read *fa-naqaḍa.* I owe this point to Professor Abbas.

239. Text: *matīn,* "strong, solid"; read *muthniyyan,* following the Cairo ed.

maternal uncles, delighted in al-Farazdaq's misfortune. He threw down the sword and began to speak, making excuses to Sulaymān [1339] and recalling how the sword of Warqāʾ glanced off the head of Khālid:

If there was ever an unreliable sword, or a fate which delayed
    the soul of someone whose destiny has yet to arrive.
Then it is the sword of the Banū ʿAbs; they struck with it,
    through the hand of Warqāʾ, and it glanced off Khālid's
    head.
Such are the swords of India; sometimes their edges have no
    effect.
Although sometimes they cut necks.[240]

Warqāʾ is Warqāʾ b. Zuhayr b. Jadhīmah al-ʿAbsī, who struck Khālid b. Jaʿfar b. Kilāb. Khālid was on top of Warqāʾ's father, Zuhayr, smiting him with the sword and felling him. Warqāʾ b. Zuhayr approached and struck Khālid, but the blow had no effect, and so the former recited:

When I saw Zuhayr under Khālid's chest,
    I approached, running, like a mother bereft of her child,
    hurrying.
May my right hand be paralyzed if I smite Khālid,
    and double armor protects him from me.[241]

Al Farazdaq recited at the same session:

Are the people surprised that I made the best of them laugh,
    God's Caliph, by whom rain is invoked?
The sword did not fail due to cowardice or bewilderment in
    the presence of the Imām; rather, his day was delayed by
    fate.
Had I struck his neck with the intent to kill,[242]
    his body would have fallen separated from his head.
[1340] (It would have rolled away from him when I smote him,

---

240. See *Dīwān al-Farazdaq*, I, 157.
241. See *Aghānī* (Beirut), XI, 84.
242. The text is ʿalā ʿAmrin. This should be amended to read ʿamdan. I owe this point to Professor Abbas.

like a stone that rolls off a slippery spot).[243]
The soul is not hastened before its preordained time of death
    by a two-handed grip, or by the sharp sword itself.[244]

Jarīr recited in connection with this:

With the sword of Abū Raghwān, the sword of Mujāshiʿ,
    you struck. But you did not strike with the sword of Ibn
    Ẓālim.
You struck with it in the presence of the Imām, and your
    hands
        trembled. So they said, "That is an inexperienced sword,
        not a cutting one."[245]

According to ʿAbdallāh b. Aḥmad—his father—Sulaymān—
ʿAbdallāh b. Muḥammad b. ʿUyaynah—Abū Bakr b. ʿAbd al-ʿAzīz
b. al-Ḍaḥḥāk b. Qays: Sulaymān b. ʿAbd al-Malik attended a funeral in Dābiq at which the corpse was buried in a field. He
picked up some of the soil and said, "How good and how fine is
this soil!" Before a week or so had passed, he was buried next to
that grave.

---

243. This verse, omitted by Ṭabarī, is supplied from *Dīwān al-Farazdaq*, I, 291,
where the text has *idhan tadahdaʾ ʿanhu ḥīna aḍribuhu kamā tadahdā ʿani-l-
zuhlūfati al-ḥajaru.*
244. See *Dīwān al-Farazdaq*, I, 291.
245. See *Naḵāʾiḍ Jarīr wa-l-Farazdaq*, I, 413, ll. 15–16.

The Caliphate of ʿUmar b. ʿAbd al-ʿAzīz

The
Events of the Year

99 (cont'd)
(AUGUST 14, 717–AUGUST 2, 718)[246]

In this year 'Umar b. 'Abd al-'Azīz b. Marwān b. al-Ḥakam was appointed as Caliph.[247]

The Reason Why Sulaymān Appointed 'Umar as Caliph[248]

According to al-Ḥārith—Ibn Sa'd—Muḥammad b. 'Umar—al-Haytham b. Wāqid: 'Umar b. 'Abd al-'Azīz was appointed as Caliph at Dābiq, on Friday, the tenth of Ṣafar, in the year 99 (September 22, 717).

According to Muḥammad b. 'Umar—Dāwūd b. Khālid b.   [1341]

---

246. For other sources on the caliphate of 'Umar b. 'Abd al-'Azīz, see Ibn Qutaybah, *Ma'ārif*, 362–63; Dīnawarī, *Akhbār*, 332; Ya'qūbī, *Ta'rīkh*, III, 45–53; Kūfī, *Futūḥ*, VII, 306–23; Mas'ūdī, *Murūj* (Beirut), III, 182–95; *FHA*, 37–64; Ibn Kathīr, *Bidāyah*, IX, 184–219.

247. See Ibn Khayyāṭ, *Ta'rīkh*, I, 322; Ya'qūbī, *Ta'rīkh*, III, 44–45; Mas'ūdī, *Murūj* (Beirut), III, 182; *FHA*, 37.

248. See Ibn Qutaybah, *Ta'rīkh*, I, 92–96; Mas'ūdī, *Murūj* (Beirut), III, 183; Ibn Kathīr, *Bidāyah*, IX, 181–83.

Dīnār—Suhayl b. Abī Suhayl—Rajāʾ b. Ḥaywah:[249] On Friday, Sulaymān b. ʿAbd al-Malik put on green robes made of silk and looked in the mirror, saying, "By God, I am a king in the prime of his manhood." Then he went out to lead the people in the Friday prayers. Upon his return, however, he fell ill. When his condition deteriorated, he entrusted the succession, in a document he wrote himself, to one of his sons, a youth who had not yet attained puberty.[250] I said to him, "What are you doing, O Commander of the Faithful? One of the things that preserves a caliph in his grave is the appointment of an upright man[251] to serve as his successor over the Muslims." Sulaymān replied, "I will ask God for guidance, and I will consider the matter, for I have not made up my mind yet."

Sulaymān tarried a day or two and then tore up the document. He called for me and asked, "What is your opinion of Dāwūd b. Sulaymān?" I replied, "He is away in Constantinople, and you do not know whether he is dead or alive." He asked me, "Whom would you propose, then?" I replied, "The decision is yours, O Commander of the Faithful." I wanted to see whom he would mention. He asked, "What is your opinion of ʿUmar b. ʿAbd al-ʿAzīz?" I replied, "By God, I know him to be a worthy, excellent man and a sincere Muslim." He said, "By God, he is exactly as you describe him." Then he said, "But if, by God, I appoint him and do not appoint anyone else, there will surely be civil strife, for (the Banū ʿAbd al-Malik) will never allow him to rule over them, unless one of them is put next in succession." Now Yazīd b. ʿAbd al-Malik was away at that moment on the pilgrimage. Sulaymān said, "Therefore, I will appoint Yazīd b. ʿAbd al-Malik to be Caliph after him; that should placate them, and they will accept him." I said, "The decision is yours."

[1342]   Then Sulaymān wrote, "In the name of God, the Merciful, the Compassionate. This is a document from the servant of God,

---

249. Abū al-Miqdām Rajāʾ b. Ḥaywah b. Khanzal al-Kindī (d. 112/730). On this figure see C. E. Bosworth, "Rajāʾ ibn Ḥaywa al-Kindī and the Umayyad Caliphs," 36–80. The translation of the following section, from p. 70 to p. 74, may be compared to that by Bosworth in the aforementioned article, pp. 52–59.

250. According to Dīnawarī, *Akhbār*, 332, Sulaymān's oldest son, Muḥammad, was twelve years old when his father died.

251. An allusion to ʿUmar, who was known as *al-rajul al-ṣāliḥ*, "the upright man." See text below, II/1375.

Sulaymān, Commander of the Faithful, to ʿUmar b. ʿAbd al-ʿAzīz. I have appointed you to be my successor to the caliphate, and you are to be succeeded by Yazīd b. ʿAbd al-Malik. Therefore, hearken to him, O people, and obey; fear God and avoid dissension, lest enemies take advantage of you." He sealed the document and sent a message to Kaʿb b. Ḥāmid al-ʿAbsī, his Commander of the Guard, saying, "Order the members of my household to assemble." Kaʿb ordered them to assemble, and they did so. After they had gathered, Sulaymān said to Rajāʾ, "Take this document of mine to them, tell them that it is my document, and order them to swear the oath of allegiance to whomever I have appointed." Rajāʾ did as he was told. When Rajāʾ said that to them they asked, "May we go in to greet the Commander of the Faithful?" He replied, "Yes." They entered, and Sulaymān said to them, "This document"—to which he was directing their attention and at which they were looking, in the hand of Rajāʾ b. Ḥaywah—"is my succession covenant, so listen, obey, and swear allegiance to the person I have named in this document." Accordingly they swore allegiance to him, individually. Then the document was taken out, still sealed, in the hand of Rajāʾ b. Ḥaywah.[252]

Rajāʾ said: After they had dispersed, ʿUmar b. ʿAbd al-ʿAzīz approached me and said, "I fear that Sulaymān has involved me in this matter. I beseech you by God, and by your deference to and your affection for me, let me know if this is the case so that I might ask to be excused now, before a situation develops in which I am unable to accomplish what I can accomplish at the present moment." Rajāʾ answered, "No, by God, I will not tell you a single word." Thus, ʿUmar went away, furious.

[1343]

Rajāʾ continued: Hishām b. ʿAbd al-Malik met me and said, "O Rajāʾ, you have a long-standing feeling of deference to and affection for me, and I owe you a debt of gratitude, so tell me about this affair. If I have been appointed, I will be aware of it; and if someone else has been appointed, I can speak up, for a man like me cannot be sold short. Tell me, and I swear to you in the name of God that I will never mention anything about this." Rajāʾ said: But I refused, saying, "By God, I will not tell you a single word of

---

252. The validity of this document, for which there were apparently no witnesses, was subsequently disputed by the jurists. See Ibn Kathīr, *Bidāyah*, IX, 197.

what has been confided to me." Hishām departed in despair, striking one hand over the other and saying, "In favor of whom have I been passed over? Will the caliphate pass out of the hands of the sons of ʿAbd al-Malik?"

Rajāʾ said: I went in to see Sulaymān and found him dying. When the agony of death came over him, I set about turning him toward the *qiblah*, but whenever he recovered his senses he would say, "The time for that has not yet arrived, Rajāʾ." I did this twice, and on the third attempt he said, "Do it now, Rajāʾ, if you wish to do something. I bear witness that there is no God but God and I bear witness that Muḥammad is His servant and His messenger."[253] I turned him toward the *qiblah* and he died. After shutting his eyes, I covered him with a green velvet coverlet and locked the door. His wife sent a messenger to me, asking, "How is he?" I replied, "He is sleeping and has covered himself." The messenger looked at him, wrapped in the coverlet. He returned and told her this report, which she accepted, imagining that he was asleep.

[1344] Rajāʾ said: I stationed a trustworthy man in front of the door and ordered him not to leave until I returned and not to let anyone go in to the Caliph. I left and sent a message to Kaʿb b. Ḥāmid al-ʿAbsī, who gathered the household of the Commander of the Faithful. When they had assembled in the mosque of Dābiq, I said, "Swear the oath of allegiance." They replied, "We have already sworn once. Why should we swear again?" I said, "This is the Commander of the Faithful's command, so swear allegiance, in accordance with his command, to the person named in this sealed document." They then swore the oath of allegiance a second time, individually.

Rajāʾ continued: When they had sworn the oath of allegiance after Sulaymān's death, and I realized that I had put the matter on a solid footing, I said, "Rise out of reverence for your master, for he has just died." They recited, "Surely we belong to God, and to him we return."[254] Then I read the document to them. When I reached the point at which ʿUmar b. ʿAbd al-ʿAzīz is mentioned, Hishām b. ʿAbd al-Malik cried out, "We will never swear alle-

---

253. That is, he died with credo of the faith (*shahādah*) on his lips.
254. Qurʾān 2:156.

giance to him." I said, "By God, then I will cut off your head. Rise and swear allegiance." Reluctantly, he stood up.

Rajā' said: While he was reciting *innā lillāhi* on account of what had happened to him, I took 'Umar b. 'Abd al-'Azīz by the arms and seated him on the pulpit. At the same time Hishām was reciting *innā lillāhi* on account of what had escaped him. When Hishām finally reached 'Umar, the latter exclaimed, "'Surely we belong to God, and to Him we return,'[255] when what I dislike has come to me,"—because he did not want to become Caliph. Meanwhile, (Hishām) was reciting, "'Surely we belong to God, and to him we return,' when I have been passed over."

Sulaymān's body was washed and wrapped in a shroud, and 'Umar b. 'Abd al-'Azīz prayed over him. When the burial ceremony had been completed, the caliphal stable of animals was brought out to 'Umar: There were slow-paced horses, swift riding horses, and mules, each animal with its own groom. 'Umar asked, "What is this?" They replied, "The Caliph's stable." He said, "My own mount will suffice." Then 'Umar mounted it and, after those animals had been sent away, he departed.[256] Someone asked, "Will you occupy the Caliph's residence?" 'Umar replied, "The family of Abū Ayyūb (that is, Sulaymān) is still living there, and my own pavilion will suffice until they leave." He therefore remained in his own living quarters until they eventually vacated the Caliph's residence. [1345]

Rajā' said: On the evening of the same day, 'Umar said, "O Rajā', summon a scribe for me." I called one. Now up to this point I was pleased with everything that he had done, that is, the actions he had taken with regard to the riding animals and Sulaymān's residence. I said to myself, "How is he going to handle writing? Will he make drafts or what?" When the scribe had taken his seat, 'Umar dictated a single letter, directly from his mouth to the hand of the scribe, without any preliminary drafts. He dictated in the finest, most eloquent and most succinct manner possible. He then decreed that copies of the letter should be sent to every land.

---

255. Qur'ān 2:156.
256. Ibn Kathīr, *Bidāyah*, IX, 183, adds: "Then he rode to Damascus with the soldiers."

Meanwhile, ʿAbd al-Azīz b. al-Walīd, who was away at the time, learned of the death of Sulaymān b. ʿAbd al-Malik. Since he was unaware of the fact that the people had sworn allegiance to ʿUmar b. ʿAbd al-ʿAzīz and that Sulaymān had designated ʿUmar as his successor, he unfurled the banner and summoned the people to acknowledge him as the next Caliph. Subsequently, when he learned that the people had sworn allegiance to ʿUmar in accordance with Sulaymān's succession covenant, he went to see ʿUmar b. ʿAbd al-ʿAzīz. ʿUmar said to him, "I have been informed that you made your supporters swear the oath of allegiance to you and that you wanted to enter Damascus." ʿAbd al-ʿAzīz replied, "Both of those things are true, but I only acted in that manner because I was told that the Caliph, Sulaymān, had not appointed a successor; I feared that the holdings of the treasury would be plundered." ʿUmar said, "If the oath of allegiance had been sworn to you[257] and if you had taken power, I would not have opposed you; indeed, I would have remained in my house." ʿAbd al-ʿAzīz said, "There is no one beside you that I would like to have seen assume power." He then swore the oath of allegiance to ʿUmar b. ʿAbd al-ʿAzīz. People invoked God's blessings upon Sulaymān because he appointed ʿUmar b. ʿAbd al-ʿAzīz as his successor and passed over his own children.[258]

[1346]   In this year, ʿUmar b. ʿAbd al-ʿAzīz sent a message to Maslamah, who was in Byzantine territory, ordering him to return together with the Muslims who were accompanying him.[259] ʿUmar sent him swift and excellent horses and considerable quantities of food; he urged the people to render assistance to Maslamah and his men. According to some sources, the number of purebred horses that he sent to him was five hundred.

In this year, the Turks attacked Ādharbayjān,[260] killing a group of Muslims and causing serious damage.[261] ʿUmar b. ʿAbd al-ʿAzīz dispatched Ibn Ḥātim b. al-Nuʿmān al-Bāhilī,[262] who killed those

---

257. Text: *bāyaʿta*; read *būyiʿta*, following the Cairo ed.
258. See note 250 above.
259. See Ibn Khayyāṭ, *Taʾrīkh*, I, 326; Kūfī, *Futūḥ*, VII, 307–11; *FHA*, 39; Ibn Kathīr, *Bidāyah*, IX, 184.
260. Ādharbayjān was a Persian province. See *EI²*, s.v. Ādharbaydjān; Le Strange, *Lands*, 159–71.
261. See Ibn Khayyāṭ, *Taʾrīkh*, I, 326.
262. Some sources give his name as ʿAbd al-ʿAzīz b. Ḥātim, others as Ḥātim b.

Turks; only a small number managed to escape. He brought fifty of them as prisoners to ʿUmar in Khunāṣirah.[263]

In this year, ʿUmar dismissed Yazīd b. al-Muhallab from Iraq.[264] He sent ʿAdī b. Arṭāt al-Fazārī to serve as governor of al-Baṣrah and its surrounding territory. He dispatched ʿAbd al-Ḥamīd b. ʿAbd al-Raḥmān b. Zayd b. al-Khaṭṭāb al-Aʿraj al-Qurashī, one of the Banū ʿAdī b. Kaʿb, to serve as governor of al-Kūfah and its surrounding territory, accompanied by Abū al-Zinād, who was ʿAbd al-Ḥamīd b. ʿAbd al-Raḥmān's scribe. ʿAdī b. Arṭāt sent Mūsā b. al-Wajīh al-Ḥimyarī in pursuit of Yazīd b. al-Muhallab.

In this year, the pilgrimage was led by Abū Bakr Muḥammad b. ʿAmr b. Ḥazm, who was ʿUmar's governor in Medina.

ʿUmar's governor in Mecca in this year was ʿAbd al-ʿAzīz b. ʿAbdallāh b. Khālid b. Asīd. Al-Kūfah and its surrounding territory were governed by ʿAbd al-Ḥamīd b. ʿAbd al-Raḥmān, while al-Baṣrah and its surrounding territory were governed by ʿAdī b. Arṭāt. Khurāsān was governed by al-Jarrāḥ b. ʿAbdallāh. The judi- [1347] ciary of al-Baṣrah was in the charge of Iyās b. Muʿāwiyah b. Qurrah al-Muzanī. As mentioned earlier, ʿAdī had initially appointed al-Ḥasan b. Abī al-Ḥasan,[265] but when the latter complained, he asked Iyās b. Muʿāwiyah to take charge of the judiciary. The judiciary of al-Kūfah in this year was reportedly in the charge of ʿĀmir al-Shaʿbī.

Al-Wāqidī had reported: Al-Shaʿbī was in charge of al-Kūfah's judiciary in the days of ʿUmar b. ʿAbd al-ʿAzīz, serving on behalf of ʿAbd al-Ḥamīd b. ʿAbd al-Raḥmān, while al-Ḥasan b. Abī al-Ḥasan al-Baṣrī was in charge of al-Baṣrah's judiciary, serving on behalf of ʿAdī b. Arṭāt. But when al-Ḥasan asked ʿAdī to excuse him from that office, the latter complied with his request and appointed Iyās in his place.

---

al-Nuʿmān. See Ibn Khayyāṭ, *Taʾrīkh*, I, 326; Yaʿqūbī, *Taʾrīkh*, III, 47; Ibn al-Athīr, *Kāmil*, V, 43; Ibn Kathīr, *Bidāyah*, IX, 183.

263. See Ibn Khayyāṭ, *Taʾrīkh*, I, 326; Ibn Kathīr, *Bidāyah*, IX, 185. Khunāṣirah is a settlement located sixty km. to the southeast of Aleppo and one hundred km. to the northeast of Ḥamāh where ʿUmar had a stronghold constructed in which he resided frequently. See *EI²*, s.v. Khunāṣira.

264. See Ibn Khayyāṭ, *Taʾrīkh*, I, 326; Yaʿqūbī, *Taʾrīkh*, III, 46; *FHA*, 39–40.

265. That is, Abū Saʿīd b. Abī al-Ḥasan Yasār al-Baṣrī, known as Ḥasan al-Baṣrī, d. 110/728. See *EI²*, s.v. Ḥasan al-Baṣrī.

The
Events of the Year

100
(August 3, 718—July 23, 719)

Among those events was the revolt of the Khārijites,[266] who rebelled against ʿUmar b. ʿAbd al-ʿAzīz in Iraq.[267]

The Revolt of the Khārijites

According to Muḥammad b. ʿUmar—Ibn Abī al-Zinād: The Ḥarūriyyah[268] in Iraq rose up in rebellion, and ʿUmar b. ʿAbd al-ʿAzīz wrote to ʿAbd al-Ḥamīd b. ʿAbd al-Raḥmān b. Zayd b. al-Khaṭṭāb, his governor in Iraq, ordering him to summon the rebels to act in accordance with the Book of God and the *sunnah* of His Prophet.[269] When they ignored his summons,[270] ʿAbd al-Ḥamīd sent an

[1348]

---

266. The Khārijites were members of the earliest religious sect in Islam. See *EI²*, s.v. Khārijites.

267. See Ibn Qutaybah, *Taʾrīkh*, I, 99–100; Masʿūdī, *Murūj* (Beirut), III, 190–93; *FHA*, 41–47; Ibn Kathīr, *Bidāyah*, IX, 187.

268. That is, the Khārijites, who are also known as the Ḥarūriyyah, after a town two miles from al-Kūfah, where they first assembled. See *EI²*, s.v. Khārijites.

269. Text: *al-ʿamal bi-kitāb allāh wa-sunnat nabīhi.* On the significance of this phrase, see Crone and Hinds, *God's Caliph*, 62.

270. Text: *fa-lammā aʿdhara fī duʿāʾihim.*

army against them, but it was defeated by the Ḥarūrīs. Upon being informed of this, ʿUmar sent Maslamah b. ʿAbd al-Malik against them leading a regiment of the Syrian army that he had equipped in al-Raqqah.[271] ʿUmar wrote to ʿAbd al-Ḥamīd as follows: "Having learned of the defeat of your army—the evil army—I have dispatched Maslamah b. ʿAbd al-Malik, who is to be given free access to the rebels." Maslamah engaged them in battle, leading the Syrian army, and it was not long before God granted him victory over them.

Abū ʿUbaydah Maʿmar b. al-Muthannā mentioned that the person who headed the revolt against ʿAbd al-Ḥamīd b. ʿAbd al-Raḥmān, in Iraq, during the caliphate of ʿUmar b. ʿAbd al-ʿAzīz, was Shawdhab—his real name was Bisṭām—one of the Banū Yashkur. His rebellion was based in Jūkhā,[272] where he commanded eighty horsemen,[273] most of them from the tribe of Rabīʿah. ʿUmar b. ʿAbd al-ʿAzīz wrote to ʿAbd al-Ḥamīd, saying, "Do not engage them in combat unless they shed blood or[274] cause corruption in the earth. But if they do act in that manner, intervene so as to prevent that. Choose a man who is strong and endowed with good judgment and send him against them with a detachment of soldiers, having charged him as I have commanded you." As a result, ʿAbd al-Ḥamīd put Muḥammad b. Jarīr b. ʿAbdallāh al-Bajalī in command of two thousand Kūfans, charging him as he had been charged by ʿUmar.

Meanwhile, ʿUmar wrote to Bisṭām, summoning him and asking him about his revolt. Bisṭām received ʿUmar's letter after Muḥammad b. Jarīr had arrived and deployed his troops opposite him, without, however, engaging him in combat or provoking him. ʿUmar's letter to Bisṭām contained the following statement: "I have been informed that you have rebelled in anger for the sake of God and His Prophet. But you have no better right to that than I do. Come to me, then, so that I may discuss the matter with you:

---

271. Capital of Diyār Muḍar in al-Jazīrah, on the left bank of the Euphrates. See *EI*, s.v. Raḳḳa; Le Strange, *Lands*, 101–3.

272. A district in the Sawād of Baghdad, between Khāniqīn and Khūzistān. See Yāqūt, *Muʿjam*, II, 179; Morony, *Iraq*, 137ff. According to Masʿūdī, the revolt took place in al-Jazīrah. See *Murūj* (Beirut), II, 190.

273. It is also reported that Bisṭām commanded either three hundred or six hundred horsemen. See *FHA*, 47.

274. Text: *aw*. Ibn al-Athīr, *Kāmil*, V, 45, has *wa*, "and."

[1349]   if we are in the right, you will join (the community) in what the people (believe); but if you are in the right, we will reconsider our position."[275] As a result, Bisṭām did not engage the Caliph's forces in combat and he wrote to 'Umar, saying, "You have been fair, and I am therefore sending you two men who will confer and debate with you."

According to Abū 'Ubaydah: One of the two men who were sent by Shawdhab to 'Umar was Mamzūj, a client of the Banū Shaybān,[276] and the other was a descendant of the Banū Yashkur.

Our source continued: It is reported that Bisṭām sent a group of men that included the aforementioned two, but that 'Umar sent a message to the group calling upon them to choose two men. They chose these two, who then went in to visit 'Umar. They engaged him in debate, saying, "Tell us about Yazīd. Why do you acknowledge him to be your successor as Caliph?"[277] 'Umar replied, "Someone else appointed him as my successor." They said, "Consider the following case: Suppose you were administering some property that belonged to someone else and you then entrusted it to someone who was unreliable. Do you think that you would have conveyed the trust to its owner?"[278]

'Umar said, "Give me three days," and the two men left. The Banū Marwān[279] were afraid that 'Umar would confiscate the properties that they owned and administered and that he would renounce Yazīd; therefore, they had someone poison his drink. He died less than three days after the two men left him.[280]

---

275. A longer version of 'Umar's letter is cited in *FHA*, 41–42.

276. Some sources give the client's name as 'Āṣim and indicate that he was an Ethiopian. See Mas'ūdī *Murūj* (Beirut), III, 190; *FHA*, 43.

277. For longer versions of this debate, see Ibn Qutaybah, *Ta'rīkh*, I, 99–100; Mas'ūdī, *Murūj* (Beirut), III, 191–92; *FHA*, 43–46; Ibn al-Athīr, *Kāmil*, V, 45–47.

278. Text: *a-turāka kunta addayta al-amānah ilā man ītamanaka*. Ibn al-Athīr, *Kāmil*, V, 48, has *a-tarāhu addā-l-ḥaqq alladhī yalzamuhu lillāhi aw tarāhu qad salama*, "Do you think that he fulfilled the obligation incumbent upon him (in the eyes) of God, or do you consider him blameless?" See also *FHA*, 46.

279. The Banū Marwān were the descendants of Marwān b. al-Ḥakam, the fourth Umayyad Caliph and father of the Marwānid branch of the Umayyad family. See *EI*, s.v. Marwān b. al-Ḥakam.

280. It is also reported that one of the two messengers acknowledged the validity of 'Umar's arguments and stayed with the Caliph, who awarded him a stipend; and that 'Umar died not three, but fifteen days later. See Ibn Qutaybah, *Ta'rīkh*, I, 100; Mas'ūdī, *Murūj* (Beirut), III, 192–93; *FHA*, 47; and Ibn al-Athīr, *Kāmil*, V, 48. The claim that 'Umar was poisoned by the Marwānids was discounted by Well-

In this year, 'Umar b. 'Abd al-'Azīz sent al-Walīd b. Hishām al-Mu'aytī and 'Amr b. Qays al-Kindī, from the army of Ḥimṣ,[281] on the summer campaign.

In this year, 'Umar b. Hubayrah al-Fazārī went to al-Jazīrah[282] in order to serve as 'Umar's governor over that province.

In this year, Yazīd b. al-Muhallab was transported from Iraq to 'Umar b. 'Abd al-'Azīz.[283]

The Capture of Yazīd b. al-Muhallab [1350]

The biographers disagree on this subject. According to Hishām b. Muḥammad—Abū Mikhnaf: When Yazīd b. al-Muhallab made his way to Wāsiṭ and then embarked on ships with the intention of sailing to al-Baṣrah, 'Umar b. 'Abd al-'Azīz sent 'Adī b. Arṭāt to al-Baṣrah to serve as governor. 'Adī dispatched Mūsā b. al-Wajīh al-Ḥimyarī, who arrested Yazīd after overtaking him at the Baṣrah bridge of the Ma'qil Canal.[284] 'Adī sent Yazīd to 'Umar b. 'Abd al-'Azīz in the custody of Mūsā b. al-Wajīh. When the prisoner arrived, 'Umar b. 'Abd al-'Azīz summoned him. Now 'Umar, who detested Yazīd and his household, used to say, "They are tyrants, and I do not approve of people like them." Yazīd b. al-Muhallab, likewise, hated 'Umar and used to say, "I suspect that he is a hypocrite." But when 'Umar came to power Yazīd learned that 'Umar was anything but a hypocrite. 'Umar summoned Yazīd and asked him about the moneys that the latter had mentioned in his letter to Sulaymān b. 'Abd al-Malik.[285] Yazīd replied, "You know what my position was in the eyes of Sulaymān. I wrote to Sulaymān only in order to augment his reputation among the people; I knew that Sulaymān would not hold me accountable for something that I said (and I did not fear that he would treat me) in an

---

hausen (*Arab Kingdom*, 311), but more recently supported by Crone and Hinds (*God's Caliph*, 76–77).

281. Ḥimṣ is a town (Ḥoms) in Syria on the eastern bank of the Orontes; it is situated midway along the route joining Aleppo and Damascus. See *EI²*, s.v. Ḥimṣ.

282. The northern part of the territory situated between the Tigris and the Euphrates. See *EI²*, s.v. al-Djazīra; Le Strange, *Lands*, 86–114.

283. See Ibn Khayyāṭ, *Ta'rīkh*, I, 326; Ya'qūbī, *Ta'rīkh*, III, 46; Kūfī, *Futūḥ*, VII, 311–22; *FHA*, 47–50; Ibn Kathīr, *Bidāyah*, IX, 188.

284. A canal in al-Baṣrah named after Ma'qil b. Yasar al-Mazanī. See Yāqūt, *Mu'jam*, V, 323–24.

285. See text above, II/1334–35, sub anno 98.

unpleasant manner."[286] ʿUmar said to him, "I see no alternative in your case but to put you in prison. Fear God and hand over whatever is in your possession, for it belongs to the Muslims and it is not in my power to abandon it." The Caliph returned Yazīd to his place of confinement.[287] Then he sent a message to al-Jarrāḥ b. ʿAbdallāh al-Ḥakamī,[288] ordering him to leave for Khurāsān (where he would serve as governor).

[1351] Meanwhile, Makhlad b. Yazīd advanced from Khurāsān, distributing stipends to the soldiers and bestowing large sums of money on the inhabitants of every district through which he passed. Then he left Khurāsān and made his way to ʿUmar b. ʿAbd al-ʿAzīz. When he went in to see the Caliph, he praised God and said, "O Commander of the Faithful, God has favored the Muslim community by putting you in charge. But we (that is, the Muhallabids) have been smitten by you. Let us not be reduced to the utmost destitution on account of your taking power. On what grounds have you imprisoned this old man? I will take responsibility for whatever he owes. Make an agreement with me for (part of) the amount that you are asking from him." ʿUmar said, "No, not unless you take responsibility for the entire amount that we seek from him." He replied, "O Commander of the Faithful, if you have clear proof, produce it, but if you do not have clear proof, accept what Yazīd says as the truth. If you do not believe him, ask him to swear the oath; if he refuses to swear, work out a compromise with him." ʿUmar said to him, "I have no alternative but to hold him accountable for the entire sum of money." When Makhlad left, ʿUmar said, "I prefer him to his father." But Makhlad died shortly thereafter. Thus, when Yazīd refused to give any of the money to ʿUmar, the latter had him dressed in a wool garment and placed on a camel. Then he said, "Take him to Dahlak."[289] When Yazīd had been taken out and paraded in front

---

286. Text: *wa-lā bi-amrin akrahuhu.* I suspect that the text is defective here. My translation follows Kūfī, *Futūḥ,* VII, 318: *wa-lā kuntu akhāfu an yaʾtiyanī min qibalihi amrun akrahuhu.*

287. Ibn al-Athīr, *Kāmil,* V, 49, adds: "in the fortress of Aleppo."

288. Abū ʿUqbah al-Jarrāḥ b. ʿAbdallāh al-Ḥakamī, an Umayyad general, called "hero of Islam" and "cavalier of the Syrians." See *EI²,* s.v. al-Djarrāḥ b. ʿAbdallāh; Crone, *Slaves,* 132, no. 16.

289. A group of islands off the west coast of the Red Sea, opposite Eritrea; Dahlak al-Kabīr, one of the largest islands, was used as a place of exile or prison by the Umayyad caliphs. See *EI²,* s.v. Dahlak.

of the soldiers, he exclaimed, "Have I no kinsmen? Why should I be transported to Dahlak? Only sinners, disquieters, and thieves are sent to Dahlak. Praise be to God! Have I no kinsmen?" Then Salāmah b. Nuʿaym al-Khawlānī approached ʿUmar and said, "O Commander of the Faithful, send Yazīd back to his place of confinement, for I fear that if you send him away, his tribe will attempt to recover him. Indeed, I know that his tribe is angry on his behalf."[290] ʿUmar therefore sent him back to prison. And it happened that Yazīd was still in prison when he learned that ʿUmar had taken ill.

[1352]

As for sources other than Abū Mikhnaf: ʿUmar b. ʿAbd al-ʿAzīz wrote to ʿAdī b. Arṭāt, ordering him to arrest Yazīd b. al-Muhallab[291] and deliver him to the soldiers at ʿAyn al-Tamr. ʿAdī b. Arṭāt sent Yazīd with Wakīʿ b. Ḥassān b. Abī Sūd al-Tamīmī, bound in chains, on a boat. When he had been brought as far as the Abān Canal,[292] some men from the tribe of Azd confronted Wakīʿ in an effort to seize Yazīd. But Wakīʿ leapt down, drew his sword and cut the ship's cable. Then he took Yazīd b. al-Muhallab's sword and swore a weighty oath[293] to the effect that he would strike off Yazīd's head unless they dispersed. Yazīd b. al-Muhallab called out to them, informing them of Wakīʿ's oath, whereupon they dispersed. Wakīʿ proceeded until he had delivered Yazīd to the soldiers at ʿAyn al-Tamr, and he then returned to ʿAdī b. Arṭāt. The soldiers who were at ʿAyn al-Tamr took Yazīd b. al-Muhallab to ʿUmar b. ʿAbd al-ʿAzīz, who threw him into prison.

Abū Jaʿfar (al-Ṭabarī) said: In this year, ʿUmar b. ʿAbd al-ʿAzīz dismissed al-Jarrāḥ b. ʿAbdallāh from Khurasan, replacing him with ʿAbd al-Raḥmān b. Nuʿaym al-Qushayrī.[294] Al-Jarrāḥ's term of office in Khurāsān had been one year and five months; he had

---

290. Text: *qad ghaḍibū lahu*. Ibn al-Athīr, *Kāmil*, V, 50, has *qad ʿaṣabū lahu*, "has rallied to his defense."

291. Text: *bi-tawjīh Yazīd b. al-Muhallab*. Ibn al-Athīr, *Kāmil*, V, 48, has *bi-infādh Yazīd b. al-Muhallab ilayhi mūthaqan*, "to deliver Yazīd b. al-Muhallab to him in shackles."

292. The Abān Canal, below Wāsiṭ, was one of the navigable waterways by means of which the Tigris flowed into the Great Swamp. See Le Strange, *Lands*, 40–41.

293. Literally: "On the condition that he divorce his wife."

294. See Balādhurī, *Futūḥ* (Cairo), III, 524; Yaʿqūbī, *Taʾrīkh*, III, 46–47; Ibn Kathīr, *Bidāyah*, IX, 188.

gone there in the year 99/717–718 and left toward the end of the month of Ramaḍān in the year 100 (March 27–April 25, 719).

The Dismissal of al-Jarrāḥ b. ʿAbdallāh

The reason for this, according to ʿAlī b. Muḥammad—Kulayb b. Khalaf—Idrīs b. Ḥanẓalah and al-Mufaḍḍal—his grandfather and ʿAlī b. Mujāhid—Khālid b. ʿAbd al-ʿAzīz: When Yazīd b. al-Muhallab left Jurjān, he designated Jahm b. Zaḥr as governor of that province.[295] But when Yazīd's fate took a turn for the worse,[296] the governor of Iraq sent someone from Iraq to serve as governor of Jurjān. The (new) governor approached Jurjān from the direction of Iraq, but Jahm b. Zaḥr seized him, together with a group of men who had accompanied him, and bound them in shackles. Then Jahm set out, leading fifty of the Yaman, headed for al-Jarrāḥ in Khurāsān, whereupon the people of Jurjān released their governor from prison. Al-Jarrāḥ said to Jahm, "Were it not for the fact that you are my paternal cousin, I would not have allowed you to do that." To which Jahm replied, "Were it not for the fact that you are my paternal cousin, I would not have come to you" (Jahm was related to al-Jarrāḥ by ties of marriage, since their respective wives were the daughters of Ḥusayn b. al-Ḥārith; the two men were also paternal cousins, because their respective fathers, al-Ḥakam and Juʿfī, were the sons of Saʿd). Al-Jarrāḥ said to Jahm, "You have defied your Imām and risen up in rebellion. Carry out a raid; perhaps, if you are successful, you can improve your position with your Caliph." He therefore sent him toward Khuttal.[297] Jahm left and, upon approaching them, he traveled in disguise together with three men, having left in command of his army his paternal cousin, al-Qāsim b. Ḥabīb, who was also the husband of his daughter, Umm al-Aswad. When he finally made his way into the presence of the leader of the Khuttal, he said to him, "Come with me so that we can speak privately." They met privately. Jahm claimed to be the son of so-and-so, whereupon the

[1353]

---

295. See text above, II/1333, sub anno 98.

296. Text: *fa-lammā kāna min amri Yazīd mā kāna.* The reference is to Yazīd's imprisonment.

297. A region on the right bank of the Oxus River, lying between the Wakhsh and the Panj Rivers. See *EI²*, s.v. Khuttalān.

leader of the Khuttal came down from his throne and gave him whatever he needed. They say: The Khuttal are the clients of al-Nuʿmān; thus, he acquired booty.

Al-Jarrāḥ then wrote to ʿUmar. He also sent a delegation that included two Arab tribesmen and a client of the Banū Ḍabbah. The latter went by the patronymic of Abū al-Ṣaydāʾ and his name was Ṣāliḥ b. Ṭarīf; he was virtuous in matters of religion. According to one source: The client was Saʿīd, the brother of Khālid or Yazīd al-Naḥwī. The two Arab tribesmen spoke, while the other delegate remained in his seat. ʿUmar asked him, "Are you not a member of the delegation?" He replied, "Yes, I am." He said, "Then what prevents you from speaking?" He said, "O Commander of the Faithful, there are twenty thousand clients who make raids without receiving any stipend or allowance, and there are a similar number of 'protected people' (ahl al-dhimmah)[298] who have converted to Islam, yet are still made to pay the tribute. Our governor is a partisan of the Arabs, a rough man who stands on the pulpit and proclaims, 'I come to you out of solicitude. Today, I am a partisan of the Arabs and, by God, one man from my tribe is dearer to me than a hundred men who are not.' His harshness reached the point that the sleeve of his coat of mail is equal in value to one-half of another's coat of mail.[299] He is, after all,[300] one of the swords of al-Ḥajjāj, who committed acts of tyranny and oppression." ʿUmar said, "Let them send messengers like you."

ʿUmar then wrote to al-Jarrāḥ, saying, "Whoever prays with you in the direction of the qiblah is to be relieved of the poll tax." As a result, many people hastened to accept Islam. Someone said to al-Jarrāḥ, "The people are rushing to accept Islam in order to avoid the poll tax, so test them by requiring that they submit to circumcision." Al-Jarrāḥ conveyed this suggestion to ʿUmar, who wrote back, "God sent Muḥammad in order to summon people to Islam, not to circumcise them."

ʿUmar said, "Find me a trustworthy man who can advise me about the situation in Khurāsān." Someone replied, "You have

[1354]

---

298. That is, non-Muslim adherents of a revealed religion. See *EI²*, s.v. *Dhimma*.
299. Text: *yablaghu niṣf dirʿihi*. The translation is conjectural.
300. Text: *baʿdu*. The reading *yuʿaddu*, "He is considered," is also possible.

already found him. You must summon Abū Mijlaz." ʿUmar then wrote to al-Jarrāḥ, saying, "Come here and bring Abū Mijlaz with you. Put ʿAbd al-Raḥmān b. Nuʿaym al-Ghāmidī in charge of military affairs in Khurāsān and put ʿUbaydallāh—or ʿAbdallāh—b. Ḥabīb in charge of fiscal affairs."

Al-Jarrāḥ then addressed the soldiers, saying, "O army of Khurāsān, I came to you wearing the clothes that are on my back and riding my own horse. I have not taken any of your wealth, except for the ornamentation on my sword." Indeed, he had nothing except a horse and a she-mule whose faces had turned white. He set out in the month of Ramaḍān (March 27–April 25), leaving ʿAbd al-Raḥmān b. Nuʿaym as his deputy. When he arrived, ʿUmar asked him, "When did you set out?" He replied, "In the month of Ramaḍān." He said, "Whoever described you as being coarse spoke the truth! Why didn't you wait there until you had broken the fast before setting out?" Al-Jarrāḥ used to proclaim, "By God, I am a partisan of the Arabs who travels during Ramaḍān in order to promote the cause of the Arabs."[301]

[1355]

Now, when al-Jarrāḥ first arrived in Khurāsān, he had written to ʿUmar, saying, "I have reached Khurāsān and found people who have become arrogantly seditious, leaping and bounding in mischief. There is nothing that they would like better than to revolt so that they might withhold what they owe God. Nothing will check them except the sword and whip, but I would not want to undertake that without your permission." ʿUmar wrote back, saying, "O son of the mother of al-Jarrāḥ, you desire sedition even more than they do! Do not apply the whip to a believer or to one of the tributaries unless he deserves it and do not inflict punishment, for you will arrive in the presence of one who 'knows the treachery of the eyes and what the breasts conceal'[302] and you will recite a Book 'that leaves nothing behind, small or great, but it has numbered it.'"[303]

When al-Jarrāḥ was preparing to leave Khurāsān on his way to ʿUmar b. ʿAbd al-ʿAzīz, he took twenty thousand dirhams—according to some sources: ten thousand—from the Public Treasury and said, "I am borrowing this until I turn it over to the

---

301. Text: *ʿaṣabī ʿaqabī yurīdu min al-ʿaṣabiyyah.* The translation is conjectural.
302. Qurʾān 40:20.
303. Qurʾān 18:49.

Caliph." He reached ʿUmar, who asked him, "When did you set out?" He replied, "At the end of the month of Ramaḍān. I owe money, so settle the debt."[304] He said, "Had you set out after you broke the fast, I would have settled it for you." As a result, his kinsmen paid for him out of their stipends.

ʿUmar b. ʿAbd al-ʿAzīz Appoints ʿAbd al-Raḥmān b. Nuʿaym and ʿAbd al-Raḥmān b. ʿAbdallāh al-Qushayrī over Khurāsān

[1356]

The reason for this, according to what was reported to me: al-Jarrāḥ b. ʿAbdallāh was dismissed from his position in Khurāsān at the time that the complaint was lodged against him. He was summoned by ʿUmar b. ʿAbd al-ʿAzīz and went to see him, as I have already reported above.[305]

According to ʿAlī b. Muḥammad—Khārijah b. Muṣʿab al-Ḍabbʿī and ʿAbdallāh b. al-Mubārak, and others: Then, when ʿUmar wanted to appoint someone as governor of Khurāsān, he said, "Find me a trustworthy man who might advise me about conditions in Khurāsān." Someone said to him, "Abū Mijlaz Lāḥiq b. Ḥumayd." The Caliph wrote a letter summoning Abū Mijlaz, who came to him. Abū Mijlaz, who was not the type of man who stands out in a crowd, went in to see ʿUmar, together with a group of people. But ʿUmar did not recognize him, and he left with the other men. Later, when ʿUmar asked about him, he was told, "He entered with the group of men and then left." ʿUmar then summoned him and said, "O Abū Mijlaz, I did not recognize you." He responded, "When you failed to recognize me, why didn't you ask about my identity?" He said, "Tell me about ʿAbd al-Raḥmān b. ʿAbdallāh." He said, "He rewards those who are competent but treats enemies with hostility. He is a military commander who acts independently and will advance boldly if he finds supporters." ʿUmar asked, "What about ʿAbd al-Raḥmān b. Nuʿaym?" He replied, "Soft, flexible, forgiving, and gentle."[306] ʿUmar said, "I prefer the one who is

---

304. Text: *wa-ʿalayya dayn fa-qḍihi*. See Balādhurī, *Futūḥ* (Cairo), III, 524, where the text is *kāna ʿalayhi dayn fa-qaḍāhu*, which Murgotten (*Origins*, II, 197) translates as "ʿUmar owed him a debt, but paid him."

305. See text above, II/1352–55.

306. Text: *ta'attā lahu*. Ibn al-Athīr, *Kāmil*, V, 52, has *wa-l-ta'annī*. The two verbs are synonymous.

forgiving and gentle." He therefore put ʿAbd al-Raḥmān b. Nuʿaym in charge of prayer and military affairs and ʿAbd al-Raḥmān al-Qushayrī—he was one of the Banū al-Aʿwar b. Qushayr—in charge of the fiscal administration. ʿUmar wrote to the army of Khurāsān as follows: "I have put ʿAbd al-Raḥmān b. Nuʿaym in charge of your military affairs and ʿAbd al-Raḥmān b. ʿAbdallāh in charge of your fiscal administration, not on the basis of any personal knowledge of them and without choosing them from a list of candidates, but rather on the basis of what was reported to me about them. If you

[1357]   are satisfied with them, praise God; but if they act in a manner that displeases you, seek help from God, for there is no power and no strength, save in God."

According to ʿAlī—Abū al-Sarī al-Azdī—Ibrāhīm al-Ṣaʾīgh: ʿUmar b. ʿAbd al-ʿAzīz wrote to ʿAbd al-Raḥmān b. Nuʿaym as follows: "Now then, if you are a sincere servant of God with regard to His servants, no reproach that anyone might utter will have any effect on you in the cause of God, for God is closer to you than the people are, and what you owe Him is greater than what you owe them. Do not commission anything in the affairs of the Muslims except that which is known to be good for them and that which promotes their welfare, and be faithful to what is entrusted to you. Beware lest you incline toward anything but what is right, for the unseen is not concealed from God.[307] And do not walk along a path that leads away from God, for there is no refuge from God, except with Him."

According to ʿAlī—Muḥammad al-Bāhilī—Abū Nuhayk b. Ziyād and others: ʿUmar b. ʿAbd al-ʿAzīz sent the document of appointment in which he put ʿAbd al-Raḥmān b. Nuʿaym in charge of military affairs in Khurāsān and Sijistān[308] in the hands of ʿAbdallāh b. Ṣakhr al-Qurashī. ʿAbd al-Raḥmān b. Nuʿaym was still in office in Khurāsān when ʿUmar b. ʿAbd al-ʿAzīz died, and he remained in office until Yazīd b. al-Muhallab was slain, at which time Maslamah appointed Saʿīd b. ʿAbd al-ʿAzīz b. al-Ḥārith b. al-Ḥakam.[309] Thus, ʿAbd al-Raḥmān's term of office was more than a year and a half; he took office in the month of Ramaḍān in

---

307. See Qurʾān 69:18.
308. The border district between Persia and Afghanistan. See *EI²*, s.v. Sistān; Le Strange, *Lands*, 334–51.
309. That is, Saʿīd Khudhaynah. See text below, II/1417ff., sub anno 102.

the year 100 (March 27–April 25, 719) and was dismissed in the year 102/720–721, after Yazīd b. al-Muhallab was slain.

According to ʿAlī: ʿAbd al-Raḥmān b. Nuʿaym's term of office in Khurāsān was sixteen months.

The Beginning of the Daʿwah[310]   [1358]

Abū Jaʿfar (al-Ṭabarī) said: In this year, that is to say, the year 100/718–719, Muḥammad b. ʿAlī b. ʿAbdallāh b. ʿAbbās sent Maysarah[311] from the land of the Sharāt[312] to Iraq, and he[313] sent Muḥammad b. Khunays, Abū ʿIkrimah al-Sarrāj, that is, Abū Muḥammad al-Ṣādiq,[314] and Ḥayyān al-ʿAṭṭār, the maternal uncle of Ibrāhīm b. Salamah, to Khurāsān. At that time, Khurāsān was governed by al-Jarrāḥ b. ʿAbdallāh al-Ḥakamī, on behalf of ʿUmar b. ʿAbd al-ʿAzīz. Muḥammad b. ʿAlī ordered them to recruit for him and for the members of his household. They met with certain people and then departed, bearing letters to Muḥammad b. ʿAlī from those people who had responded to their call. They conveyed these letters to Maysarah, who sent them on to Muḥammad b. ʿAlī. Abū Muḥammad al-Ṣādiq chose for Muḥammad b. ʿAlī the following twelve chiefs: Sulaymān b. Kathīr al-Khuzāʿī; Lāhiz b. Qurayẓ al-Tamīmī; Qaḥṭabah b. Shabīb al-Ṭāʾī; Mūsā b. Kaʿb al-Tamīmī; Khālid b. Ibrāhīm Abū Dāwūd, one of the Banū ʿAmr b. Shaybān b. Dhuhl; al-Qāsim b. Mujāshiʿ al-Tamīmī; ʿImrān b. Ismāʿīl Abū al-Najm, a client of the family of Abū Muʿayṭ; Mālik b. al-Haytham al-Khuzāʿī; Ṭalḥah b. Zurayq al-

---

310. *Daʿwah* refers to propaganda for an ʿAbbāsid descendant of the Prophet's family. See *EI*², s.v. Daʿwa; Maqdisī, *Badʾ*, VI, 59–60; Ibn Kathīr, *Bidāyah*, IX, 189; Cahen, "Points de vue"; F. Omar, *The Abbāsid Caliphate*, 67–74; Sharon, *Black Banners*, 73–99; Lassner, *Islamic Revolution*, 62ff.

311. Abū Riyāḥ Maysarah al-Nabbāl (or al-Raḥḥāl), a client of the Azd (or of the Banū Asad). See Sharon, *Black Banners*, 134, 149–50.

312. Text: *arḍ al-sharāt*, a reference to the homeland of the ʿAbbāsids in Jordan. See Ibn al-Athīr, *Kāmil*, V, 53; Sharon, *Black Banners*, index, s.v. Ḥumaymah.

313. The subject here could be either Muḥammad or Maysarah. See text below, II/1434, sub anno 102, where Maysarah is specifically mentioned. But according to Dīnawarī, *Akhbār*, 334, and Ibn Kathīr, *Bidāyah*, IX, 189, it was Muḥammad b. ʿAlī who sent Abū ʿIkrimah and Ḥayyān al-ʿAṭṭār to Khurāsān. See *Akhbār al-dawlah* for the fullest version of this report.

314. Abū ʿIkrimah al-Sarrāj Muḥammad b. Ṣāliḥ b. Dīnār al-Madanī, d. 168/784–85. See Dhahabī, *Kāshif*, III, 53.

Khuzāʿī; 'Amr b. A'yan Abū Ḥamzah, a client of the Khuzāʿah;
Shibl b. Ṭahmān Abū 'Alī al-Harawī, a client of the Banū Ḥanīfah;
and 'Īsā b. A'yan, a client of the Khuzāʿah. Abū Muḥammad al-
Ṣādiq also chose seventy men, and Muḥammad b. 'Alī wrote a
letter to them so that they might have a plan of action to follow.[315]

[1359]   In this year, the pilgrimage was led by Abū Bakr b. Muḥammad
b. 'Amr b. Ḥazm. This was related to me by Aḥmad b. Thābit—
the person he mentioned—Isḥāq b. 'Īsā—Abū Ma'shar. The same
was reported by al-Wāqidī.

The governors of the garrison towns in this year were the same
as in the previous year, as mentioned above,[316] with the exception of Khurāsān, for its governors, at the end of the year, were
'Abd al-Raḥmān b. Nu'aym, who was in charge of prayer and
military matters, and 'Abd al-Raḥmān b. 'Abdallāh, who was in
charge of the fiscal administration.

---

315. Compare text below, II/1988, sub anno 130, where Ṭabarī mentions a
second list of twelve chiefs. References to 'Abbāsid propaganda in the years following A.H. 100 have been collected by Wellhausen, *Arab Kingdom*, 506–14. The
problem of the organization of the *Da'wah* is discussed in Sharon, *Black Banners*,
153–200.
316. See text above, II/1346–47, sub anno 99.

The
Events of the Year

101

(JULY 24, 719—JULY 11, 720)

These events include the escape of Yazīd b. al-Muhallab from the prison of ʿUmar b. ʿAbd al-ʿAzīz.[317]

The Escape of Yazīd b. al-Muhallab

According to Hishām b. Muḥammad—Abū Mikhnaf: ʿUmar b. ʿAbd al-ʿAzīz, upon being addressed on behalf of Yazīd b. al-Muhallab at the time that he wanted to banish him to Dahlak—that is, when someone said to him, "We fear that his tribe will attempt to recover him"—sent Yazīd back to prison,[318] where he remained until he learned that ʿUmar had taken ill. At this point, Yazīd began to plot his escape from prison, due to his fear of Yazīd b. ʿAbd al-Malik, whose in-laws, the family of Abū ʿAqīl,[319] had been tortured by him.[320] Umm al-Ḥajjāj, the daugh-

---

317. See Ibn Khayyāṭ, *Taʾrīkh*, I, 328; Yaʿqūbī, *Taʾrīkh*, III, 52; Kūfī, *Futūḥ*, VII, 322. Azdī, *Taʾrīkh*, 3; *FHA*, 50; Ibn Kathīr, *Bidāyah*, IX, 191; Wellhausen, *Arab Kingdom*, 313.
318. See text above, II/1351, sub anno 100.
319. The text specifies ʿUqayl.
320. See text above, II/1282, sub anno 96.

ter of Muḥammad b. Yūsuf, the brother of al-Ḥajjāj b. Yūsuf, was married to Yazīd b. 'Abd al-Malik and she bore him al-Walīd b. Yazīd, who would later be slain.[321]

[1360]   Yazīd b. 'Abd al-Malik had sworn to God that if God would enable him to overcome Yazīd b. al-Muhallab, he would cut off one of his limbs. Fearing such an outcome, Yazīd b. al-Muhallab sent a message to his clients, who prepared some camels for him. Now 'Umar had taken ill in Dayr Simʿān,[322] and when his illness became more severe Yazīd called for his camels, which were brought to a spot near the prison. When it became clear to Yazīd that 'Umar was seriously ill, he slipped out of the prison and set off on foot until he reached the place that he had agreed upon with his clients.[323] But he did not find them there, and his comrades-in-flight became anxious and annoyed.[324] Yazīd said to them, "Do you think that I am going to return to prison? No, by God, I will never return." Finally, the camels arrived, and he mounted and set off, accompanied by his wife, 'Ātikah, the daughter of al-Furāt b. Muʿāwiyah al-ʿĀmiriyyah, one of the Banū al-Bakkā, who rode in the enclosure of the camel litter. He traveled for a while and when he had gone a certain distance he wrote to 'Umar b. 'Abd al-'Azīz as follows: "By God, if I knew that you were going to live, I would not have left my place of confinement; but I do not trust Yazīd b. 'Abd al-Malik." 'Umar exclaimed, "O God, if Yazīd (b. al-Muhallab) wishes evil on this community, ward off his evil deed, and turn this hostile action back on his own neck." Yazīd b. al-Muhallab proceeded until he passed by Ḥadath al-Zuqāq,[325] where al-Hudhayl b. Zufar, accompanied by tribesmen from the Qays, was present. The Qaysīs pursued Yazīd b. al-Muhallab at the point where he had passed by them and managed to capture part of his traveling apparatus and some of his

---

321. Umm al-Ḥajjāj had been tortured by Yazīd b. al-Muhallab, despite Yazīd b. 'Abd al-Malik's efforts to intervene on behalf of his wife. See Ibn al-Athīr, *Kāmil*, V, 57. On al-Walīd b. Yazīd, see text below, II/1775ff., sub anno 126.

322. Site of a Christian monastery near Damascus named after Simon Peter. See Yāqūt, *Muʿjam*, II, 517; *EI²*, s.v. Dayr Samʿān.

323. Yazīd reportedly secured his release from prison by bribing both the guards and the governor of Aleppo. See *FHA*, 50; Ibn al-Athīr, *Kāmil*, V, 58.

324. Ibn Kathīr, *Bidāyah*, IX, 191, states that Yazīd escaped with a group of people, including his wife.

325. A site in the Palmyra Desert. See *EI²*, s.v. al-Ḥadath.

young slaves. But al-Hudhayl b. Zufar sent after the Qaysīs, and
when they had come back, he asked, "Tell me what you want. Do
you seek blood revenge from Yazīd b. al-Muhallab or from one of
his kinsmen?" They replied, "No." He asked, "Then what do you   [1361]
want? He is merely a man who fled from captivity out of fear for
his life."

Al-Wāqidī maintained that Yazīd b. al-Muhallab did not escape
from prison until after ʿUmar's death.

In this year ʿUmar b. ʿAbd al-ʿAzīz died.[326]

[The Death of ʿUmar b. ʿAbd al-ʿAzīz][327]

According to Aḥmad b. Thābit—the person he mentioned—Isḥāq
b. ʿĪsā—Abū Maʿshar: ʿUmar b. ʿAbd al-ʿAzīz died on the twenty-
fifth of Rajab in the year 101 (February 10, 720). Muḥammad b.
ʿUmar reported likewise.

According to al-Ḥārith—Ibn Saʿd—Muḥammad b. ʿUmar—
ʿAmr b. ʿUthmān: ʿUmar b. ʿAbd al-ʿAzīz died on the twentieth of
Rajab in the year 101 (February 5, 720).

According to Hishām—Abū Mikhnaf: ʿUmar b. ʿAbd al-ʿAzīz
died on Friday the twenty-fifth of Rajab, in Dayr Simʿān, in the
year 101 (February 10, 720). He was thirty-nine years and a few
months old and had been Caliph for two years and five months.
He died in Dayr Simʿān.

According to al-Ḥārith—Aḥmad b. Saʿd—Muḥammad b.
ʿUmar—his paternal uncle, al-Haytham b. Wāqid: I was born in the
year 97/715–716, and ʿUmar b. ʿAbd al-ʿAzīz was appointed as
Caliph in Dābiq on Friday the nineteenth of Ṣafar in the year 99
(October 1, 717). I have three dīnars that were distributed by
him.[328] He died in Khunāṣirah on Wednesday the twenty-fifth of   [1362]
Rajab in the year 101 (February 10, 720) after an illness that lasted
for twenty days. He had been Caliph for two years, five months,

---

326. See Ibn Khayyāṭ, *Taʾrīkh*, I, 328; Yaʿqūbī, *Taʾrīkh*, III, 52; Kūfī, *Futūḥ*, VII,
323; Masʿūdī, *Murūj* (Beirut), III, 182; *FHA*, 63–64; Ibn Kathīr, *Bidāyah*, IX, 193,
212.
327. The rubric, which is not in the Leiden ed., is added from the Cairo ed.
328. Text: *fa-aṣābanī min qismihi*, which may also mean, "that were minted
by him."

and four days. He died at the age of thirty-nine years and a couple of months and was buried in Dayr Sim'ān.

Some sources report: He was thirty-five years and five months old on the day he died. According to other sources: He was forty years old.

Hishām reported: 'Umar died at the age of forty years and a few months. His patronymic was Abū Ḥafṣ. The following verses were addressed to 'Umar by al-'Uwayf after the two of them had witnessed a funeral procession together:

Answer me, Abū Ḥafṣ. Did you meet Muḥammad
    at his pool, giving good tidings to those who were behind
    you?
You are a man whose two hands are *both* useful.
    Your left hand is better than the right of others.

His mother was Umm 'Āṣim, the daughter of 'Āṣim b. 'Umar b. al-Khaṭṭāb. He was known as "The Umayyad with the scar on his forehead" because one of his father's riding animals had wounded him in the face.

According to al-Ḥārith—Ibn Sa'd—Sulaymān b. Ḥarb—al-Mubārak b. Faḍālah—'Ubaydallāh b. 'Umar—Nāfi': I frequently used to hear Ibn 'Umar[329] say, "Would that I knew who from among the children of 'Umar will have a sign on his face. That one will fill the world with justice."

According to Manṣūr b. Abī Muzāhim—Marwān b. Shujā'—Sālim al-Afṭas: When 'Umar b. 'Abd al-'Azīz was a child in Damascus, he was kicked by an animal and carried to his mother, Umm 'Āṣim, the daughter of 'Āṣim b. 'Umar b. al-Khaṭṭāb, who [1363] took him in her arms and wiped the blood from his face. His father came in to see her while she was taking care of the boy, and she turned to him and scolded him, blaming him for the accident, saying, "You have destroyed my son! Why didn't you make sure that he had a servant or a nurse to protect him from something like this?" He said to her, "Be quiet, Umm 'Āṣim. All is well that ends well, since he is destined to be 'The Umayyad with the scar on his forehead.' "

---

329. That is, 'Abdallāh b. 'Umar b. al-Khaṭṭāb, who died in 73/693. See *EI²*, s.v. 'Abdallāh b. 'Umar.

Aspects of His Character

According to ʿAlī b. Muḥammad—Kulayb b. Khalaf—Idrīs b. Ḥanẓalah and al-Mufaḍḍal—his grandfather and ʿAlī b. Mujāhid—Khālid: When ʿUmar b. ʿAbd al-ʿAzīz became Caliph, he wrote to Yazīd b. al-Muhallab as follows: "Now then, Sulaymān was one of God's servants upon whom God bestowed His blessing and then took him away. He designated me as his successor and he designated Yazīd b. ʿAbd al-Malik—if he is still alive—to succeed me. The office that God has entrusted and allotted to me is not easily borne. Were it my desire to take many wives and acquire wealth, then the sums that He has already given me are greater than that attained by any of his creatures.[330] But I fear, in connection with the office for which I have been chosen, a difficult reckoning and a painful questioning, except for whatever defense from trial God may grant me, in His mercy. Those at our end have sworn the oath of allegiance, so now let those at your end do the same."

The letter was brought to Yazīd b. al-Muhallab, who showed it to Abū ʿUyaynah. After the latter had read it, (Yazīd) said, "I will not be one of his governors." Abū ʿUyaynah asked, "Why not?" He replied, "This is not the way that members of his household have spoken in the past, and he does not intend to follow their example." Nevertheless, the soldiers swore the oath of allegiance after Yazīd called on them to do so. He said: ʿUmar then wrote to Yazīd, saying, "Appoint someone as your representative in Khurāsān and come to me." He designated his son, Makhlad, as his representative. [1364]

According to ʿAlī—ʿAlī b. Mujāhid—ʿAbd al-Aʿlā b. Manṣūr—Maymūn b. Mihrān: ʿUmar wrote to ʿAbd al-Raḥmān b. Nuʿaym as follows: "Indeed, Action (ʿamal) and Knowledge (ʿilm) are closely related,[331] so be one who is knowledgeable of God and one who acts on His behalf. There have been people who were knowledgeable but did not act; their knowledge was detrimental to them."

---

330. Text: *kāna fī-lladhī aʿṭānī min dhālika mā qad balagha bī afḍal mā ba-lagha bi-aḥad min khalqihi.*

331. The Arabic words for "action" and "knowledge," *ʿamal* and *ʿilm*, have the same three-letter roots.

According to Muṣʿab b. Ḥayyān—Muqātil b. Ḥayyān: ʿUmar wrote to ʿAbd al-Raḥmān as follows: "Now then, act like a man who knows that God will not repair the deeds of those who cause corruption."

According to ʿAlī—Kulayb b. Khalaf—Ṭufayl b. Mirdās: ʿUmar wrote to Sulaymān b. Abī al-Sarī as follows: "Establish inns in your lands so that whenever a Muslim passes by, you will put him up for a day and a night and take care of his animals; if he is sick, provide him with hospitality for two days and two nights; and if he has used up all of his provisions and is unable to continue, supply him with whatever he needs to reach his hometown." When Sulaymān received ʿUmar's letter, the people of Samarqand said to him, "Qutaybah deceived us, defrauded us, and seized our land.[332] But now that God has made justice and equity to triumph, grant us permission to send a delegation to the Commander of the Faithful in order to present our grievances. If we are in the right, then the land will be given back to us, and we are certainly in need of that." He gave his permission, whereupon they sent a group of their people to visit ʿUmar, who then wrote [1365] on their behalf to Sulaymān b. Abī al-Sariyy: "The people of Samarqand have complained to me about the injustice they were made to suffer and the mistreatment they received from Qutaybah, who expelled them from their land. Therefore, when my letter reaches you, have the judge sit and consider their complaint. If he decides in their favor, expel (the Arabs) to their campgrounds, thereby restoring the status quo to what it had been prior to Qutaybah's conquest of Samarqand."[333]

Sulaymān therefore ordered Jumayʿ b. Ḥāḍir al-Qāḍī al-Nājī to carry out a judicial investigation. He decreed that the Arabs of Samarqand should be sent back to their campgrounds and that the two sides should fight on equal terms, so that there would either be a new peace treaty or victory by force. The army of al-Sughd[334]

---

332. Qutaybah b. Muslim had conquered Samarqand in the year 93/711–12, turning the city into an Arab garrison town. See text above, II/1249ff., sub anno 93.

333. See Balādhurī, *Futūḥ* (Cairo), III, 519.

334. Al-Sughd (also spelled al-Ṣughd) is the name of a district in Transoxiana comprising the lands east of Bukhārā from Dabūsiyah to Samarqand, the latter being its capital. See Yāqūt, *Muʿjam*, III, 222–23; *EI*², s.v. Soghd; Le Strange, *Lands*, 460–73.

said, "But we are satisfied with the old agreement and we will not initiate hostilities." The two sides came to terms on that basis. The wise people[335] among them said, "These tribesmen have mixed with us, and we dwell with them. They trust us and we trust them. But if a judgment is rendered in our favor, we will return to war, and we do not know who will be victorious; and if the judgment is not in our favor, we will have brought hostility into the struggle."[336] Therefore, they left things as they were. They were satisfied and they did not fight.

'Umar wrote to 'Abd al-Raḥmān b. Nu'aym ordering him to recall the Muslims who were in Transoxiana, together with their women and children. But they refused, saying, "Marw does not suffice us." 'Abd al-Raḥmān wrote to 'Umar about this, and 'Umar wrote back to him saying, "By God, I have already fulfilled my obligation. Therefore, do not send the Muslims on any more military campaigns. Let them be satisfied with the victories that God has already granted them."[337]

Our source continued: He also wrote to 'Uqbah b. Zur'ah al-Ṭā'ī, whom he had put in charge of the fiscal administration, after al-Qushayrī: "Sovereignty has several pillars, without which it will not endure: The governor is a pillar; the judge is a pillar; the head of the Public Treasury is a pillar; and I am the fourth pillar. There is no Muslim frontier that is of greater concern to me or that I consider to be as important as the Khurāsān frontier. Therefore, collect the tribute in its entirety and guard it without committing any injustice: If it proves to be sufficient to cover their stipends, that is the path of God; if not, write to me and I will transfer the money to you, thereby making it possible for you to pay them their stipends in full measure." 'Uqbah arrived and determined that the tribute they collected was greater than the stipends to which they were entitled. He therefore wrote to 'Umar notifying him of this, and 'Umar wrote back to him saying, "Distribute the surplus among the needy." [1366]

---

335. The text specifies *ahl al-Rayy*, "the people of al-Rayy." This should be amended to *ahl al-ra'i*. I owe this point to Professor Abbas.

336. Text: *qad ijtalabnā 'adāwah fī-l-munāza'ah*, which could also mean "introduced animosity."

337. See Ya'qūbī, *Ta'rīkh*, III, 47, where it is reported that 'Umar praised the Muslims for their decision to remain in Transoxiana.

According to 'Abdallāh b. Aḥmad b. Shabbawayh—his father—Sulaymān—'Abdallāh—Muḥammad b. Ṭalḥah—Dāwūd b. Sulaymān al-Ju'fī: 'Umar b. 'Abd al-'Azīz wrote as follows: "Greetings from the servant of God, 'Umar, the Commander of the Faithful, to 'Abd al-Ḥamīd. Now then, the army of al-Kūfah has been stricken by trial, hardship, and deviation from the judgments of God, as well as by corrupt customs that were imposed on them by evil governors. The foundation of religion is justice and the performance of good deeds, and there is nothing more important to you than your soul. Remember that even the smallest sin is significant. Do not treat uncultivated land like cultivated land, nor cultivated land like uncultivated land. Examine the uncultivated land, take from it whatever it can bear, and improve it so that it will flourish. Nothing should be taken from cultivated land, except the rate of the tribute. Take it gently, leaving the peasants[338] unruffled. Do not take as tribute anything but the weight of seven.[339] The following levies are not permitted: tolls;[340] the wages of mint officials; presents at the Nawrūz and Mihrajān festivals;[341] and fees for official papers, for couriers, for housing, and for weddings. No tribute shall be levied on those peasants who convert to Islam.[342] Follow my instructions in this matter, for I have commissioned you to carry out what I was commissioned to do by God. Furthermore, do not hasten, on your own initiative, to cut off the arm of the thief or to crucify someone until you have consulted with me on the matter. Finally, consider the request of women and children who desire to go on pilgrimage and immediately pay them one hundred dirhams by means of which they may perform the pilgrimage. Farewell."

[1367]

---

338. Text: *ahl al-arḍ*.

339. Text: *wazn sab'ah*, that is, a dīnar weighing seven *mithqāl*s. See Balādhurī, *Futūḥ* (Cairo), III, 571ff.

340. Text: *āyīn*. On this term, see Wellhausen, *Arab Kingdom*, 303.

341. The spring and autumn festivals of Nawrūz and Mihrajān were the pivots of the Sassanian administrative and ceremonial year. Public audiences were held, and gifts were presented to the monarch on both occasions. The requirement for gifts at Nawrūz and Mihrajān was revived by 'Abdallāh b. Darrāj, perhaps in his capacity as royal agent, who added ten million dirhams in gifts to the income from taxes. See Morony, *Iraq*, 73; *EI*[1], s.vv. Nawrūz and Mihrgān.

342. See Gibb, "The Fiscal Rescript of 'Umar II," 1–16.

According to ʿAbdallāh b. Aḥmad b. Shabbawayh—his father—
Sulaymān—ʿAbdallāh—Shihāb b. Sharīʿah al-Mujāshiʿī: ʿUmar b.
ʿAbd al-ʿAzīz included the wives and children of the soldiers who
received stipends (in the Dīwān). Lots were cast among them, and
those on whom the lot fell were assigned one hundred (dirhams),
while those on whom the lot did not fall were assigned forty. He
distributed money to the poor people of al-Baṣrah, giving each
man three dirhams and giving the chronically ill fifty dirhams
each.

He said: And I think he also awarded stipends to children upon
weaning.[343]

According to ʿAbdallāh—his father—al-Fuḍayl—ʿAbdallāh: I
was told that ʿUmar b. ʿAbd al-ʿAzīz wrote to the Syrian army as
follows: "Peace upon you, and the mercy of God. Now then,
whoever contemplates death frequently speaks little, while he
who knows that death is certain is satisfied with a little.
Farewell."

According to ʿAlī b. Muḥammad: Abū Mijlaz said to ʿUmar:
"You have put us in a wasteland,[344] so send us money." He
replied, "O Abū Mijlaz, you have reversed the matter." He said,
"O Commander of the Faithful, does the money belong to us or to
you?" ʿUmar said, "Indeed, it belongs to you when the amount
you collect does not cover your stipends." He said, "But you have
neither carried it to us, nor carried us to it,[345] and you have put
one part of it upon the other." He said, "I will have it carried to
you, God willing." But he fell ill that very night and died.

ʿAbd al-Raḥmān b. Nuʿaym's tenure of office in Khurāsān was
sixteen months.

Abū Jaʿfar (al-Ṭabarī) said: In this year, ʿUmārah b. Ukaymah al-
Laythī, whose patronymic was Abū al-Walīd, died at the age of
seventy-nine.

[1368]

---

343. Text: *rizq al-faṭm.* On this practice, see Balādhurī, *Futūḥ* (Cairo) III, 562.
344. Text: *bi-munqaṭaʿi-l-turāb.*
345. Text: *wa-lā naḥmiluhu ilayka*—"and we have not carried it to you"; read
wa-lā taḥmilunā ilayhi, as suggested in footnote (g) of the Leiden text. I owe this
point to Professor Abbas.

A Supplement to the Biography of 'Umar b. 'Abd al-'Azīz That Is Not Part of Abū Ja'far's [al-Ṭabarī's] Book, to the Beginning of the Caliphate of Yazīd b. 'Abd al-Malik b. Marwān

According to 'Abdallāh b. Bakr b. Ḥabīb al-Sahmī: We were told by a man in the mosque of al-Junābidh[346] that 'Umar b. 'Abd al-'Azīz delivered a sermon to the people in Khunāṣirah in which he said:

[1369]

O people, you were not created in vain, nor will you be left to yourselves.[347] Rather, you will return to a place in which God will descend in order to judge among you and distinguish between you. Destitute and lost are those who forsake the all-encompassing mercy of God, and they will be excluded from Paradise, the borders of which are as wide as the heavens and the earth. Don't you know[348] that protection, tomorrow, will be limited to those who feared God (today), and to those who sold something ephemeral for something permanent, something small for something great, and fear for protection? Don't you realize that you are the descendants of those who have perished, that those who remain will take their place after you, and that this will continue until you are all returned to God?[349] Every day you dispatch to God, at all times of the day, someone who has died,[350] his term having come to an end. You bury him in a crack in the earth and then leave him without a pillow or a bed. He has parted from his loved ones, severed his connections with the living, and taken up residence in the earth, whereupon he comes face to face with the accounting. He is mortgaged to his deeds: He needs his accomplishments, but not the material things he left on earth.

---

346. One of the districts of Nīshāpūr. See Yāqūt, *Mu'jam*, II, 165.

347. See Qur'ān 75:36.

348. Text: *a-lā wa-'lamū*. The translation follows Ibn Kathīr, *Bidāyah*, IX, 199, where the text is *a-lam ta'lamū*: "Don't you know?"

349. Text: *ilā khayri-l-wārithīn*. Literally, "to the best heir," applied to God, who causes those who worship him to inherit Paradise.

350. Text: *wa-fī kulli yawmin tushayyi'ūna ghādiyan wa-rā'iḥan ilā-llāhi qad qaḍā naḥbahu*. The expression *qad qaḍā naḥbahu* is Qur'ānic. See Qur'ān 33:23.

Therefore, fear God before death descends and its appointed times expire.[351] I swear by God that I say these words to you knowing that I myself have committed more sins than any of you; I therefore ask God for forgiveness and I repent. Whenever we learn that one of you needs something, I try to satisfy his need to the extent that I am able. Whenever I can provide satisfaction to one of you out of my possessions, I seek to treat him as my equal and my relative, so that my life and his life are of equal value. I swear by God that had I wanted something else, namely, affluence, then it would have been easy for me to utter the word, aware as I am of the means for obtaining this. But God has issued an eloquent Book and a just example (*sunnah*) by means of which He guides us to obedience and proscribes disobedience.

He lifted up the edge of his robe and began to cry and sob, causing the people around him to break into tears. Then he stepped down. That was the last sermon he gave before he died, may God have mercy on him.[352]

According to Khalaf b. Tamīm—ʿAbdallāh b. Muḥammad b. Saʿd: I learned that when one of ʿUmar b. ʿAbd al-ʿAzīz's sons died, one of his governors wrote to him in an effort to console him over the loss of his son.[353] ʿUmar said to his scribe, "Answer him in my name," whereupon the scribe began to sharpen a reed pen. Then ʿUmar said to the scribe, "Make the pen very thin because in that way the papyrus will last longer and the words will be more concise.[354] Write, 'In the name of God the Merciful, the Compassionate, now to the matter at hand. We had prepared

[1370]

---

351. Text: *qabla nuzūl al-mawt wa-nqiḍāʾ mawāqiʿihi*, or "before death descends and overtakes you"; read *mawāqitihi*, following Ṭabarī, *Addenda et Emendanda*, vol. 14, DCXCI.

352. For variant versions of this sermon, see Ibn ʿAbd al-Ḥakam, *Sīrah*, 43–45, 132–33; Ibn Kathīr, *Bidāyah*, IX, 199.

353. See Ibn Kathīr, *Bidāyah*, IX, 208, where the son is identified as ʿAbd al-Malik b. ʿUmar.

354. ʿUmar was known for the scrupulous attention he paid to the proper use of public funds. Elsewhere we find him quibbling with the governor of Medina about the latter's consumption of candle wax and wicks. See Ibn ʿAbd al-Ḥakam, *Sīrah*, 64ff.

ourselves for this event, so that when it occurred, we did not reject it.[355] Farewell.' "

According to Manṣūr b. Muzāḥim—Shuʿayb, that is, Ibn Ṣaf-wān—Ibn ʿAbd al-Ḥamīd: ʿUmar b. ʿAbd al-ʿAzīz said:

> He who gives sincere advice to his brother in matters of religion and looks out for the well-being of the latter's daily affairs has fulfilled his brotherly obligation and carried out the duty that was incumbent upon him. Fear God. Accept these words, for they are offered as sincere advice to you with regard to your religion; and cling fast to them, for they constitute a warning that will save you in the afterlife. The sustenance has been apportioned; therefore, let no believer exceed[356] what has been apportioned to him, and be united in seeking the good. In contentment there is abundance, subsistence, and sufficiency. The term of this life is in your necks, and Gehenna lies before you. What you see will pass away, what has been is as if it never was, and all will soon be dead. You have seen the stages of the dying man, both when he is in the agony of death, and then after his demise when he has tasted death and the people all around him are saying, "He has passed away, may God have mercy on his soul." You have witnessed the hasty manner in which he is removed, and the division of his estate, when his face is lost, his memory forgotten, and his doorway forsaken, as if he had not mixed with those who keep their word, nor inhabited the lands. Therefore, beware the horror of a day on which not so much as the weight of an ant on the scale will be despised.[357]

According to Sahl b. Maḥmūd—Ḥarmalah b. ʿAbd al-ʿAzīz—his father—one of ʿUmar b. ʿAbd al-ʿAzīz's sons: ʿUmar ordered us to

---

355. Text: *lam nadhkurhu*: "We did not mention it"; read *lam nunkirhu*, following the Cairo ed.

356. Text: *yaghdira*, "betray"; the text should be amended to read *yaʿduwa*. I owe this point to Professor Iḥsan Abbas.

357. See Qurʾān 4:40, 10:61, and 34:3.

buy the plot for his grave, so we bought it from the monk. He   [1371]
said: One of the poets[358] recited:

Now that 'Umar's death has been announced to me, I say:
    May the mainstay of justice and religion be not far away.
The people have left behind, in the tomb that they dug
    in Dayr Sim'ān, the balance of the scales.

According to 'Abd al-Raḥmān b. Mahdī—Sufyān: 'Umar b. 'Abd al-'Azīz said: "He who acts without knowledge[359] causes more corruption than good, and he who does not consider his speech to be part of his actions sins repeatedly. Satisfaction is scarce, and the true believer should rely on patience: God never bestowed a blessing upon one of His servants and then took it away from him, giving him patience in return for that which was taken away, except that the replacement was better than what was taken away from him." Then he recited the following verse: "Surely the patient will be paid their wages in full without reckoning."[360]

'Abd al-Raḥmān b. Nu'aym received the following letter from him: "Do not destroy a church, synagogue, or fire temple with   [1372] respect to which an agreement has been concluded with you, and do not permit the construction of a new church or fire temple.[361] Do not drag the lamb to its place of slaughter or sharpen the knife over the head of the animal. Do not combine two prayers without an excuse."

According to 'Affān b. Muslim—'Uthmān b. 'Abd al-Ḥamīd—his father—Fāṭimah, the wife of 'Umar b. 'Abd al-'Azīz, said: He became extremely uncomfortable one night, and we stayed up with him. The next morning I instructed one of his servants, by the name of Marthid, saying, "Marthid, stay with the Commander of the Faithful so that if he needs anything you will be close at hand."

---

358. The authorship of this poem is disputed. Mas'ūdī, *Murūj* (Beirut), III, 195, records a variant version of the poem in which al-Farazdaq is specified as the author. Ibn al-Athīr, *Kāmil*, V, 59, identifies the poet as Kuthayyir 'Azzah (d. 105/723).

359. Text: *'amila 'alā ghayr 'ilm*—a pun. See text above, II/1364, note 331.

360. Qur'ān 39:10.

361. On the status of non-Muslim places of worship in Muslim lands, see *EI*[2], s.vv. Dhimma, Kanīsa.

Then we left, and our heads were throbbing[362] because we had stayed up so late. At midday I awoke and went to him, but I found Marthid sleeping outside of his room. I woke him up, saying, "Marthid, who told you to leave?" He said, "(The Caliph) did. He said, 'Marthid, leave me for by God I see something that is neither human nor jinn.' As I left, I heard him reciting this verse: 'That is the Last Abode; we appoint it for those who desire not exorbitance in the earth, nor corruption. The issue ultimate is to the godfearing.' "[363] Marthid said: When I reentered the room, I found that he had turned his face toward the *qiblah* and closed his eyes. He was dead, may God have mercy on him.[364]

---

362. Text: *fa-ḍarabnā bi-ruʾūsinā*. Literally this means "we were striking our heads."

363. Qurʾān 28:83.

364. This is the end of the supplement. Ibn ʿAbd al-Ḥakam preserves a variant version of ʿUmar's deathbed scene in which Maslamah b. ʿAbd al-Malik is reported to have been present. See *Sīrah*, 116–117.

The Caliphate of Yazīd b. ʿAbd al-Malik b. Marwān

The
Events of the Year

IOI (cont'd)
(July 24, 719–July 11, 720)[365]

In this year Yazīd b. ʿAbd al-Malik b. Marwān—his patronymic was Abū Khālid—came to power. He was twenty-nine years old at the time, according to Hishām b. Muḥammad. Upon assuming the caliphate, he dismissed Abū Bakr b. Muḥammad b. ʿAmr b. Ḥazm as governor of Medina, replacing him with ʿAbd al-Raḥmān b. al-Ḍaḥḥāk b. Qays al-Fihrī. According to al-Wāqidī, the latter arrived on a Wednesday toward the end of the month of Ramaḍān (April 10, 720). ʿAbd al-Raḥmān put Salamah b. ʿAbdallāh b. ʿAbd al-Asad al-Makhzūmī in charge of the judiciary. [1373]

According to Muḥammad b. ʿUmar—ʿAbd al-Jabbār b. ʿUmārah—Abū Bakr b. Ḥazm: When ʿAbd al-Raḥmān b. al-Ḍaḥḥāk arrived in Medina to replace me, I went in to see him. I greeted him, but he didn't welcome me. I said, "This matter (that is, the governorship of Medina) is one over which the Quraysh will not award

---

365. For other sources on the caliphate of Yazīd b. ʿAbd al-Malik b. Marwān, see Ibn Qutaybah, *Maʿārif*, 364; Dīnawarī, *Akhbār*, 334–36; Yaʿqūbī, *Taʾrīkh*, III, 53–58; Azdī, *Taʾrīkh*, 5–21; Masʿūdī, *Murūj* (Beirut), III, 195–204; *FHA*, 64–81; Ibn Kathīr, *Bidāyah*, IX, 219–33.

the Helpers (Anṣār)[366] jurisdiction."[367] Then I returned to my residence. I was afraid of him—he was a reckless young man—and indeed he let me know that he was saying, "Only old age prevents Ibn Ḥazm from coming to me, and I am aware of his deception." I realized then that my fears had materialized and when I was sure that he had uttered that statement, I said to my informant, "Tell him, 'It is not my custom to deceive, and I do not like those who do. The governor imagines that he is going to remain in power forever. But how many governors and caliphs have occupied this residence before you and then left it, so that now all that is left of them is stories, for better or for worse? Fear God and do not pay attention to what is said by a transgressor or an envious person.'"

Relations between the two men continued to deteriorate until a man from the Banū Fihr and another from the Banū al-Najjār appealed to Ibn al-Ḍaḥḥāk to resolve a dispute between them. Abū Bakr had previously rendered a decision in favor of the Najjārī and against the Fihrī with regard to some land, of which they each owned one-half. Abū Bakr had awarded the land to the Naj[1374]   jārī. The Fihrī sent to the Najjārī and to Abū Bakr b. Ḥazm, calling on them to present themselves before Ibn al-Ḍaḥḥāk. The Fihrī complained about Abū Bakr b. Ḥazm, saying, "He took my property out of my hands and awarded it to this Najjārī." Abū Bakr responded, "I beg God's forgiveness, but you know that I examined the dispute between you and your co-owner for several days, after which I decided to dispossess you of your land. Furthermore, I sent you to the legal scholars (muftīs) who advised me in the matter, Saʿīd b. al-Musayyab[368] and Abū Bakr b. ʿAbd al-Raḥmān b. al-Ḥārith b. Hishām, and you questioned them." The Fihrī said, "Indeed, but their word is not binding on me." At this point, Ibn al-Ḍaḥḥāk felt beaten and he interjected, saying, "Stand up."

---

366. The term Anṣār designates Muḥammad's Medinese supporters in distinction from his Meccan following, known as the "emigrants" (muhājirūn). See EI2, s.v. Anṣar.

367. This is a conjectural translation. Text: hādha shayʾun lā tamlikuhu qurayshun al-anṣāra; read li-l-anṣāri, following the Cairo ed. ʿAbd al-Raḥmān was a Qurashī, while Abū Bakr was one of the Helpers.

368. This dispute must have occurred at least six years earlier, since Saʿīd b. al-Musayyab, one of the first specialists in religious law whose activity can be regarded as historical, died in 95/713–14. See EI2, s.v. Fikh.

They stood up, and he said to the Fihrī, "You acknowledge to him that you questioned the *muftī*s about their judgment, but then you say to me, 'Give me my land back.' You are a fool! Leave, for you are not entitled to anything."

But Abū Bakr continued to fear Ibn al-Daḥḥāk. Subsequently, Ibn Ḥayyān[369] asked Yazīd to allow him to retaliate against Abū Bakr, who had administered the *ḥadd* punishments to him on two occasions. Yazīd said, "I won't allow it, for that man was chosen and trusted by the members of my household. I will, however, appoint you as governor of Medina." He said, "I do not want that, for if I were to punish him by virtue of my authority, that would not constitute retaliation." Yazīd then wrote to ʿAbd al-Rahmān b. al-Daḥḥāk as follows: "Now to the matter at hand. Investigate Ibn Ḥazm's punishment of Ibn Ḥayyān: If the punishment was a result of an obvious transgression, don't concern yourself with it; and if the punishment was a result of a matter that was subject to dispute, don't concern yourself with it; but if the punishment was a result of some other cause, allow Ibn Ḥayyān to retaliate against him."

ʿUthmān brought the letter to ʿAbd al-Rahmān b. al-Daḥḥāk, who said, "You have not accomplished anything. Do you think that Ibn Ḥazm punished you as a result of something that was not subject to dispute?" Then ʿUthmān said to ʿAbd al-Rahmān, "If you want to do me a favor, now is the time to do so." He said, "Now you have achieved your objective." ʿAbd al-Rahmān sent for Ibn Ḥazm and administered the *ḥadd* punishment to him twice, on a single occasion, without asking him a single question. Then Abū al-Maghrā'[370] b. Ḥayyān[371] returned, saying, "I am Abū al-Maghrā'[372] b. al-Ḥayyān [*sic*]. By God, I have not had any relations with women from the day that Ibn Ḥazm did what he did to me until this very day. Today, I shall resume my relations with women."[373]

[1375]

---

369. ʿUthmān b. Ḥayyān al-Murrī, a former governor of Medina. See text above, II/1281.
370. Text: al-Maʿzā; read al-Maghrā', following the Cairo ed.
371. That is, ʿUthmān b. Ḥayyān. See note 369, above.
372. See note 370 above.
373. See Yaʿqūbī, *Taʾrīkh*, III, 56.

Abū Jaʿfar (al-Ṭabarī) said: In this year, Shawdhab the Khārijite was slain.[374]

The Slaying of Shawdhab the Khārijite

We have already mentioned the report about the delegation that Shawdhab sent to ʿUmar b. ʿAbd al-ʿAzīz in order to argue about his revolt against the Caliph.[375] According to Maʿmar b. al-Muthannā, when ʿUmar died, ʿAbd al-Ḥamīd b. ʿAbd al-Raḥmān, desirous of winning the favor of Yazīd b. ʿAbd al-Malik, wrote to Muḥammad b. Jarīr ordering him to attack Shawdhab and his men. Now at that moment, Shawdhab, whose two messengers had not yet returned, was unaware of ʿUmar's death. Thus, when the Khārijites saw Muḥammad b. Jarīr preparing for battle, Shawdhab sent to him, asking, "What prompts you to engage in hostilities prior to the expiration of the time period upon which we had agreed? Did we not promise one another not to fight ʿuntil Shawdhab's two messengers return?'" But Muḥammad replied, saying, "We cannot leave you in this state."

Sources other than Abū ʿUbaydah: The Khārijites said: These people would not have acted in this manner but that the righteous man[376] has died.

[1376]   According to Maʿmar b. al-Muthannā: Shawdhab went forth into battle against them, and the two sides engaged in combat. Several of the Khārijites were wounded, but they killed many of the Muslims.[377] The latter turned and fled, with the Khārijites in hot pursuit, until they reached the wooden houses of al-Kūfah, where they took refuge with ʿAbd al-Ḥamīd. Muḥammad b. Jarīr himself was wounded on the buttocks. Afterwards, Shawdhab returned to his camp where he remained, waiting for the return of his two messengers. They arrived and informed him of the demands they had made upon ʿUmar and of the fact that he had died.

Yazīd confirmed ʿAbd al-Ḥamīd as governor of al-Kūfah and

---

374. See Azdī, *Taʾrīkh*, 6–8; *FHA*, 64–65; Ibn Kathīr, *Bidāyah*, IX, 219.
375. See text above, II/1347ff.
376. That is, ʿUmar b. ʿAbd al-ʿAzīz. See note 251, above.
377. Text: *ahl al-qiblah*. On this term see *EI²*, s.v. Ahl al-Ḳibla. Note, however, that Azdī, *Taʾrīkh*, 7, and Ibn al-Athīr, *Kāmil*, V, 68, have *ahl al-Kūfah*, "the Kūfan army."

sent Tamīm b. al-Ḥubāb on his behalf, with two thousand soldiers. Tamīm sent a message to the Khārijites in which he informed them that Yazīd would not leave them intact on the same terms as ʿUmar had. But they cursed him and they cursed Yazīd, whereupon Tamīm attacked them. But they slew him and put his men to flight: some of them took refuge in al-Kūfah, while the others made their way back to Yazīd.[378] Then Yazīd sent against them Najdah b. al-Ḥakam al-Azdī, leading a military division, but they slew him and put his men to flight. Next he sent against them al-Shaḥḥāj b. Wadāʿ, leading two thousand soldiers. The two sides exchanged messages, and then the Khārijites slew al-Shaḥḥāj. But several of their men were slain, including Hudbah al-Yashkurī, the paternal cousin of Bisṭām, who was a pious man; and Abū Shaybān[379] Muqātil b. Shaybān, whom they considered to be a virtuous man. Abū Thaʿlabah Ayyūb b. Khawalī[380] recited the following, elegizing them:

We left Tamīm in the dust, torn to pieces,   [1377]
    mourned by his wife and his kinsmen.
Qays abandoned Tamīm and Mālik,
    just as al-Shaḥḥāj was abandoned by his kinsmen
    yesterday.
He came from Ḥarrān carrying a standard,
    seeking to overcome the command of God, but God
    overcame him.
O Hudbah, to war, O Hudbah to the muster,
    O Hudbah to the tenacious adversary who attacks him!
O Hudbah! How many a cornered man[381] have you rescued,
    when his Fate had delivered him to the spears?
Abū Shaybān was the best fighter[382]
    to be sought after. His strength was feared by those who
    fought him.

---

378. Yazīd was in Damascus.
379. Text: Shubayl; read Shaybān, as in the sixth verse of the poem that follows; and as in Azdī, *Taʾrīkh*, 7.
380. Azdī, *Taʾrīkh*, 7, gives his name as Thaʿlabah b. Ayyūb b. Khawalī b. Bayham.
381. Text: *mulḥam*. Ibn al-Athīr, *Kāmil*, V, 69, has *muljim*.
382. Text: *muqātil*, a pun on Abū Shaybān's name, Muqātil.

He triumphed and met God with many good deeds to his
   credit.
      His slayer smote him with the sword while he was fighting
      in the path of God.
He provisioned himself with implements of this world: armor,
      mail,
      and a sharp sword whose edges did not betray him.
And a short-haired sturdy horse, as if it were,
      when it attacks, (a bird of prey,) full-feathered with crooked
      claws.[383]

[1378] When Maslamah entered al-Kūfah, the residents of the city
complained to him about Shawdhab, who had terrified them and
slain many of their men. Maslamah summoned Saʿīd b. ʿAmr al-
Ḥarashī, who was a horseman, put him in command of ten thousand men, and sent him against Shawdhab, who was at his camp.
Confronted by these insurmountable forces, Shawdhab said to his
men, "For those of you who are seeking God, the time to die as a
martyr has arrived; as for those of you who only came out because
of this world, know that this world has come to an end, while
everlasting life is to be found in the next abode." Upon hearing
this, they smashed the sheaths of their swords and attacked, repeatedly putting Saʿīd and his men to flight, so that he was afraid
of being disgraced. Then he rebuked his men, saying, "Woe to
you,[384] are you fleeing from such a small number of men? O
Syrians, beware of a distressing day!"

Our source continued: The Syrians attacked the Khārijites,
crushing them to pieces, leaving not one of them alive. They slew
Bisṭām—that is, Shawdhab—and his horsemen, including al-
Rayyān b. ʿAbdallāh al-Yashkurī, who was among those who were
submissive to God.[385] His brother, Shimr b. ʿAbdallāh, recited the
following elegy:

I was distressed about chiefs and horsemen
   from the Banū Shaybān who kindled the fire of war.

---

383. See Azdī, *Taʾrīkh*, 8.
384. Text: *lā abā lakum*, literally, "may you have no father." This proverbial
expression is used as an imprecation. See Lane, *Lexicon*, pt. 1, pp. 10–11.
385. Text: *min al-muḥiththīn*, "one of the instigators"; read *min al-mukhbitīn*,
following the Cairo ed.

The accidents of time detained and destroyed them,
    leaving me by myself, brotherless.
Sad, with grief ringing in my heart,
    like a fire, because of my deep feelings for the loss of al-
    Rayyān.
And (about) horsemen who sold their souls to God,
    from the Yashkur, proving themselves knights in battle.

Ḥassān b. Jaʿdah recited the following elegy:

O eye! Shed copious tears on your own,
    and cry for Bisṭām's men, and for Bisṭām.
As long as you live, you will never see the likes of them,
    none more pious or more perfect, gentle and wise.
They took their equals as an example during their time of   [1379]
    difficulty,
    and had no wish to hold back from enemies.
Until they went to meet the one on whose behalf they had
    rebelled,
    leaving us landmarks and signposts as an inheritance.
Verily I know that they have been made to dwell in rooms
    of Paradise, where they will live in eternity, and obtained
    there servants.
May God water the lands where they met their deaths
    with abundant spring rains!

Abū Jaʿfar (al-Ṭabarī) said: In this year, Yazīd b. al-Muhallab
reached al-Baṣrah and took control of the city. He arrested Yazīd
b. ʿAbd al-Malik's governor, ʿAdī b. Arṭāt al-Fazārī, threw him into
prison, and renounced his allegiance to Yazīd b. ʿAbd al-Malik.[386]

Yazīd b. al-Muhallab Renounces His Allegiance to Yazīd b. ʿAbd al-Malik

Having already mentioned the report of Yazīd b. al-Muhallab's
escape from the prison in which he had been confined by ʿUmar b.

---

386. See Ibn Khayyāṭ, *Taʾrīkh*, I, 328; Yaʿqūbī, *Taʾrīkh*, III, 54; Kūfī, *Futūḥ*, VIII,
1–11; Azdī, *Taʾrīkh*, 8–10; Masʿūdī, *Murūj* (Beirut), III, 199–200; *FHA*, 51–60; Ibn
Kathīr, *Bidāyah*, IX, 219–20; Wellhausen, *Arab Kingdom*, 312ff.

ʿAbd al-ʿAzīz,[387] I will discuss here his actions following his escape in the year 101/719–20. On the very day that ʿUmar b. ʿAbd al-ʿAzīz died, the oath of allegiance was sworn to Yazīd b. ʿAbd al-Malik. Upon being informed of Yazīd b. al-Muhallab's escape, the Caliph wrote to ʿAbd al-Ḥamīd b. ʿAbd al-Raḥmān, ordering him to search for the fugitive and confront him. The Caliph also wrote to ʿAdī b. Arṭāt, informing him of Yazīd's escape; he ordered ʿAdī to prepare for the confrontation and to arrest those members of Yazīd's household who were in al-Baṣrah.

According to Hishām b. Muḥammad—Abū Mikhnaf: ʿAdī b. Arṭāt arrested several of Yazīd's brothers and threw them into prison: al-Mufaḍḍal, Ḥabīb, and Marwān, the sons of al-Muhallab. Meanwhile, Yazīd b. al-Muhallab advanced until he passed by Saʿīd b. ʿAbd al-Malik b. Marwān.[388] Yazīd said to his men, "Let's block his way, seize him, and take him with us." But his men replied, "No. Rather, advance with us and leave him alone." He marched forward, climbing up above Quṭquṭānah.[389]

ʿAbd al-Ḥamīd b. ʿAbd al-Raḥmān dispatched Hishām b. Musāhiq b. ʿAbdallāh b. Mukhrimah b. ʿAbd al-ʿAzīz b. Abī Qays b. ʿAbd Wudd b. Naṣr b. Mālik b. Ḥisl b. ʿĀmir b. Luwayy al-Qurashī, leading a segment of the Kūfan army that included the security force, the notables, and the powerful people. ʿAbd al-Ḥamīd instructed Hishām as follows, "Set off until you come face to face with Yazīd, who will today pass by the shore of al-ʿUdhayb."[390] Hishām traveled a short distance but then returned to ʿAbd al-Ḥamīd and asked him, "Shall I bring him to you dead or alive?" He replied, "That's up to you." This statement greatly astonished those who heard it. Hishām made his way to al-ʿUdhayb, where he set up camp at a point not far from where Yazīd was located. But Hishām and his men avoided attacking Yazīd, who marched off in the direction of al-Baṣrah. The poet recited, referring to Yazīd:

Ibn al-Muhallab traveled without stopping,

---

387. See text above, II/1359ff.

388. Sulaymān b. ʿAbd al-Malik's brother, who would later serve as governor of Mosul and Palestine respectively. He died in 132/749–50. See Crone, *Slaves*, 129.

389. Located near al-Kūfah, facing the desert. See Yāqūt, *Muʿjam*, IV, 374.

390. A body of fresh water between al-Qādisiyyah and al-Maghīthah, four miles from the former and thirty-two miles from the latter. See Yāqūt, *Muʿjam*, IV, 92.

while Dhū al-Qaṭīfah, from the Kinānah, rested during the
night.
He took the left side, thus taking the wise course,
    and he did not approach the fortresses of Quṭquṭānah.[391]

Dhū al-Qaṭīfah refers to Muḥammad b. ʿAmr, (whose father,
ʿAmr) b. al-Walīd b. ʿUqbah b. Abī Muʿayṭ is known as Abū Qaṭī-
fah. He was given the name Dhū al-Qaṭīfah because his beard,
face, and chest were very hairy. Muḥammad is also known as
Dhū al-Shāmah ("The one with the birthmark").

When Yazīd b. al-Muhallab drew near, Hishām b. Musāhiq returned to ʿAbd al-Ḥamīd, and Yazīd then marched toward al-   [1381]
Baṣrah. Meanwhile, ʿAdī b. Arṭāt had rallied the Baṣran army, dug
a trench around the city, and put al-Mughīrah b. ʿAbdallāh b. Abī
ʿAqīl al-Thaqafī in command of the Baṣran cavalry.

ʿAbd al-Malik b. al-Muhallab said to ʿAdī b. Arṭāt, who was
from the Banū Fazārah: "Take my son, Ḥumayd, and put him in
prison in my place. I give you my solemn pledge that I will divert
Yazīd from al-Baṣrah and make him retreat to Fārs, where he will
seek a promise of safe-conduct for himself and be far removed
from you." But ʿAdī refused. When Yazīd arrived with his soldiers,
al-Baṣrah was surrounded with men, for Muḥammad b. al-Muhallab, who was not one of those who had been imprisoned, had
assembled some men and youths from his household together
with some of his clients and gone out to rendezvous with Yazīd.
He advanced with a detachment of cavalry that struck fear in the
hearts of those who saw it.

ʿAdī had summoned the army of al-Baṣrah and put one man in
command of each tribal division (khums): He put al-Mughīrah b.
Ziyād b. ʿAmr al-ʿAtakī in command of the Azd; Muḥriz b.
Ḥumrān al-Saʿdī, from the Banū Minqar, in command of the Banū
Tamīm; and ʿImrān b. ʿĀmir b. Mismaʿ, from the Banū Qays b.
Thaʿlabah, in command of the Bakr b. Wāʾil. But Abū Minqar, a
tribesman from the Qays b. Thaʿlabah, said, "We will not be
victorious unless the the Banū Mālik b. Mismaʿ carry the standard." ʿAdī then summoned Nūḥ b. Shaybān b. Mālik b. Mismaʿ
and put him in command of the Bakr b. Wāʾil; he summoned

---

391. See Kūfī, Futūḥ, VIII, 2–3.

[1382]   Mālik b. al-Mundhir b. al-Jārūd and put him in command of the ʿAbd al-Qays; and he summoned ʿAbd al-Aʿlā b. ʿAbdallāh b. ʿĀmir al-Qurashī and put him in command of the Ahl al-ʿĀliyah. The ʿĀliyah are composed of the following tribes: Quraysh, Kinānah, Azd, Bajīlah, Khathʿam, all of Qays ʿAylān, and Muzaynah. In al-Kūfah the Ahl al-ʿĀliyah are known as the "Ahl al-Madīnah fourth-division" (rubʿ), and in al-Baṣrah they are known as the "Ahl al-ʿĀliyah fifth-division" (khums). In al-Kūfah there were, at first, five divisions, but Ziyād b. ʿUbayd reorganized them into four.

According to Hishām—Abū Mikhnaf: Yazīd b. al-Muhallab advanced, but every horseman and tribal unit that he encountered turned away from him, allowing him to continue. Finally, he was confronted by al-Mughīrah b. ʿAbdallāh al-Thaqafī, who was leading the cavalry. Muḥammad b. al-Muhallab attacked him with his horsemen, but al-Mughīrah and his men moved out of his way. Yazīd proceeded to his house, where the people came to visit him in turns. He began to send messages to ʿAdī b. Arṭāt, saying, "If you deliver my brothers to me, I will conclude a peace agreement with you with regard to al-Baṣrah. I will leave you and the city alone so that I might acquire what I want from Yazīd b. ʿAbd al-Malik."[392] But ʿAdī rejected his offer. Earlier, Ḥumayd b. ʿAbd al-Malik b. al-Muhallab had gone to see Yazīd b. ʿAbd al-Malik, who sent him back, accompanied by Khālid b. ʿAbdallāh al-Qasrī and by ʿUmar b. Yazīd al-Ḥakamī. They were carrying a promise of safe-conduct for Yazīd b. al-Muhallab and his household.[393]

Yazīd b. al-Muhallab began to award stipends to the soldiers who joined him, distributing pieces of gold and silver, thereby causing the soldiers to be well-disposed toward him. ʿImrān b. ʿĀmir b. Mismaʿ joined him because he was angry with ʿAdī b. Arṭāt for taking the standard—that is, the standard of the Bakr b. Wāʾil—from him and giving it to his paternal cousin. Also joining Yazīd

[1383]   were the tribes of Rabīʿah, the remainder of Tamīm, Qays, and many individual soldiers, including ʿAbd al-Malik and Mālik, the

---

392. Yazīd wanted a guarantee of safe-conduct. See Kūfī, Futūḥ, VIII, 3, where the parallel passage has, "so that I might acquire a guarantee of safe-conduct." When Yazīd b. al-Muhallab arrived in al-Baṣrah after escaping from prison, he wrote to the new Caliph asking for a promise of safe-conduct. See FHA, 52.

393. ʿUmar reportedly awarded the promise on the condition that Yazīd stay put. See FHA, 67.

two sons of Mismaʿ. There were also some soldiers from the Syrian army with him.

ʿAdī, on the other hand, could offer each man only two dirhams. He would say, "I cannot give you a single dirham from the Public Treasury without the authorization of Yazīd b. ʿAbd al-Malik. Be content with this until such authorization is granted." Al-Farazdaq recited in connection with this:

I suspect that the "two-dirham men" are driven
    to death by their Fate and by their destined ends.
The most sensible one among them is he who remains inside
    his house,
        certain that the end is inevitable.[394]

The Banū ʿAmr b. Tamīm split off from ʿAdī's men and established themselves in al-Mirbad.[395] Yazīd b. al-Muhallab sent against them one of his clients, known as Dāris, who attacked them and put them to flight. Al-Farazdaq recited with regard to this:

The 'Reds'[396] scattered when Dāris shouted,
    for they could not endure the sharp swords.
God repaid Qays for ʿAdī as a reproach.
    Couldn't they hold fast until the fighting broke out?[397]

After the soldiers had rallied to him, Yazīd b. al-Muhallab marched to the cemetery of the Banū Yashkur, located midway between him and the fortress, where he set up camp. The Banū Tamīm, the Qays, and the Syrian army approached him, and the two sides fought for a little while. Muḥammad b. al-Muhallab attacked them and struck Miswar b. ʿAbbād al-Ḥabaṭī with his sword, smashing the nosepiece of his helmet, and then quickly thrust the sword into his nose. He also attacked Huraym b. Abī Ṭaḥmah[398] b. Abī Nahshal b. Dārim, grabbing his belt and throwing him off his horse. When (Huraym) fell between him and the

[1384]

---

394. See *Dīwān al-Farazdaq*, I, 421; Kūfī, *Futūḥ*, VIII, 4; Ibn al-Athīr, *Kāmil*, V, 72.

395. The Mirbad of al-Baṣrah was the famous caravan quarter at the western end of the city. See Yāqūt, *Muʿjam*, V, 97–99; Le Strange, *Lands*, 45.

396. The 'Reds' are the Persian *"mawālī"* (clients).

397. See *Dīwān al-Farazdaq*, II, 224; Kūfī, *Futūḥ*, VIII, 5–6.

398. Read *Ṭaḥmah*, as in the text; the Cairo ed. has *Ṭalḥah*. See Caskel, *Ǧamharah*, II, 287; Kūfī, *Futūḥ*, VIII, 5, n. 2.

horse, (Muḥammad) exclaimed, "What a futile attempt! Your paternal uncle is heavier than that."[399] The soldiers fled, pursued by Yazīd b. al-Muhallab, who followed them until he approached the fortress. There, they engaged them in battle, with ʿAdī himself going out to fight Yazīd. Several of ʿAdī's men were slain, including al-Ḥārith b. Muṣarrif al-Awdī, one of the nobles of the Syrian army who had been a horseman under al-Ḥajjāj, Mūsā b. al-Wajīh al-Ḥimyarī—later al-Kalāʿī, and Rāshid the Muʾadhdhin. ʿAdī's forces fled.

Yazīd's brothers, who were in ʿAdī's prison, heard the shouts getting closer and the arrows falling inside the fortress. ʿAbd al-Malik b. al-Muhallab said to them, "I see the arrows falling inside the fortress and hear the shouts coming closer. Although I think that Yazīd has triumphed, I fear that the Muḍarīs, that is, the Syrians who are with ʿAdī, will come and slay us before Yazīd can reach us here in the room. Therefore, barricade the door and throw some furniture against it."[400] They obeyed his instructions. Shortly thereafter they were approached by ʿAbdallāh b. Dīnār, a client of Ibn ʿUmar[401] who was the commander of ʿAdī's guards. He and his men tried to force their way in, but the Muhallabids had thrown some furniture[402] against the door and were leaning on it. The others tried, unsuccessfully, to push in

[1385]   the door, but abandoned them when the soldiers told them they had to hurry.

Yazīd b. al-Muhallab advanced and occupied the house of Sālim b. Ziyād b. Abī Sufyān,[403] which was adjacent to the fortress. Ladders were brought forward, and it was not long before ʿUthmān[404] stormed the fortress. ʿAdī b. Arṭāt was captured and brought out, smiling. Yazīd said to him, "Why are you laughing?

---

399. The context here suggests that it is Muḥammad who attacks Huraym and throws him off his horse, although the subjects could be reversed, as in Kūfī, *Futūḥ*, VIII, 5, where Muḥammad fails in his attempt to throw Huraym from his horse, whereupon it is the latter who laughs and exclaims, "What a futile attempt, O nephew! Your paternal uncle is heavier than you think."

400. Text: *thiyāb*, which literally means "clothing." Ibn al-Athīr, *Kāmil*, V, 73, specifies *al-raḥl*, "saddlebags."

401. Text: ʿAmir; read ʿUmar, following the Cairo ed.

402. Text: *matāʿ*.

403. Ibn al-Athīr, *Kāmil*, V, 73, specifies Sulaymān b. Ziyād b. Abīhi. According to Kūfī, *Futūḥ*, VIII, 6, the house belonged to Umm Muḥammad bt. ʿAbdallāh b. ʿUthmān al-Thaqafī.

404. ʿUthmān b. al-Mufaḍḍal. See *FHA*, 58.

By God, two things ought to prevent you from laughing. First, the fact that you fled from a noble death and surrendered like a woman, that is the first thing; second, the fact that you have been brought to me like a runaway slave that is dragged back to its masters. You have no covenant or pact with me, so what makes you so confident that I will (not) cut off your head?" 'Adī replied: "You have, indeed, overpowered me. But I know that your survival depends on mine and that there is a price on the head of whoever might slay me. You have seen the armies of God in the West,[405] and you are aware of how God helps those people in every single place where treachery and disloyalty prevail. Make amends, then, for your hasty actions and your mistakes by repenting and asking for forgiveness before the sea casts its waves over you, because if you ask for forgiveness later, it will not be granted. Furthermore, if you sue for peace after I have sent the army against you, you will find them keeping their distance from you, but so long as the army has not been sent against you, they will not deny you anything that you may request, namely, safe passage for yourself, your family and your property."

Yazīd replied as follows:

> As for your statement, "Your survival depends on mine"—may God not keep me alive longer than the time it takes a frightened bird to sip water if that is the case. And as for your statement, "There is a price on the head of whoever slays you"—by God, suppose I had in my control ten thousand soldiers from the Syrian army who were all of greater status than you, and I cut off their heads in one spot; they would not be as frightened and terrified by those slayings as they would be by my threat to abandon and oppose them. Furthermore, were I to ask them to shed their blood in vain for me, to give me control of their treasures, and to secure for me a great portion of their sovereignty, in exchange for terminating the war between us, they would certainly comply. Therefore, do not delude yourself: the army would forget you if news of us[406] reached them, and whatever they devise or machinate will

[1386]

---

405. That is, the Umayyad armies in Syria.

406. The text is *akhyārunā*, "our best men." This should be amended to read *akhbārunā*. I owe this point to Professor Abbas.

be only for themselves; they will not remember you, nor will they pay any attention to you. Finally, as for your statement, "Make amends for your deed, ask for forgiveness, and do this and do that"—by God, I did not ask for your advice, and you are neither my friend nor a trusted adviser. Indeed, what you have said is a redundancy uttered out of weakness. Take him away!

But an hour or so after they had taken ʿAdī away, Yazīd said, "Bring him back." When they had brought him back, Yazīd said, "I would not have imprisoned you had you not imprisoned and tortured the Banū Muhallab, despite our request that you treat them gently. But you did not ease your oppression, torture, and opposition." After hearing this statement, ʿAdī manifested a greater sense of security, and he mentioned what Yazīd had said to everyone who visited him.

A man named al-Samaydaʿ al-Kindī, from the Banū Mālik b. Rabīʿah—he was a resident of ʿUmān—held the beliefs of the Khārijites.[407] As Yazīd's and ʿAdī's forces were lining up in rows, he emerged and seceded, taking with him many of the Qurʾān reciters.[408] A group from Yazīd's forces and a group from ʿAdī's forces said, "We accept the judgment of al-Samaydaʿ." Yazīd then [1387] sent a message to al-Samaydaʿ, inviting him to join forces with him. He accepted the summons, and Yazīd appointed him governor of al-Ubullah,[409] where he turned his attention to perfumes and pleasure. When Yazīd b. al-Muhallab was victorious, the leaders of the Baṣran army, from the tribes of Qays, Tamīm, and Mālik b. al-Mundhir, fled, joining ʿAbd al-Ḥamīd b. ʿAbd al-Raḥmān in al-Kūfah. Some of them made their way to Syria. Al-Farazdaq recited:

My life for a group from the Tamīm who followed one another
    to Syria rather than accept the judgment of al-Samaydaʿ.
Would they accept the judgment of a Ḥarūrī,[410] who has
    strayed from the true religion,

---

407. On the Khārijites, see note 266 above.

408. Text: al-qurrāʾ. For a speculative view of the meaning of this term, see Shaban, *Islamic History*, 23, 51; cf. Juynboll, "The Qurrāʾ in Early Islamic History," 113–129; and Hinds, "Kūfan Political Allignments," 358ff.

409. A town located four *farsakh*s (24 km.) from al-Baṣrah, between the main course of the Tigris and one of the channels. See Barthold, *Geography*, 203.

410. That is, a Khārijite. See note 268, above.

more erroneous and more deviant than an ass with its ear
cut off?[411]

To which Khalīfah al-Aqṭaʿ responded:

His judgment was sought neither because he sent a delegation
    to ask for it,
    nor because of an opportunity from which some desirable
    outcome was expected.
Rather, they traveled to get it, by day and by night,
    on the baldest buttocks that can be seen on a day of
    wearisome travel.
For fear that the enemy would catch up with them,
    they would camp only every fourth or fifth night.

Al-Ḥawārī b. Ziyād b. ʿAmr al-ʿAtakī set out with the intention
of reaching Yazīd b. ʿAbd al-Malik, fleeing from Yazīd b. al-
Muhallab. He encountered Khālid b. ʿAbdallāh al-Qasrī and ʿAmr b.
Yazīd al-Ḥakamī, who were traveling with Ḥumayd b. ʿAbd al-
Malik b. al-Muhallab. They were returning from Yazīd b. ʿAbd al-   [1388]
Malik with a promise of safe-conduct for Yazīd b. al-Muhallab and
everything that he wanted[412] from the Caliph. Al-Ḥawārī greeted
the two men, who asked him about the latest events. But when he
saw Ḥumayd b. ʿAbd al-Malik (b. al-Muhallab) with them, he took
them aside, privately. "Where are you going?" he asked. "To Yazīd
b. al-Muhallab," they replied. "We have brought him everything
that he wanted." Al-Ḥawārī said, "You cannot do anything for
Yazīd, and he cannot do anything for you. He has defeated his
enemy, ʿAdī b. Arṭāt, slain many men, and imprisoned ʿAdī. Turn
back, both of you!" At that moment, a tribesman from the Bāhilah
named Muslim b. ʿAbd al-Malik passed by without stopping to
greet them. They called after him and asked him to account for
himself, but he still would not stop. Al-Qasrī said, "Shouldn't you
bring him back and administer one hundred lashes?" But his
companion said to him, "Let him go,"[413] and they waited until he
disappeared.

---

411. See *Dīwān al-Farazdaq*, I, 409.
412. Text: *arādahu;* the Cairo ed. has the dual form, *arādāhu*, "(everything
that) the two of them wanted." On this mission, see note 392, above.
413. Text: *gharribhu ʿanka;* the Cairo ed. reads *ʿazzibhu ʿanka*, "leave him
alone."

Al-Ḥawārī b. Ziyād continued on his way to Yazīd b. ʿAbd al-Malik, and the two men turned back, taking Ḥumayd b. ʿAbd al-Malik (b. al-Muhallab) with them. Ḥumayd said to them, "I adjure you by God not to violate the mission on which you were sent by the Caliph, for Yazīd (b. al-Muhallab) is well disposed toward you, although that one[414] and the members of his household have always been our enemies. I adjure you by God not to listen to what he says." But they rejected Ḥumayd's plea and took him with them. Eventually, they delivered him to ʿAbd al-Raḥmān b. Sulaym[415] al-Kalbī, who had been sent to Khurāsān by Yazīd b. ʿAbd al-Malik to serve as his governor there. When ʿAbd al-Raḥmān learned that Yazīd b. al-Muhallab had renounced his allegiance to Yazīd b. ʿAbd al-Malik, he wrote to the Caliph as follows: "Holy war against those who have opposed you is dearer to me than my appointment in Khurāsān, for which I have no need. Therefore, count me among those whom you are sending to me in order to fight against Yazīd b. al-Muhallab." ʿAbd al-Raḥmān sent Ḥumayd b. ʿAbd al-Malik (b. al-Muhallab) to Yazīd (b. ʿAbd al-Malik).

[1389]

ʿAbd al-Ḥamīd b. ʿAbd al-Raḥmān b. Zayd b. al-Khaṭṭāb arrested Khālid b. Yazīd b. al-Muhallab, who was in al-Kūfah, and Ḥammāl b. Zaḥr al-Juʿfī, neither of whom had uttered a word against the Caliph—although they were aware of the fact that the Banū al-Muhallab had thrown off allegiance to him. He put them in chains and sent them to Yazīd b. ʿAbd al-Malik, who imprisoned them, together (in Damascus); they died there, never having left the prison.

Yazīd b. ʿAbd al-Malik sent some soldiers from the Syrian army to al-Kūfah in order to reassure (the Kūfans), to commend them for their obedience, and to promise to increase their stipends. Included among those who were sent was al-Quṭāmī[416] b. al-Ḥusayn, that is, Abū al-Sharqī—al-Sharqī's proper name is al-Walīd. When al-Quṭāmī learned that Yazīd b. al-Muhallab had thrown off allegiance to the Caliph, he recited:

Perhaps my eye might see Yazīd,
    leading a large, powerful army.

---

414. Probably al-Ḥawārī b. Ziyād, who was from the tribe of ʿAtīk.
415. Text: Sulaymān; read Sulaym, following the Cairo ed.
416. The alternative vocalization—al-Qaṭāmī.

(An army) which lets you hear the earth reverberating noisily.
    (Yazīd) is not sordid, weak, or envious,[417]
Nor a coward in battle, trembling in fear.[418]
    You see the crowned ones prostrating themselves to him,
Bowing down, submissive, overpowered,
    while others welcomed (him) with welcoming delegations.
He violates neither the pact nor the stipulations
    of people who were of a kingly and good breed.
Every day you see them celebrating a holiday,
    having slaughtered their enemies deliberately.

Subsequently, al-Quṭāmī traveled to al-ʿAqr, where he witnessed the fighting between Yazīd b. al-Muhallab and Maslamah
b. ʿAbd al-Malik.[419] Yazīd b. al-Muhallab exclaimed, "How great
is the discrepancy between al-Quṭāmī's poetry and his actions!"

Yazīd b. ʿAbd al-Malik sent al-ʿAbbās b. al-Walīd,[420] leading   [1390]
four thousand horsemen without any infantry, hurrying toward
al-Ḥīrah in an effort to get there before Yazīd b. al-Muhallab did.
Then, Maslamah b. ʿAbd al-Malik and regiments of the Syrian
army advanced and seized al-Jazīrah along the bank of the Euphrates. The Baṣran army rallied to Yazīd b. al-Muhallab, who appointed his own governors over al-Ahwāz,[421] Fārs, and Kirmān.
These provinces were governed by al-Jarrāḥ b. ʿAbdallāh al-
Ḥakamī—until he was recalled by ʿUmar b. ʿAbd al-ʿAzīz; (then)
by ʿAbd al-Raḥmān b. Nuʿaym al-Azdī, who was in charge of
prayer, and by ʿAbd al-Raḥmān al-Qushayrī, who had been put in
charge of the fiscal administration by Yazīd b. ʿAbd al-Malik.

Mudrik b. al-Muhallab advanced, reaching Raʾs al-Mafāzah.[422]
Then ʿAbd al-Raḥmān b. Nuʿaym sent an agent to say to the Banū
Tamīm, "Mudrik b. al-Muhallab seeks to stir up war among you.
But you live in a peaceful and obedient country and you care for

---

417. Text: *ḥasūdan*. The Cairo ed. reads *ḥayūdan*, "turning away."

418. Text: *ʿadīdan*, "equal"; read *riʿdīdan*, following the Cairo ed.

419. See text below, II/1395ff., sub anno 102.

420. Al-ʿAbbās b. al-Walīd was an Umayyad general, son of the Caliph, al-Walīd
I. See *EI²*, s.v. al-ʿAbbās b. al-Walīd.

421. An administrative district between al-Baṣrah and Fārs. See Yāqūt, *Muʿjam*,
I, 284–86; *EI²*, s.v. al-Ahwāz.

422. Al-Mafāzah (the wilderness) is the name of the Great Desert of Khurāsān
that stretches across the high plateau of Iran from northwest to southeast. It is
approximately eight hundred miles long. See Le Strange, *Lands*, 322–28; Barthold,
Geography, 133–35.

the unity of the community." They set out at night in order to confront Mudrik. But the Azd learned of this, and approximately two thousand of their horsemen set out and intercepted the Banū Tamīm before they reached Raʾs al-Mafāzah. The Azd asked the Banū Tamīm, "What has brought you here, and what has caused you to come to his place?" They made some excuses without acknowledging that they had come out in order to slay[423] Mudrik b. al-Muhallab. The Azd said to them, "We know that you have come out to confront our leader. Look, there he is, nearby. What do you want?"

Then the Azd left and joined up with Mudrik b. al-Muhallab at Raʾs al-Mafāzah. They said to him, "You are dearer to us and more esteemed than any man. Your brother has revolted, declaring war on the Caliph. If God grants him victory, that will be good for us, for we are the quickest to come to you, O family of al-Muhallab, and the most ready to do that. In the other case, by God, there shall be no solace for you in our misfortune." Upon hearing this, Mudrik resolved to leave. The following was recited by Thābit Quṭnah, that is, Thābit b. Kaʿb, from the tribe of Azd, from al-ʿAtīk:[424]

[1391]

Did you not see that the Dawsar protected their brother,
  when the Tamīm had massed to slay him?
They saw the blue spearheads surrounding him,
  and a tribe whose sacred precincts are inviolable.
(I mean) Dawsar's two branches: Shunūʾah and ʿUmrān b.
  Ḥazm.
  There the glory and the most noble descent lie.
They did not attack, but were held back
  by the spears of the Azd and its long-standing invincibility.
We turned Mudrik back truly and properly,
  without any wound on his face from you.
With horses, like divining arrows, let free with their riders
  on a piece of land whose parts are rich with grass.

---

423. Text: *li-yutlifū*. The Cairo ed. reads *li-yutliffū*, probably a typographical error for *li-yatalaqqaw*, "to meet." Azdī, *Taʾrīkh*, 8, has *li-liqāʾi*, "to confront."

424. Thābit Quṭnah was a poet and cavalier who was a companion of Yazīd b. al-Muhallab. See Ibn Qutaybah, *Shiʿr*, II, 630–31, no. 117; *Aghānī* (Beirut), XIV, 247–65.

On their backs are every haughty and mighty Dawsarī
    who does not flee or leave his place in battle.
By means of them fools are put right by reproach,
    until you begin to see fools restrained by wise censure.[425]

According to Hishām—Abū Mikhnaf—Mu'ādh b. Sa'd: When
the army of al-Baṣrah had assembled, Yazīd stood before them and
praised God. After informing them that he was summoning them
to the Book of God and the *sunnah* of His Prophet, Muḥammad,[426] he incited them to holy war, claiming that those who
fought in the holy war against the Syrian army would receive a
greater reward than those who fought against the Turks and the
Daylamīs.[427]

Our source continued: I entered the mosque with al-Ḥasan al-
Baṣrī, whose hand was on my shoulder.[428] He asked me, "Look
around. Do you recognize anyone?" I replied, "No, by God, I
don't." Al-Ḥasan said, "By God, these people are transgres-
sors."[429] We then made our way forward until we reached the
pulpit. I heard (Yazīd) mention the Book of God and the *sunnah* of
His Prophet. Then al-Ḥasan raised his voice and exclaimed, "By
God, we have seen you as both governor and governed, and that
does not suit you." At that, we jumped on al-Ḥasan, grabbing his
hand and covering his mouth, and made him sit down. By God,   [1392]
we were sure that Yazīd had heard him, even though he did not
pay any attention to him and continued his sermon. Our source
said: Then we went out to the gate of the mosque where, lo and
behold, al-Naḍr b. Anas b. Mālik[430] was standing at the gate,
saying, "O servants of God, what prevents you from responding
to the Book of God and the *sunnah* of His Prophet? By God, none
of us has seen the likes of that one (that is, Yazīd) since the day
you were born—except during the caliphate of 'Umar b. 'Abd

---

425. See al-A'shā, *Dīwān*, 340.

426. It was customary for rebels of the Umayyad period, whatever their sec-
tarian stance, to make a call to the Book of God and the precedent of the Prophet;
the collocation stood for justice. See Crone and Hinds, *God's Caliph*, 61, 66.

427. Turks and Daylamīs were non-Muslims.

428. The context suggests that al-Ḥasan had gone blind, a point that I am unable
to corroborate.

429. Text: *al-a'tā'*. The Cairo ed. reads *al-ghuthā'*, "the scum of the the earth."

430. For information on this figure, see al-Dhahabī, *Kāshif*, III, 203, no. 5926.

al-ʿAzīz." Al-Ḥasan exclaimed, "Praise be to God. Al-Naḍr b. Anas, too, has testified (in favor of Yazīd)."

According to Hishām—Abū Mikhnaf—al-Muthannā b. ʿAbdallāh: Al-Ḥasan al-Baṣrī passed by the soldiers, who had arranged themselves in two rows and raised the standards and spears in anticipation of Yazīd's emergence. They were saying, "Yazīd has summoned us to the example of the two ʿUmars."[431] Al-Ḥasan said, "Only yesterday Yazīd was striking off the heads of those whom you see here and sending them to the Marwānids, seeking thereby to win the approval of the Umayyads. But when he became angry, he lifted up a stick, tied some rags to it, and said, 'I have thrown off allegiance to (the Marwānids), so you do the same.'" Those people said, "Yes." Then al-Ḥasan said, "I summon you to the example of the two ʿUmars, which requires that chains be put on (Yazīd's) legs and that he be sent back to the prison in which ʿUmar had imprisoned him." After hearing this, some soldiers who supported al-Ḥasan said to him, "By God, it appears, Abū Saʿīd, as if you approve of the Syrian army." To which he replied, "I approve of the Syrian army! May God afflict them and render them hideous! Are they not the ones who desecrated the sacred precinct of the Messenger of God, slaughtering its inhabitants for three days and three nights, declaring them lawful for their Nabataeans and Copts, carrying off free, pious women, and not holding back from violating the honor of any sacred thing? Then they went to God's sacred house and destroyed the Kaʿbah, lighting fires amidst its stones and coverings. May the curse of God and the evil of the (Last) Abode be upon them!"[432]

[1393]

Our source continued: Then Yazīd left al-Baṣrah, having appointed Marwān b. al-Muhallab as his governor. Taking weapons and the contents of the Public Treasury with him, he set out for Wāsiṭ. Now, as he was turning in the direction of Wāsiṭ he sought the counsel of his officers, saying, "Give me your advice, for the Syrian army is advancing quickly in this direction." Ḥabīb[433]—and others—advised him as follows: "We think that you should

---

431. That is, ʿUmar b. al-Khaṭṭāb and Abū Bakr, or ʿUmar b. al-Khaṭṭāb and ʿUmar b. ʿAbd al-ʿAzīz.

432. The Syrian troops of the Umayyads ravaged Mecca in 64 (683) and 74 (694). See EI², s.v. Kaʿba.

433. Ḥabīb b. al-Muhallab was Yazīd's brother.

leave (al-Baṣrah) and go to Fārs, where you can seize the mountain roads and passes and draw near to Khurāsān. In this way, you will outlast the enemy, so that when the army of al-Jibāl[434] is deployed around you,[435] you will control the fortresses and strongholds." He replied, "I do not agree with your recommendation, which is unacceptable to me. You seek to turn me into a bird on a mountaintop."

Then Ḥabīb said to him:

The plan that should have been adopted at the outset is no longer feasible. When you took control of al-Baṣrah, I ordered you to send horsemen led by members of your household back to al-Kūfah, where ʿAbd al-Ḥamīd b. ʿAbd al-Raḥmān (is the governor). Earlier, you passed by him with seventy foot soldiers, and he was unable to defeat you. He would have had even less success against a large number of your horsemen. In this way, we would have beaten the Syrian army to al-Kūfah, where the great majority of its eminent people accept you; indeed, most of them would prefer to be governed by you than by the Syrians. But since you did not obey me, I now advise you as follows: send some of your most accomplished horsemen to al-Jazīrah, together with the members of your household. Let them make their way there quickly and occupy one of its fortresses. You yourself should follow them. Thus, when the Syrian army approaches, looking for you, they will not escape any of your regiments in al-Jazīrah. As they advance toward you, they will be bogged down with your cavalry, who will keep them away from you until you come to them, at which point you will be joined by those of your tribesmen who are in Mosul.[436] The armies of Iraq and of the frontiers will be deployed

[1394]

---

434. Al-Jibāl is the broad mountain region stretching across from the plains of Iraq in the west to the Great Desert of Khurāsān in the east. See Yāqūt, *Muʿjam*, II, 99–100; Le Strange, *Lands*, 185; *EI²*, s.v. Djibāl.

435. This is a conjectural translation. The text is *yanfaḍḍūna ilayka*, literally, "scattered around you." Compare Kūfī, *Futūḥ*, VIII, 12 (*wa-ahl al-jibāl maʿaka*, "and the army of al-Jibāl will be with you"); Azdī, *Taʾrīkh*, 9 (*yanhadūna ilayka*, "they will hasten toward you"); Ibn al-Athīr, *Kāmil*, V, 76 (*yaʾtūna ilayka*, "they will come to you").

436. The capital of the Diyār Rabīʿah, located on the west bank of the Tigris, opposite the ancient Niniveh. See *EI*, s.v. Moṣul.

around you,[437] and you will engage them in battle in a land of abundance and cheap prices,[438] having put all of Iraq behind you.

He said, "I do not want to divide my forces." When he arrived in Wāsiṭ, he remained there only a few days.

According to Abū Jaʿfar (al-Ṭabarī): In this year, ʿAbd al-Raḥmān b. al-Ḍaḥḥāk b. Qays al-Fihrī led the pilgrimage. This was related to me by Aḥmad b. Thābit—his source—Isḥāq b. ʿĪsā—Abū Maʿshar. A similar report was transmitted by Muḥammad b. ʿUmar.

ʿAbd al-Raḥmān b. al-Ḍaḥḥāk was the governor of Medina on behalf of Yazīd b. ʿAbd al-Malik, while Mecca was governed by ʿAbd al-ʿAzīz b. ʿAbdallāh b. Khālid b. Asīd. In al-Kūfah, ʿAbd al-Ḥamīd b. ʿAbd al-Raḥmān served as governor, and al-Shaʿbī was in charge of the judicial administration. Al-Baṣrah had been taken over by Yazīd b. al-Muhallab. ʿAbd al-Raḥmān b. Nuʿaym was in charge of Khurāsān.

---

437. Text: *yanfaḍḍu ilayka*. Azdī, *Taʾrīkh*, 10, reads *yanqaḍḍu ilayka*, "will rush to you." See note 435 above.

438. Text: *fī arḍin rafīʿati-l-siʿr*, "a land of high prices." The text should be amended to read *fī arḍin rafīghati-l-siʿr*. I owe this point to Professor Abbas.

The
Events of the Year

102

(July 12, 720—June 30, 721)

One of the events of this year was the march undertaken by al-ʿAbbās b. al-Walīd b. ʿAbd al-Malik and Maslamah b. ʿAbd al-Malik in the direction of Yazīd b. al-Muhallab, having been sent to fight him by Yazīd b. ʿAbd al-Malik.   [1395]

In this year, Yazīd b. al-Muhallab was slain in the month of Ṣafar (August 11–September 8).[439]

The Slaying of Yazīd b. al-Muhallab

According to Hishām—Abū Mikhnaf—Muʿādh b. Saʿīd: Yazīd b. al-Muhallab decided to leave Wāsiṭ in order to confront Maslamah b. ʿAbd al-Malik and al-ʿAbbās. He designated his son, Muʿāwiyah, as his representative in that city, entrusting him with the Public Treasury, the coffers, and the prisoners of war, and he dispatched an advance party headed by his brother, ʿAbd al-Malik.

---

439. See Ibn Khayyāṭ, *Taʾrīkh*, I, 332; Yaʿqūbī, *Taʾrīkh*, III, 54–55; Kūfī, *Futūḥ*, VIII, 11–25; Azdī, *Taʾrīkh*, 10–14; *FHA*, 65–74; Ibn Kathīr, *Bidāyah*, IX, 220; Wellhausen, *Arab Kingdom*, 316–19.

Then he set out and, after passing by Fam al-Nīl,[440] he set up camp at al-ʿAqr.[441] Meanwhile, Maslamah advanced, marching along one of the banks of the Euphrates until he reached al-Anbār,[442] where, after laying a bridge over the river, he crossed over at a point near a village known as Fāriṭ.[443] Then he advanced until he encountered Yazīd b. al-Muhallab.

Yazīd's brother, ʿAbd al-Malik, who had been sent ahead in the direction of al-Kūfah, was confronted in Sūrā[444] by al-ʿAbbās b. al-Walīd. The two armies engaged in battle after arranging themselves in ranks. The Baṣran army charged, putting (the Syrians) to flight. With al-ʿAbbās were some soldiers from the Banū Tamīm and Qays, who had fled from Yazīd, from al-Baṣrah; indeed, there were a good number of them with al-ʿAbbās, including Ḥuraym b. Abī Ṭaḥmah al-Mujāshiʿī. When the Syrian army was put to flight in that manner, Ḥuraym b. Abī Ṭaḥmah called out to them, "O Syrians, fear God, fear God, and do not abandon us!" ʿAbd al-Malik's soldiers had forced them to the river. In response, they called out to him, "Don't worry. It is customary for the Syrian army to feign defeat at the outset of battle. But assistance is on its way."

[1396]

Then the Syrian army gained the offensive, exposing ʿAbd al-Malik's forces and putting them to flight. Among those slain was al-Mantūf, a client of the Bakr b. Wāʾil. Al-Farazdaq recited the following lines in an attempt to incite the Bakr b. Wāʾil:

The Bakr b. Wāʾil weep for al-Mantūf,
    but they don't let anyone cry for the two sons of Mismaʿ.
Two youths who grew up amid the fires of war and
    accomplished
    noble deeds before their beards began to grow.
Were Mālik and Ibn Mālik alive,

---

440. A town in the Sawād of al-Kūfah. See Yāqūt, *Muʿjam*, V, 334–39, s.v. al-Nīl.

441. ʿAqr of Babel was near Karbalāʾ, in the administrative district of al-Kūfah. See Yāqūt, *Muʿjam*, IV, 136; Wellhausen, *Arab Kingdom*, 316, n. 1.

442. A town on the east bank of the Euphrates, near the ʿĪsā Canal. See *EI²*, s.v. al-Anbār; Wellhausen, *Arab Kingdom*, 316, n. 1.

443. There is no entry in Yāqūt's geographical dictionary for this village.

444. An old Jewish town on the upper Sūrā Canal, near the site of the later Qaṣr Ibn Hubayrah. See Yāqūt, *Muʿjam*, III, 278; Le Strange, *Lands*, 70–72.

then they would have lit two fires whose flames would
have risen high.[445]

The two sons of Misma' were Mālik b. Misma' and 'Abd al-
Malik b. Misma', who were slain by Mu'āwiyah b. Yazīd b. al-
Muhallab. In response to al-Farazdaq, al-Ja'd b. Dirham,[446] a client of (Suwayd b. Ghafalah)[447] from the tribe of Hamdān, recited
the following lines:

We weep for al-Mantūf because he aided his tribe,
    but we do not weep for the two dead ones who disgraced
    their father.[448]
The two of them sought the ruin of the Bakr b. Wā'il,
    and the strength of Tamīm, had their home been attacked.
May they not find any comfort from God for even an hour,
    and may the eyes of the mourner who cries for them
    continue to shed tears forever.
Should we cry for them deceitfully, if ever we cry,
    when they met their death having deceived us too?

[1397]

'Abd al-Malik b. al-Muhallab rejoined his brother in al-'Aqr,
where he ordered 'Abdallāh b. Ḥayyān al-'Abdī to cross over the
river to the side where the Ṣarāt al-Aqṣā[449] is located—there was
a bridge between the two places. 'Abdallāh, together with his
troops and one of Yazīd's units, set up camp there and dug a
trench (around the camp). But Maslamah, accompanied by Sa'īd b.
'Amr al-Ḥarashī, crossed over the water—some authorities maintain that it was al-Waḍḍāḥ who crossed over—and the two sides
came face to face.

Meanwhile, Yazīd was joined by a large number of soldiers
from al-Kūfah and from al-Jibāl, and soldiers from the frontiers
were making their way towards him. He put 'Abdallāh b. Sufyān
b. Yazīd b. al-Mughaffal al-Azdī in command of the Kūfan con-

---

445. See *Dīwān al-Farazdaq*, II, 203.
446. See *EI*², s.v. Ibn Dirham.
447. The lacuna in the text is filled in by the editor of the Cairo ed.
448. The text, *al-shā'idayn*, should be amended to read *al-shā'inayn*. I owe this
point to Professor Abbas.
449. The Ṣarāt Canal branched off from the 'Īsā Canal just above the town of al-
Muḥawwal. Yāqūt mentions two canals by this name, the Greater and Smaller
Ṣarāt. See *Mu'jam*, III, 399–400; Le Strange, *Lands*, 66–67.

tingents that had joined him, as well as of the Medinese contingent; he put al-Nuʿmān b. Ibrāhīm b. al-Ashtar al-Nakhaʿī in command of the contingent from the Madhḥij and Asad; he put Muḥammad b. Isḥāq b. Muḥammad b. al-Ashʿath in command of the contingent from the Kindah and Rabīʿah; and he put Ḥanẓalah b. ʿAttāb b. Warqāʾ al-Tamīmī in command of the contingent from the Tamīm and Hamdān. He brought all of them together with al-Mufaḍḍal b. al-Muhallab.[450]

[1398]

According to Hishām b. Muḥammad—Abū Mikhnaf—al-ʿAlāʾ b. Zuhayr:[451] By God, we were sitting with Yazīd that day when suddenly he asked, "Do you think that they have one thousand soldiers?"[452] To which Ḥanẓalah b. ʿAttāb replied, "Yes, by God. They probably have four thousand." He said, "By God, they have never attacked with even a thousand men. By God, I reckon that there are one hundred and twenty thousand soldiers listed in my military register. But by God, I wish that I had my tribesmen from Khurāsān with me at this hour, instead of them."

According to Hishām—Abū Mikhnaf: Then he stood up on that day, inciting us for battle. Later, he said, as he put it to us, "Those soldiers will not be turned away from their misguided actions except by a thrust into their eyes[453] and a blow on the head with the sword." Then he added, "I have been told about this yellow locust"—that is, Maslamah b. ʿAbd al-Malik—"and that she-camel slaughterer from Thamūd,"[454] that is, al-ʿAbbās b. al-Walīd, who had blue eyes and red skin, his mother being a Greek. "By God, Sulaymān wanted to negate his lineage until I intervened on his behalf, whereupon the Caliph allowed him to adhere to his lineage. But now I learn that the two of them have no other objective but to search for me throughout the land. By God, were they to gather all of mankind,[455] while I was by myself, I would not quit the field of

---

450. Perhaps this should read: "under the command of al-Mufaḍḍal."

451. Text: Ruhayr; read Zuhayr, following the Cairo ed.

452. Text: *alf sayf yuḍrabu bihi.* Literally: "a thousand swords capable of being struck."

453. Text: *ʿuyūnihim.* Kūfī, *Futūḥ,* VIII, 15, has *nuḥūrihim,* "their throats," which makes better sense.

454. The tribe of Thamūd, which disappeared from Arabia some time before the appearance of Islam, was punished because one of its members had hamstrung a sacred camel. See *EI,* s.v. Thamūd.

455. Text: *ahl al-arḍ,* literally, "peasants."

battle until victory had been achieved by one side or the other."
They said, "We fear that you will impose hardships upon us, just as
'Abd al-Raḥmān b. Muḥammad[456] did." Yazīd said, "'Abd al-
Raḥmān b. Muḥammad brought shame upon his family and upon
his noble reputation. Was he able to exceed his appointed time?"
Then he stepped down.

Our source continued: We were joined by 'Āmir b. al-'Amaythal, a soldier from the Azd, who had combined several military
units. He came to Yazīd and swore the oath of allegiance to him.
The wording of the oath of allegiance sworn to Yazīd was as
follows: "You swear allegiance to the Book of God and to the
sunnah of His Prophet that no army will pillage our country or
our headquarters and that we will never again be subject to the
behavior of that sinner al-Ḥajjāj. We accept the allegiance of anyone who will swear on these terms and we will engage in holy war
against anyone who refuses, putting God between him and us."
Then he would ask, "Do you swear allegiance to us?" If they
responded affirmatively, he would accept allegiance from them.

Meanwhile, 'Abd al-Ḥamīd b. 'Abd al-Raḥmān had ordered his
troops to set up camp in al-Nukhaylah.[457] He sent some men to
the water, and they broke through the bank of the river, flooding
the area between al-Kūfah and Yazīd b. al-Muhallab, so as to
prevent him from reaching the city. 'Abd al-Ḥamīd also estab-   [1399]
lished observation points and lookouts in the vicinity of al-Kūfah
in order to prevent the Kūfan army from joining Yazīd.

'Abd al-Ḥamīd sent Maslamah a military unit from al-Kūfah
commanded by Sayf b. Hāni' al-Hamdānī. After flattering the
soldiers and praising them for their fidelity, Maslamah exclaimed,
"By God, how few are the number of those who have come to us
from al-Kūfah!" 'Abd al-Ḥamīd learned of this and he sent a second, larger unit commanded by Sabrah b. 'Abd al-Raḥmān b.
Mikhnaf al-Azdī. When Sabrah arrived, Maslamah praised him,
saying, "This man's household has obedience and heroic deeds.
Attach to him all of the soldiers from the Kūfan army that are
here." Then Maslamah sent a message to 'Abd al-Ḥamīd b. 'Abd al-

---

456. That is, 'Abd al-Raḥmān b. Muḥammad b. al-Ash'ath, who led a revolt
against al-Ḥajjāj in 80–82 or 83/699–700 or 702. See text above, II/1042ff., sub
anno 80; EI², s.v. Ibn al-Ash'ath; Crone, Slaves, 110–11.
457. A town in Iraq, near al-Kūfah. See EI, s.v. al-Nukhaila.

Raḥmān, dismissing him. In his place, he appointed Muḥammad b. ʿAmr b. al-Walīd b. ʿUqbah, who is known as Dhū al-Shāmah.[458]

Yazīd b. al-Muhallab summoned the chiefs of his army and addressed them as follows: "I have decided to assemble twelve thousand soldiers and to send them with Muḥammad b. al-Muhallab. They will attack Maslamah by night, taking with them packsaddles and containers for use in filling in their trench. They will engage the enemy in battle at the trench throughout the night, during which time I will be sending reinforcements to Muḥammad. The next morning I will rush out to them, leading the soldiers, and we will engage them in battle. I hope that God will grant us victory over them."

But al-Samaydaʿ objected, "We have summoned (the Syrians) to the Book of God and to the *sunnah* of His Prophet, Muḥammad, and they claim to have accepted this from us. Thus, we should not engage in deceit or treachery, nor should we wish any evil upon them until they reject what they claim to have accepted from us."

Abū Ruʾbah, the leader of a group of Murjiʾites,[459] who was accompanied by his supporters, said, "Al-Samaydaʿ is correct. That is the proper course." But Yazīd exclaimed, "Alas! Do you really believe that the Umayyads will act in accordance with the Book and the *sunnah* when they have neglected both for as long as they have been around? They say[460] to you, 'We accept you,' and they claim not to want to exercise their authority except in accordance with your orders and your instructions. But, in fact, they seek to drive you away from them so that they might engage in treachery. Therefore, do not let them deceive you first. Beat them to it. I have had experience with the Marwānids and, by God, none of them is more devious or more deeply immersed in falsehood[461] than that yellow locust"—that is, Maslamah. But

[1400]

---

458. Dhū al-Shāmah means: "the one with the birthmark." See text above, II/1380, sub anno 101.

459. The Murjiʾites were an early Islamic sect that advocated postponement (*irjāʾ*) of any decision about a grave sinner. See *EI*, s.v. al-*Murdjiʾa*. On Abū Ruʾbah, see Wellhausen, *Arab Kingdom*, 317.

460. Text: *lam yaqūlū*, "they did not say"; read *yaqūlū*, following the Cairo ed.

461. Text: *abʿada ghawran*. Ibn al-Athīr, *Kāmil*, V, 80, has *abʿada ghadaran*, "more treacherous."

they said, "We do not agree to act in that manner until they reject
what they claim to have accepted from us." Meanwhile, Marwān
b. al-Muhallab was in al-Baṣrah, inciting the soldiers to go to war
against the Syrian army and sending soldiers to Yazīd. Al-Ḥasan
al-Baṣrī, on the other hand, was imploring the soldiers not to rise
with Yazīd b. al-Muhallab.

According to Abū Mikhnaf—'Abd al-Ḥamīd al-Baṣrī: Al-Ḥasan
al-Baṣrī was saying at that time:

> O people, stay in your homes[462] and restrain your-
> selves.[463] Fear God, your Lord, and do not kill one another
> on account of this transient world or on account of greed
> for trifling things that will not survive for the people who
> seek them, for God is not pleased with them because of
> their personal acquisitions. There never was a civil war
> except that most of the rebels were preachers, poets, fools,
> drifters, and conceited men. No one is safe from that (that
> is, civil war), except the unknown person who is hidden[464]
> and the God-fearing person who is well-known. Therefore,
> let the hidden person among you adhere to the truth and
> let him hold himself back from the things of this world
> over which the people are contending with one another. By
> God, let him be satisfied with God's good opinion of him,
> as a sign of honor, and let that be sufficient for him in place
> of the things of this world. As for the person among you
> who is well-known and distinguished, he avoids the things
> of this world over which his peers vie with one another,
> seeking thereby to please God. Oh, how happy and right-   [1401]
> eous he is, and how greatly will God magnify his reward
> and lead him along His path! Tomorrow, that is to say, on
> the Day of Resurrection, that person will have the greatest
> satisfaction and will be the one most welcomed by God.

When Marwān b. al-Muhallab was informed of al-Ḥasan's statement, he stood up, as was his custom, to deliver the sermon. After
ordering the soldiers to be diligent and to assemble together, he
said to them, "I have learned that that errant, hypocritical

---

462. Text: *rijālakum*, "your men"; read *riḥālakum*, following the Cairo ed.
463. Text: *wa-kuffū aydiyakum*, a Qur'ānic expression. See Qur'ān 4:77.
464. Text: *khafiyy*. Kūfī, *Futūḥ*, VIII, 13, reads *ḥaqīr*, "despicable."

shaykh"—he did not mention his name—"is discouraging the soldiers. By God, if his neighbor had stolen a piece of wood from the roof of his house, the neighbor's nose would still be bleeding. Does he deny to us and to the people of our town the right to seek our welfare[465] and to refute injustices that we have suffered? By God, if he does not stop mentioning us and likening us to the vile ones of al-Ubullah and the Nabataeans of the Baṣran Euphrates—people who have no connection to us and who have not received a favor from a single one of us, I shall finish him off harshly."[466]

When al-Ḥasan was informed of Marwān's remarks, he said, "By God, it does not displease me that God should honor me by chastising him."[467] Then some soldiers who were his supporters said, "If he were to have evil designs on you, and you wanted us to, we would defend you." To which he replied, "In that case I would cause you to do the thing that I have forbidden you to do. I have ordered you not to kill one another for the sake of someone else. (And now it is as if) I am calling on you to kill one another for my sake."[468] Marwān b. al-Muhallab was informed of this, and he became more violent with them, frightened them, and made demands on them, forcing them to disperse. Al-Ḥasan continued to make speeches, but Marwān b. al-Muhallab avoided him.

On Friday, the fourteenth of Ṣafar (August 25), eight days after Yazīd b. al-Muhallab and Maslamah had first encountered one another, Maslamah ordered al-Waḍḍāḥ to take the Waḍḍāḥiyyah regiment in boats and to set fire to the bridge; he complied with the order. Maslamah then emerged from his camp and, after preparing the Syrian army, he marched forward with them in the direction of Yazīd b. al-Muhallab. He stationed Jabalah b. Makhramah al-Kindī on his right flank and al-Hudhayl b. Zufar b. al-

[1402]

---

465. Text: *khayranā*. The Cairo ed. reads *ḥaqqanā*.
466. Text: *la-unḥiyanna ʿalayhi mibradan khashanan*, literally, "I will finish him off with a rough file." See Kūfī, *Futūḥ*, VIII, 13: *illā nālahu minnā mā yakrahu*, "We will see that he comes to an unpleasant end"; Ibn Kathīr, *Bidāyah*, IX, 221, reads *la-afʿalanna wa-la-afʿalanna*, "I will do this and that (to him)."
467. Text: *mā akrahu an yukrimanī-llāhu bi-hawānihi*. Compare Kūfī, *Futūḥ*, VIII, 14: *fa-innī akrahu an yukrimanī rabbī bi-hawāni Marwān b. al-Muhallab*," It displeases me that my master should honor me by chastising Marwān b. al-Muhallab."
468. Text: *dūnī*. Kūfī, *Futūḥ*, VIII, 14, has *li-ajlī*, "because of me."

Ḥārith al-ʿĀmirī on his left. Al-ʿAbbās stationed Sayf b. Hāniʾ al-Hamdānī on his right flank and Suwayd b. al-Qaʿqāʿ al-Tamīmī on his left. Maslamah was in command of the soldiers. Yazīd b. al-Muhallab emerged from his camp, having put Ḥabīb b. al-Muhallab on his right flank and al-Mufaḍḍal b. al-Muhallab on his left flank. The Kūfan army was with al-Mufaḍḍal, who was in command of it; with him also were a substantial number of horsemen from the tribe of Rabīʿah. He was adjacent to al-ʿAbbās b. al-Walīd.

According to Abū Mikhnaf—al-Ghanawī—Hishām—I suspect that al-Ghanawī is al-ʿAlāʾ b. al-Minhāl: One of the Syrians went out, challenging his opponents to a single combat, but no one accepted his challenge. Then Muḥammad b. al-Muhallab stepped forward and attacked him. The Syrian protected himself with his hand—he was wearing a glove made of iron—but Muḥammad stabbed him, tearing the iron glove, and quickly thrust the sword into his hand.[469] As the man held on to his horse's neck, Muḥammad advanced and stabbed him, saying, "A reaping hook would have served you better."[470] According to one source, that man was Ḥayyān al-Nabaṭī.[471]

Al-Waḍḍāḥ approached the bridge and set fire to it, sending smoke billowing in the air. Meanwhile, the war had begun and the two sides were engaged in light fighting. But when the soldiers saw the smoke and were told that the bridge had been set on fire, they fled. After learning that the soldiers had fled, Yazīd [1403] exclaimed, "What have they fled from? Is this the type of battle from which one flees?" Someone said to him, "When they were told that the bridge had been set on fire, not a single one of them held firm in battle." He said, "May God render them hideous! (They are like) an insect that flies off when some smoke is di-

---

469. That the unnamed Syrian was the standard-bearer of the Syrian army is suggested by the fact that he was the first to attack Yazīd's army; also he was wearing an iron glove. It was customary for one army to try to cut down the flag of the other by either severing or severely wounding the hand of the standard-bearer. For further details on this aspect of Islamic warfare, see Juynboll, "The Qurʾān Reciter on the Battlefield and Concomitant Issues," 25–26.

470. That is, you are better suited for farming than for fighting duels. See Kūfī, Futūḥ, VIII, 17.

471. Nabataeans were viewed as peasants. On Ḥayyān, see text above, II/1290ff., sub anno 96.

rected towards it." He emerged together with his supporters, his clients, and his fellow tribesmen, saying, "Strike off the heads of the deserters." They complied with his order until there were many heads, which he accepted from them in huge piles. Then he said, "Leave them alone for by God I hope that God will never again cause me to occupy the same spot as they do. Leave them alone, may God expose them to hardships.[472] (They are like) sheep attacked by a wolf." Yazīd would never consider fleeing from battle.

Earlier, while in Wāsiṭ before arriving in al-ʿAqr, Yazīd had been approached by Yazīd b. al-Ḥakam b. Abī al-ʿĀṣ[473]—his mother was the daughter of al-Zibriqān al-Saʿdī—who recited:

Verily, the kingship of the Marwānids has come to an end.
    If you have not noticed that, then notice it now.

Yazīd said, "I hadn't noticed." Then Yazīd b. al-Ḥakam b. Abī al-ʿĀṣ al-Thaqafī recited:

Live as a king or die with dignity, for if you die
    with your sword unsheathed in your hand, you will be
    forgiven.

He said, "That may be."
When Yazīd went out to his forces and was confronted by the rout, he asked al-Samaydaʿ, "Who was right—you or I? Didn't I tell you what the army had in mind?" He replied, "Yes, by God, you were right. I am here with you and I will not leave you. I am at your command." He said, "If you will not leave me, then attack," so he attacked, leading his forces. Then someone came to Yazīd b. al-Muhallab and announced that Ḥabīb had been slain.

According to Hishām—Abū Mikhnaf—Thābit, a client of Zuhayr b. Salamah al-Azdī: I testify that when Yazīd was informed of Ḥabīb's death, I heard him say, "Life is not worth living without Ḥabīb! By God, I have always hated life after a defeat and, by God, this only increases my hatred. Advance!" By God, we

[1404]

---

472. Text: *yuraḥḥimuhumu-llāhi*, "may God have mercy on them." This should be amended to read *barramahumu-llāhi*. I owe this point to Professor Abbas.

473. Yazīd b. al-Ḥakam was an Umayyad poet who died in 105/723. See Sezgin, *GAS*, II, 332.

knew that Yazīd was desperate, and those who did not want to fight began to withdraw and slip away in secret. Nevertheless, a substantial number of soldiers remained with Yazīd as he approached his destiny. Whenever he passed the cavalry, he put them to flight; the units of the Syrian army turned away from him and from the path of his soldiers. Abū Ru'bah al-Murji'ī approached Yazīd and said, "The soldiers have fled." I was listening to him as he was indicating this to him. Abū Ru'bah asked, "Do you want to go to Wāsiṭ, a fortified city where you might remain until reinforcements arrive from the army of al-Baṣrah and until the armies of 'Umān and al-Baḥrayn[474] arrive by sea? You can dig a trench (around the city)." Yazīd replied, "What a bad suggestion! Are you suggesting that to *me*? Death would be far easier for me." Abū Ru'bah said, "I am afraid for you, for reasons that are known to you. Do you not see the iron mountains around you?" He was gesturing at him. Yazīd said to him, "I don't care whether they are mountains of iron or mountains of fire! Leave us if you do not want to fight." Our source added: Yazīd quoted the verses of Ḥārithah b. Badr al-Ghudānī.[475] Abū Ja'far (al-Ṭabarī) said: That is a mistake. The verses are by al-A'shā:[476]

Is it with death that some people[477] threaten me,   [1405]
    when I see that those who cower in death suffer anyway?
A death I die not powerless is not
    a shame when the soul is taken away by its death.[478]

Yazīd b. al Muhallab advanced toward Maslamah, riding his gray horse, oblivious to everyone else. When he drew near, Maslamah went to his horse in order to mount it.[479] But the Syrian

---

474. 'Umān and al-Baḥrayn are on the mainland of eastern Arabia, embracing the oases of Qaṭif and Ḥajar. See *EI*², s.v. al-Baḥrayn.

475. Ḥārithah b. Badr al-Ghudānī was a poet and notable of the Tamīmī clan of the Banū Ghudānah, at al-Baṣrah; he died in 64/684 or 66/686. See *EI*², s.v. Ḥārithah b. Badr al-Ghudānī.

476. Maymūn b. Qays al-A'shā was a prominent poet of the tribe of Qays b. Tha'labah; he died ca. A.D. 625. See *EI*², s.v. al-A'shā; *Aghānī* (Beirut), IX, 104–25.

477. Text: 'ibād; the Cairo ed. has 'ubād, referring to the Banū 'Ubād.

478. See Kūfī, *Futūḥ*, VIII, 19.

479. It is reported that Yazīd challenged Maslamah to a single combat, but that he declined on the recommendation of his supporters. See Kūfī, *Futūḥ*, VIII, 17–18.

cavalry attacked Yazīd and his forces, slaying Yazīd b. al-Muhallab. Al-Samaydaʿ and Muḥammad b. al-Muhallab were also slain.

There was a man from the tribe of Kalb, from the Banū Jābir b. Zuhayr b. Janāb al-Kalbī, by the name of al-Qaḥl b. ʿAyyāsh, who, when he saw Yazīd, said, "O Syrians, by God, there is Yazīd, and by God, either I will slay him or he will slay me. He has soldiers with him, so who will attack with me and engage his forces so that I might reach him?" Some of his comrades said to him, "We will attack with you." They did. All of them attacked, and they fought one another for a while. When the dust rose, the two sides cleared themselves away from Yazīd, who lay dead, and from al-Qaḥl b. ʿAyyāsh, who was on the point of death. Al-Qaḥl signaled to his comrades with his head, showing them the spot where Yazīd lay, and said to them, "I slew him."[480] Then he pointed at himself so as to indicate that he had been mortally wounded by Yazīd. Maslamah passed by al-Qaḥl b. ʿAyyāsh, who was lying on the ground next to Yazīd, and al-Qaḥl said, "I think that (Yazīd) is the one who mortally wounded me." A client of the Banū Murrah brought forward Yazīd's head, and someone asked him, "Did you slay him?" He replied, "No." The head was brought to Maslamah, who could not identify it for sure. Al-Ḥawārī b. Ziyād b. ʿAmr al-ʿAtakī said to him, "Order that his head be washed and wrapped in a turban." When this was done, Maslamah recognized it. He sent his head to Yazīd b. ʿAbd al-Malik, with Khālid b. al-Walīd b. ʿUqbah b. Abī al-Muʿayṭ.

[1406]

According to Abū Mikhnaf—Thābit, a client of Zuhayr: After Yazīd was slain and the army defeated, al-Mufaḍḍal b. al-Muhallab continued to fight the Syrian army, unaware of the fact that Yazīd was dead and the soldiers routed. He was riding a powerful, low-built horse, and in front him was a horse covered with a coat of mail. Every time he attacked it, it turned back and withdrew; then he withdrew. He would attack with soldiers from his forces so that he was in the middle of the army and then he would return to a spot behind his forces. Whenever he saw one of us turn his head, he would point to him with his hand, thereby

---

480. It is also reported that Yazīd b. al-Muhallab was slain by al-Hudhayl b. Zufar b. al-Ḥārith al-Kilābī. See Ibn al-Athīr, *Kāmil*, V, 83.

indicating that he should not turn his head, so that the soldiers would direct their faces exclusively against their enemy.

Our source continued: We fought for a while. It was as if I were looking at 'Āmir b. al-'Amaythal al-Azdī as he brandished his sword, reciting:

The mother of the newborn child knew
    that I am not afraid to use the blade of the sword.

By God, we fought for an hour or so, and the horsemen from Rabī'ah were put to flight. By God, I don't think that any of the Kūfan forces persevered greatly or fought vehemently. Then al-Mufaḍḍal stood before the Rabī'ah, brandishing a sword, and called out to them, "O tribe of Rabī'ah, attack, attack! By God, you never fled before, nor were you ignoble. That is not your custom. So do not let the Iraqi army be attacked from your side today. O Rabī'ah, my soul for you, persevere for a while." Then they rallied around him and came back to him and, lo, your little rally[481] took place.

We assembled, wanting to attack them, until al-Mufaḍḍal [1407] came. But someone asked him, "What are you doing here? Yazīd, Ḥabīb, and Muḥammad have all been slain, and the soldiers fled long ago." The news spread among the soldiers, who then scattered, whereupon al-Mufaḍḍal set out on the road to Wāsiṭ. I never saw an Arab of his stature who was more willing to engage in the actual fighting and to smite with his sword, or better at arraying his comrades for battle.

According to Abū Mikhnaf—Thābit, a client of Zuhayr. I passed by the defensive trench and, behold, above it was a wall on which men armed with arrows were standing. I was wearing a coat of mail, and they called out, "O you, wearing the coat of mail, where are you going?" The coat of mail that I was wearing was extremely heavy, and as soon as I had passed beyond them, I dismounted and threw off the coat of mail so as to lighten my horse's burden.

---

481. This is a conjectural translation. The text is *kuwayfatuka*. Yāqūt mentions a place by the name of Kuwayfah ("little al-Kūfah") near Bazīqiyyah. See *Mu'jam*, IV, 496.

The Syrian army reached Yazīd b. al-Muhallab's camp, where Abū Ruʾbah, the leader of the Murjiʾites, engaged them in combat for an hour or so, until most of (the Murjiʾites) had gone. The Syrians captured approximately three hundred men, and Maslamah sent them to Muḥammad b. ʿAmr b. al-Walīd, who imprisoned them. When Muḥammad b. ʿAmr received a letter from Yazīd b. ʿAbd al-Malik ordering him to slay the prisoners, he said to al-ʿUryān b. al-Haytham, the commander of his guard, "Take them out in groups of twenty and thirty."

Our source continued: Approximately thirty men from the Banū Tamīm stood up and said, "We led the soldiers in flight. Fear God and give us precedence. Send us out before the others (are slain)."[482] Al-ʿUryān said to them, "Go out, in the name of God."[483] He brought them out to the square and sent a message to Muḥammad b. ʿAmr, informing him that he had brought them out (and informing him) of what they had said. But Muḥammad replied that al-ʿUryān should slay them.

According to Abū Mikhnaf—Najīḥ, Abū ʿAbdallāh, a client of Zuhayr: "By God, I was looking at them as they were exclaiming, 'O God, we led the soldiers in flight, and this is our reward!'" No sooner had he finished with them than a messenger arrived with a letter from Maslamah in which he pardoned the prisoners and forbade their being slain. Ḥājib b. Dhubyān, from the Banū Māzin b. Mālik b. ʿAmr b. Tamīm, recited:

[1408]

By my life, (the tribe of) Muʿayṭ has waded in our blood
with their swords until they were covered with muck.
The tribes have never been burdened with anything graver than
(shedding) forbidden blood,
or retaliation, when retaliation was sought.
All of you forbade shedding the blood of those who brandished
their swords against you,
but murder was committed against the cavaliers of your
group.

---

482. The Banū Tamīm may have expected to be spared because their flight facilitated the victory of the Syrian army.

483. Text: ʿalā-smi-llāhi, which is equivalent to bismi-llāhi. The functions of ʿalā and bi overlap to a certain extent in classical Arabic. See Hopkins, Studies, 125 (no. 119); Lane, Lexicon, pt. 5, p. 2145.

Al-'Uryān protected the cavaliers of his tribe with their bodies.
How strange! Where is integrity and justice?[484]

Al-'Uryān used to say, "By God, it was neither my intention nor
wish (to slay) them, until they said, 'Give us precedence. Send us
out.' I brought them out and dutifully informed the person who
was charged with slaying them (that is, Muḥammad b. 'Amr), but
he rejected their plea and issued the order to slay them. By God,
despite what happened, I would not want a fellow tribesman to be
killed in place of them. If they blame me, I am not one who heeds
their reproach. So do not blame me excessively."[485]

[1409]

Maslamah advanced towards al-Ḥīrah, where he set up camp.
With him were approximately fifty prisoners whom he had kept
with himself rather than send to al-Kūfah. When the soldiers saw
that he intended to slay them, al-Ḥusayn b. Ḥammād al-Kalbī
approached him and asked to be given three prisoners as a gift:
Ziyād b. 'Abd al-Raḥmān al-Qushayrī, 'Utbah b. Muslim, and Is-
mā'īl, a client of the family of the Banū 'Aqīl b. Mas'ūd. Maslamah
gave the three prisoners to al-Ḥusayn and complied with his followers' requests for the other prisoners.

When the news of Yazīd's defeat reached Wāsiṭ, Mu'āwiyah b.
Yazīd b. al-Muhallab took out thirty-two prisoners who were in
his possession and slew them. Among those slain were 'Adī b.
Arṭāt; Muḥammad b. 'Adī b. Arṭāt; Mālik and 'Abd al-Malik, the
sons of Misma'; 'Abdallāh b. 'Azrah al-Baṣrī; 'Abdallāh b. Wā'il;
and Ibn Abī Ḥāḍir al-Tamīmī, from the Banū Usayyid b. 'Amr b.
Tamīm.[486] These men had said to him, "Woe to thee! We think
that you are killing us only because your father was slain. But
killing us will be of no use to you in this world and it will be to
your disadvantage in the next." But he slew all of the prisoners
with the exception of Rabī' b. Ziyād b. al-Rabī' b. Anas b. al-
Rayyān.[487] When he passed over him, some men asked, "Did you
forget him?" He replied, "I did not forget him, but I will not slay
him for he is a noble shaykh from my tribe with a good reputation

---

484. See Kūfī, *Futūḥ*, VIII, 20–21.
485. Text: *wa-lā tukabbir 'alayya*, "But do not praise me." This should be
amended to read *fa-lā yukaththar 'alayya*." I owe this point to Professor Abbas.
486. See Ibn Khayyāṭ, *Ta'rīkh*, I, 332–33; Ya'qūbī, *Ta'rīkh*, III, 54; Azdī, *Ta'rīkh*,
12; *FHA*, 74; Ibn Kathīr, *Bidāyah*, IX, 221.
487. Text: al-Raffān; read al-Rayyān, following the Cairo ed.

and a mighty family. I cannot doubt his affection and I have no fear that he will turn against us."

Thābit Quṭnah recited, on the subject of the slaying of ʿAdī b. Arṭāt:

The slaying of al-Fazārī and his son, ʿAdī, did not make me
    happy,
    and I did not want Ibn Mismaʿ to be slain.
But, O Muʿāwiyah, it was a mistake,
    by which you misplaced my order.

[1410]   Muʿāwiyah (b. Yazīd) marched to al-Baṣrah carrying with him the Public Treasury[488] and the coffers. When al-Mufaḍḍal b. al-Muhallab arrived, the entire Muhallab family was gathered in al-Baṣrah. Fearing that they would suffer the same fate as Yazīd, they prepared seagoing vessels, taking on all necessary provisions.

Earlier, Yazīd b. al-Muhallab had sent Wadāʿ b. Ḥumayd al-Azdī to serve as the governor of Qandābīl,[489] saying to him, "I am going out to face the enemy and when I encounter them, I will not quit the field of battle until one side or the other prevails. If I am victorious, I will bestow honors upon you; if not, you will be in Qandābīl, so that the members of my household can go to you and fortify themselves there until such time as they are able to secure a guarantee of safe-conduct for themselves. As for me, I have chosen you for my household from all of my tribesmen and I trust that you will live up to my faith in you." Yazīd made him swear weighty oaths that he would serve as a faithful counselor to his household if they took refuge with him in their hour of need.

When the Muhallabids gathered in al-Baṣrah after the defeat, they loaded their families and their possessions on the seagoing vessels and put out to sea. Upon reaching al-Baḥrayn, they were told by Harim b. al-Qarār al-ʿAbdī, who had been appointed governor of that province by Yazīd: "I advise you not to leave your boats, upon which you are dependent for your survival, for I fear that if you disembark from these boats, the soldiers will capture

---

488. Text: al-māl. See text below, II/1411, where a parallel passage reads bayt al-māl.

489. The capital of a district known as Nudhah in the province of Sind, Qandābīl is on the road from Bālis to Quṣdār. See EI², s.v. al-Ḳandābīl; Barthold, Geography, 75; Yāqūt, Muʿjam, IV, 402.

you and bring you to the Marwānids." So they sailed on until they
were opposite Kirmān, where they disembarked from the boats
and loaded their families and possessions on horses and mules.

Earlier, Muʿāwiyah b. Yazīd b. al-Muhallab had arrived in al-
Baṣrah, carrying the coffers and the Public Treasury, acting as if [1411]
he wanted to become the head of the family. But the Muhallabids
assembled and said to al-Mufaḍḍal, "We accept you as our leader
and our chief, even though you are only a young man of tender
years, like one of your family's young slaves." Al-Mufaḍḍal continued to serve as their chief until they reached Kirmān, where he
was joined by large numbers of runaway soldiers.

Maslamah b. ʿAbd al-Malik sent Mudrik b. Ḍabb al-Kalbī in
pursuit of the Muhallabids and the runaway soldiers. Mudrik
caught up with al-Mufaḍḍal b. al-Muhallab in Fārs after the latter
had been joined by the runaway soldiers. He pursued them, finally overtaking them in ʿAqabah,[490] where they attacked him, engaging him in a heated battle. Slain along with al-Mufaḍḍal b. al-
Muhallab were al-Nuʿmān b. Ibrāhīm b. al-Ashtar al-Nakhaʿī and
Muḥammad b. Isḥāq b. Muḥammad b. al-Ashʿath. Taken prisoner
were Ibn Ṣūl, the King of Quhistān,[491] and al-ʿĀliyah, al-Mufaḍḍal's concubine. ʿUthmān b. Isḥāq b. Muḥammad b. al-Ashʿath
was severely wounded, but he fled to Ḥulwān,[492] where he was
slain when someone identified him; his head was sent to Maslamah in al-Ḥīrah.

Some soldiers who had supported Yazīd b. al-Muhallab came
back and asked for a guarantee of safe-conduct, which they received. Among these were Mālik b. Ibrāhīm b. al-Ashtar and al-
Ward b. ʿAbdallāh b. Ḥabīb al-Saʿdī, from the tribe of Tamīm, who
had been present with ʿAbd al-Raḥmān b. Muḥammad at all of the
battles and wars in which he had participated. Muḥammad b.
ʿAbdallāh b. ʿAbd al-Malik b. Marwān requested the guarantee of
safe-conduct for al-Ward from Maslamah b. ʿAbd al-Malik, who [1412]
was both his paternal uncle and his father-in-law, and Maslamah

---

490. This town is possibly ʿAqabah of al-Ṭīn, in Fārs. See Yāqūt, *Muʿjam*, IV,
134. Alternatively, the text could mean, "finally overtaking them at a mountain
pass (ʿaqabah)."

491. The mountainous region in the southern part of Khurāsān. See Barthold,
Geography, 209; *EI²*, s.v. al-Ḳūhistān.

492. See note 19, above.

agreed to his request. But when al-Ward came to him, Maslamah stopped him and rebuked him, while standing. He said, "You are disobedient, rebellious, hypocritical, and cowardly whenever there is a civil strife; one day you side with the weaver of the Kindah, the next with the sailor of the Azd.[493] You do not deserve to receive a guarantee of safe-conduct." Then he left.

The guarantee of safe-conduct for Mālik b. Ibrāhīm b. al-Ashtar was requested by al-Ḥasan b. ʿAbd al-Raḥmān b. Sharāhīl—Sharāhīl's nickname was Rustam al-Ḥaḍramī. When Maslamah came and looked at Mālik, al-Ḥasan b. ʿAbd al-Raḥmān al-Ḥaḍramī said to him, "This is Mālik b. Ibrāhīm b. al-Ashtar." Maslamah told Mālik to leave, whereupon al-Ḥasan said to Maslamah, "May God cause you to prosper! Why don't you rebuke him as you did his comrade?" Maslamah said, "I hold your family in too high esteem for that, and you are dearer and more loyal to me than the family of Muḥammad b. ʿAbdallāh." Al-Ḥasan said, "But we want you to swear at him for, by God, compared to al-Ward b. ʿAbdallāh, his ancestors are of greater rank, and he has had a worse influence on the Syrian army." Several months later al-Ḥasan said, "Maslamah left Mālik alone out of envy lest our companion become distinguished. He wanted to show us that he held him in great contempt."

The Muhallabids, together with the runaway soldiers who had taken refuge with them, continued their journey until reaching Qandābīl. Meanwhile, Maslamah recalled Mudrik b. Ḍabb al-Kalbī and sent Hilāl b. Aḥwaz al-Tamīmī, from the Banū Māzin b. ʿAmr b. Tamīm, to search for them. Hilāl caught up with them (as they were about to enter) Qandābīl.[494] The Muhallabids wanted to enter Qandābīl, but were prevented from doing so by Wadāʿ b. Ḥumayd. Hilāl b. Aḥwaz had written to Wadāʿ, who did not, (at first), abandon the Muhallabids. (After receiving the letter, however, Wadāʿ) left them.[495] The Muhallabids became aware of the

---

493. The phrase "the weaver of the Kindah" refers to Ibn al-Ashʿath, who led a revolt against al-Ḥajjāj; see note 456, above. The phrase "the sailor of the Azd" refers to Yazīd b. al-Muhallab; see text above, II/1287, sub anno 96.

494. See Ibn Khayyāṭ, *Taʾrīkh*, I, 334; Balādhurī, *Futūḥ* (Cairo), III, 540; Yaʿqūbī, *Taʾrīkh*, III, 54–55; Azdī, *Taʾrīkh*, 15; Masʿūdī, *Murūj* (Beirut), III, 200–1; *FHA*, 74.

495. This is a conjectural translation. The text is: *wa-lam yubāyin āl al-Muhallab fa-yufāriquhum.* See Ibn al-Athīr, *Kāmil*, V, 86, where the subject of the verb *yubāyin* is Hilāl b. Aḥwāz.

fact that Wadāʿ had abandoned them when they assembled and lined up in military ranks. Wadāʿ b. Ḥumayd was on the right flank and ʿAbd al-Malik b. Hilāl on the left—both of them were Azdīs. Hilāl b. Aḥwaz waved the peace flag at them, whereupon Wadāʿ b. Ḥumayd and ʿAbd al-Malik b. Hilāl joined them. The soldiers dispersed, leaving the Muhallabids by themselves.

When Marwān b. al-Muhallab witnessed this, he started to make his way to the women, but al-Mufaḍḍal asked him, "Where are you going?" He replied, "I am going to our women, whom I intend to slay so that they will never fall into the hands of those sinners." Al-Mufaḍḍal exclaimed, "Woe to you! Would you slay your sisters and the women of your household? By God, they are not in any danger from them." He convinced him not to slay them. Then they charged with their swords and fought until they were all slain,[496] except for Abū ʿUyaynah b. al-Muhallab and ʿUthmān b. al-Mufaḍḍal, both of whom escaped and joined up with the Khāqān, Rutbīl.[497] Their women and children were sent, together with the heads of the slain men, to Maslamah, who was in al-Ḥīrah; Maslamah conveyed the heads to Yazīd b. ʿAbd al-Malik, who sent them to al-ʿAbbās b. al-Walīd b. ʿAbd al-Malik, the governor of Aleppo.[498] When the heads had been set out on display, al-ʿAbbās went out to look at them and said to his men, "This is the head of ʿAbd al-Malik and this is the head of al-Mufaḍḍal. By God, it is as if he were sitting here talking to me."

Maslamah swore, "Verily, I will sell their women and children while they are in Dār al-Rizq (the Abode of Sustenance)."[499] Then al-Jarrāḥ b. ʿAbdallāh said, "I will buy them from you in order to relieve you from your oath." He bought them from him for one hundred thousand (dirhams). Maslamah said, "Give me the mon-

[1413]

[1414]

---

496. Ibn al-Athīr, *Kāmil*, V, 86, adds: "They are: al-Mufaḍḍal, ʿAbd al-Malik, Ziyād, and Marwān, the sons of Muhallab; Muʿāwiyah b. Yazīd b. al-Muhallab and al-Minhāl b. Abī ʿUyaynah b. al-Muhallab; and ʿAmr and al-Mughīrah, the two sons of Qabīṣah b. al-Muhallab. Their heads were carried away; in the ear of each one was a chit bearing his name."

497. Text: Khāqān wa-Rutbīl, "The Khāqān and Rutbīl." The term Khāqān is a title meaning "supreme ruler"; it applies to the heads of the various Turkish confederations. Rutbīl (or Zanbīl) was the name of the Turkish ruler of Zābulistān. See *EI²*, s.v. Khāḳān; Ṭabarī, *Index*, s.v. Rutbīl; Gibb, *Arab Conquests*, 41.

498. See *EI²*, s.v. Ḥalab.

499. The sale of Muslims as slaves is contrary to Islamic law. Dār al-Rizq seems to have been a depot for provisions in both al-Kūfah and al-Baṣrah; in the latter, it was adjacent to Zābūqah. See Ṭabarī, Index; Yāqūt, *Muʿjam*, III, 41.

ey." Al-Jarrāḥ replied, "Take it whenever you want." But Maslamah did not take any (money) from al-Jarrāḥ, who released the women and children, except for nine boys whom he sent to Yazīd b. ʿAbd al-Malik. They were brought to Yazīd, and he beheaded them.[500]

Thābit Quṭnah recited the following elegy when he learned that Yazīd b. al-Muhallab had been slain:

O Hind,[501] how long a night have I spent!
    Even the shortest night has become too long.
As if, when the Pleiades were high overhead,
    I was given an adder's spittle[502] or poison to drink.
One day embittered the sweetness of life,
    turning my hair white though I was still a youth.
(That is the day when) your father's sons were killed while I
      was far away
    and could not see them. They departed nobly.
No, by God, I shall never forget Yazīd,
    or the dead who were slain unlawfully.
I hope to slay Yazīd[503] one day in retaliation for your brother,
    or else slay Hishām in retaliation for him.
I hope to lead the horses until they are disheveled,
    lean and lank, pounding the hillsides.
I will very shortly surprise the Ḥimyar with them in the
      morning,
    and the ʿAkk, and frighten with those two the Judhām.
And we will give the Madhḥij and the tribe of Kalb
    long draughts of deadly poison to drink.
(I mean) our kinsmen who mistreat us and
    regularly put us to the test year after year.[504]
Were it not for them and the crime they committed against us,
    he would have become, in the midst of us, a king and hero.

---

500. Kūfī, *Futūḥ*, VIII, 22, mentions eighty men who were slain by order of the Caliph. Azdī, *Taʾrīkh*, 15, mentions fourteen prisoners who were slain in retaliation for ʿAdī b. Arṭāt and his comrades.

501. That is, Hind bt. al-Muhallab, Yazīd's sister.

502. Text: *luʿāb aswad*. Literally, "black drivel."

503. That is, Yazīd b. ʿAbd al-Malik.

504. Text: *ʿāman bi-ʿāmā*. This should be amended to read *ʿāman fa-ʿāmā*. I owe this point to Professor Abbas.

He also recited the following elegy for Yazīd b. al-Muhallab:

The length of this night has refused to come to an end,
    and concern stirred your captivated heart.
I stayed awake, while Umm Khālid[505] slept alongside me.
    I couldn't sleep for a full year.
Because of the deceased whose loss crushed the tribe.   [1415]
    When the Fates summoned him, he responded and
    submitted.
Because of a king, O friend, in al-ʿAqr, to whose
    cavalry detachments cowardice was attributed,
    who met his death with his well-known emblem (of
    courage).
He was slain, but I was not present. Had I been present,
    I would have put on the garments of mourning[506] if the
    tribe did not observe a day of mourning.
In the vicissitudes of time, O Hind, know
    that someone who seeks to retaliate has to bide his time
    because he has to go about it carefully.
Perhaps, if the wind blows me
    in the direction of Ibn Abī Dhibbān,[507] he will repent.
O Maslamah, if our spears reach you,
    with them we will make you taste the venom of black
    serpents—O Maslamah.[508]
And if al-ʿAbbās[509] should ever stumble,
    we will repay him for what he did that day.
In retaliation. Yet we will not exceed what he did
    to us, and even then Ibn Marwān[510] would be the
    wrongdoer.
You will know, if your foot slips,
    and some people reveal the shame they want to suppress,

---

505. Umm Khālid is either Thābit Quṭnah's wife or concubine.
506. Text: *tassalaytu*, "I would have been consoled"; read *la-sallabtu*, following Ibn al-Athīr, *Kāmil*, V, 88.
507. Ibn Abī Dhibbān is either Yazīd b. ʿAbd al-Malik b. Marwān (see Ṭabarī, *Glossary*, s.v. Ibn Abī Dhibbān), or his brother, Maslamah (see Azdī, *Taʾrīkh*, 14, n. 1).
508. Text: *muslamā*, "having been given up to destruction." This should be amended to read *maslamā*. I owe this point to Professor Abbas.
509. Al-ʿAbbās b. al-Walīd.
510. Yazīd b. ʿAbd al-Malik b. Marwān.

[1416]   Who the transgressor is who drags mischief to his household,
>   whether the causes of a matter are clear or obscure.
Verily, we are inclined to clemency out of generosity—after
>   we see ignorance from the extravagance of a base person.
Verily, we have established ourselves in frontier fortresses
>   in which no one resides except for a large military
>   regiment.
We see that the neighbors have needs and deference,[511]
>   when such a neighbor's deference is not considered by
>   other people.
Verily, we feed the guest from the highest part of the camel's
>   hump,
>   when the offers of those who can offer are made
>   reluctantly.
When the cold wind brings forth incessant ice,
>   on the backs of tired grey mares that stand still without
>   eating fodder.
Our father is the father of the 'Helpers,' ʿAmr b. ʿĀmir,[512]
>   and they gave birth to ʿAwf, Kaʿb, and Aslam.[513]
There was considerable glory in Ghassān,
>   a glory that was old and considered magnificent.

In the year in which Maslamah b. ʿAbd al-Malik concluded the
conflict with Yazīd b. al-Muhallab, Yazīd b. ʿAbd al-Malik gave
[1417]   him joint control over the governorships of al-Kūfah, al-Baṣrah,
and Khurāsān.[514] Having been charged with these assignments by
Yazīd, Maslamah appointed Dhū al-Shāmah Muḥammad b. ʿAmr
b. al-Walīd b. ʿUqbah b. Abī Muʿayṭ as governor of al-Kūfah.

Now, after the Muhallabids had left al-Baṣrah, control of that
city was taken—according to some authorities—by Shabīb b. al-
Ḥārith al-Tamīmī, who managed its affairs. But when al-Baṣrah
was put under Maslamah's jurisdiction, he appointed ʿAbd al-
Raḥmān b. Sulaym al-Kalbī as his governor there; and he put

---

511. The text is *ḥājan wa-ḥurmatan*. See Azdī, *Taʾrīkh*, 14: *ḥaqqan wa-ḥur-matan*, "rights and deference"; Ibn al-Athīr, *Kāmil*, V, 88: *ḥaqqan wa-dhim-matan*, "rights and protection."
512. See text above, I/1132; Caskel, *Ǧamharah*, II, 169, s.v. ʿAmr b. ʿĀmir.
513. See Caskel, *Ǧamharah*, I, 176.
514. See Ibn Khayyāṭ, *Taʾrīkh*, I, 332; Dīnawarī, *Akhbār*, 334; FHA, 75.

'Umar b. Yazīd al-Tamīmī in charge of the police and the militia.
'Abd al-Raḥmān b. Sulaym wanted to review the Baṣran army,[515]
but when he revealed his plan to 'Umar b. Yazīd, the latter said to
him, "Do you want to review the Baṣran army when you have
neither proceeded towards a fortress in Kuwayfah,[516] nor staffed
it with your supporters?[517] By God, if the soldiers of the Baṣran
army were to throw stones at you and your forces, I fear that they
would kill us. Wait ten days so that we can prepare ourselves for
that." 'Umar then sent a messenger to Maslamah, informing him
of 'Abd al-Raḥmān's plan, whereupon Maslamah sent 'Abd al-
Malik b. Bishr b. Marwān to serve as governor of al-Baṣrah, and he
confirmed 'Umar b. Yazīd's position as head of the police and the
militia.

Abū Ja'far (al-Ṭabarī) recounted: In this year, Maslamah b. 'Abd
al-Malik dispatched Sa'īd b. 'Abd al-'Azīz b. al-Ḥārith b. al-Ḥakam
b. Abī al-'Āṣ, who is known as Sa'īd Khudhaynah, (to serve as
governor of Khurāsān).[518] He was given this nickname, according
to some authorities, because he was a soft, easy, man who lived in
comfort and luxury. He arrived in Khurāsān, riding a Bukhtiyyah
camel,[519] with a knife hanging from his belt. When the King of   [1418]
Abghar[520] went in to see him, Sa'īd was wearing dyed garments
and was surrounded by dyed cushions. The King emerged and was
asked, "How did you find the governor?" He replied, "He is a
khudhaynah whose hair style resembles that of Sukaynah."[521]
This is why he was given the nickname "Khudhaynah." The
word *khudhaynah* means "the wife of the *dihqān*," (hence,) "the
mistress of the house." Maslamah appointed Sa'īd Khudhaynah as
governor of Khurāsān because the latter was his son-in-law, for
Sa'īd was married to Maslamah's daughter.

---

515. Ibn al-Athīr, *Kāmil*, V, 89, adds: "in order to kill them."
516. See note 481 above.
517. Text: *wa-tudkhilu taḥtāju ilayhi*; read *wa-tudkhilu man taḥtāju ilayhi*,
following the Cairo ed.
518. See Ibn Khayyāṭ, *Ta'rīkh*, I, 335; Balādhurī, *Futūḥ* (Cairo), III, 524–25;
Dīnawarī, *Akhbār*, 334; Ya'qūbī, *Ta'rīkh*, III, 55; Wellhausen, *Arab Kingdom*,
451–52.
519. A Bukhtiyyah camel is a species of camel of Turkoman or Bactrian breed.
See Lane, *Lexicon*, pt. 1, p. 158.
520. A district of Samarqand. See Yāqūt, *Mu'jam*, I, 74; Le Strange, *Lands*, 466.
521. Text: *khudhayniyyah limmatuhu sukayniyyah*. Sukaynah bt. al-Ḥusayn
b. 'Alī had a special hair style that was named for her.

Maslamah Appoints Saʿīd Khudhaynah as Governor of Khurāsān

When Maslamah appointed Saʿīd Khudhaynah as governor of Khurāsān, the latter dispatched to that province, prior to his own departure, Sawrah b. al-Ḥurr, who was from the Banū Dārim. According to some authorities, Sawrah arrived there one month before Saʿīd did. Saʿīd also appointed Shuʿbah b. Zuhayr al-Nahshalī as governor of Samarqand. Shuʿbah set out for that province, accompanied by twenty-five members of his household, taking the road to Āmul[522] and reaching Bukhārā,[523] where he was joined by two hundred men. Then he reached al-Sughd,[524] the inhabitants of which had renounced Islam during the administration of ʿAbd al-Raḥmān b. Nuʿaym al-Ghāmidī, who had served as governor for eighteen months. Subsequently, they returned to the terms of the peace treaty. Shuʿbah delivered a speech to the army of al-Sughd in which he denounced the Arab inhabitants of the province and accused them of cowardice, saying, "I do not see a wounded man among you, nor do I hear anyone groaning." They made excuses to him, attributing cowardice to their governor, ʾIlbāʾ b. Ḥabīb al-ʿAbdī, who was in charge of military affairs. Then, when Saʿīd arrived, he arrested and imprisoned the governors of ʿAbd al-Raḥmān b. ʿAbdallāh al-Qushayrī, who had been appointed during the caliphate of ʿUmar b. ʿAbd al-ʿAzīz. ʿAbd al-Raḥmān b. ʿAbdallāh al-Qushayrī appealed to him on behalf of them, but Saʿīd responded, "They are accused of stealing money from the tribute." ʿAbd al-Raḥmān offered to assume liability for the stolen money—the security for them was seven hundred thousand (dirhams)—but Saʿīd did not collect the sum from him.

[1419]

Next, as is reported by ʿAlī b. Muḥammad, Saʿīd was informed that eight men—including Jahm b. Zaḥr al-Juʿfī, ʿAbd al-ʿAzīz b. ʿAmr b. al-Ḥajjāj al-Zabīdī, al-Muntajiʿ b. ʿAbd al-Raḥmān al-Azdī, and al-Qaʿqāʿ al-Azdī—who had been appointed as governors by

---

522. A town in Khurāsān situated three miles from the left bank of the Oxus. See *EI*², s.v. Āmul.

523. See *EI*², s.v. Bukhārā.

524. See note 334 above.

Yazīd b. al-Muhallab, had in their possession monies that they had stolen from the levies belonging to the Muslims. He sent for them and imprisoned them in the Marw citadel.[525] Someone said to him, "These men will not pay up unless you raise your hand against them,"[526] so he sent for Jahm b. Zaḥr, who was brought from the Marw citadel on a donkey and put on display in front of al-Fayḍ b. ʿImrān. Al-Fayḍ stood before him and struck him on the nose, whereupon Jahm said to him, "O sinner, why didn't you do that when they brought you to me, drunk on wine, and I administered the *ḥadd* punishment to you?" Angered by Jahm, Saʿīd administered two hundred lashes to him. The merchants praised God when Jahm b. Zaḥr received his beating. Saʿīd then ordered that Jahm and the other seven men who were in the prison were to be handed over to Warqāʾ b. Naṣr al-Bāhilī,[527] but when Warqāʾ asked to be excused from that job, Saʿīd complied with his request.

[1420]

ʿAbd al-Ḥamīd b. Dithār—or ʿAbd al-Malik b. Dithār—and al-Zubayr b. Nushayṭ, a client of the tribe of Bāhilah and husband of Saʿīd Khudhaynah's mother, said, "Give us control over their imprisonment."[528] Warqāʾ agreed, and they slew Jahm, ʿAbd al-ʿAzīz b. ʿAmr, and al-Muntajiʿ, after torturing them; they tortured al-Qaʿqāʿ and several others to the point of death. They were still in prison when the Turks and the Soghdian army attacked, at which point Saʿīd ordered the release of those who remained. Saʿīd used to exclaim, "May God render al-Zubayr hideous, for he slew Jahm."

In this year, the Muslims carried out raids against the Soghdians and the Turks; this was the year in which the battle took place at the fortress of al-Bāhilī.

In this year, Saʿīd Khudhaynah dismissed Shuʿbah b. Ẓuhayr as governor of Samarqand.[529]

---

525. Text: *quhunduz Marw*. On the Arabic term *quhunduz*, see Yāqūt, *Muʿjam*, IV, 419.

526. Text: *tabsuṭu ʿalayhim*, a Qurʾānic expression. See Qurʾān 5:11, 60:2.

527. Warqāʾ had reportedly served as commander of the guard in Khurāsān under Qutaybah b. Muslim. See text above, II/1292, sub anno 96.

528. Text: *maḥābisahum*; the Cairo ed. has *maḥāsibahum*, "(Let us settle) the score with them."

529. See Ibn Kathīr, *Bidāyah*, IX, 222–23; Gibb, *Arab Conquests*, 61.

Saʿīd's Dismissal of Shuʿbah and the Battle at the Fortress of al-Bāhilī

According to ʿAlī b. Muḥammad—his aforementioned authorities: When Saʿīd Khudhaynah arrived in Khurāsān, he summoned a group of *dihqān*s and asked them to recommend the names of men that he might send out to the districts. They recommended a group of Arabs, whom he then appointed. Subsequently, however, he began to receive complaints about them. One day, when the people had come to see him, he said, "I arrived in this province not knowing anything about its inhabitants, so I asked for advice, and a certain group was recommended to me. I inquired about them and, after receiving positive reports, I appointed them. I adjure you to inform me about my governors!"

[1421]   Then the people praised them. But ʿAbd al-Raḥmān b. ʿAbdallāh al-Qushayrī said, "Had you not adjured us, I would have desisted, but now that you have adjured us I can say that you sought counsel from polytheists who recommended to you people who would be amenable to themselves and their likes. This is all that we know about them." At that, Saʿīd steadied himself on his elbow[530] and then sat up straight. Then he recited, " 'Take the abundance, and bid to what is honorable, and turn away from the ignorant.'[531] Leave!"

Our source continued: Saʿīd dismissed Shuʿbah b. Zuhayr from al-Sughd, putting ʿUthmān b. ʿAbdallāh b. Muṭarrif b. al-Shikhkhīr in command of the military administration and Sulaymān b. Abī al-Sarī, a client of the Banū ʿUwāfah, in charge of the fiscal administration. He appointed Maʿqil b. ʿUrwah al-Qushayrī as his governor in Herat,[532] whereupon Maʿqil set out for that city. The soldiers, who considered Saʿīd to be a weak man, gave him the nickname "Khudhaynah," and the Turks therefore became eager to defeat Saʿīd. The Khāqān of the Turks rallied his men and sent them to al-Sughd. The commander of the Turks was a certain

---

530. Text: *ittakā*. The Cairo ed. has *ittakaʾa*, which means the same thing.
531. Qurʾān 7:199.
532. One of the principal cities of Khurāsān and a great trading center, strategically located on the trade routes linking the Mediterranean Sea with India and China. See *EI*², s. v. Harāt; Yāqūt, *Muʿjam*, V, 396–97.

Kūrṣul.[533] They advanced to the Bāhilah fortress, where they set
up camp.

Some sources say: One of the great *dihqān*s wanted to marry a
Bāhilī woman who was in that fortress; he sent her a proposal of
marriage. When she refused, he raised up an army in the hope of
capturing the inhabitants of the fortress and seizing the woman.

Kūrṣul advanced and surrounded the inhabitants of the fortress,
in which there were one hundred families. Fearing that ʿUthmān
b. ʿAbdallāh, the governor of Samarqand at the time, would be
slow to send them reinforcements, they sued the Turks for peace
in exchange for forty thousand (dirhams); they also gave the
Turks seventeen men as hostages. Meanwhile, ʿUthmān b. ʿAbdallāh called for volunteers. Al-Musayyab b. Bishr al-Riyāḥī responded to the summons; in addition, four thousand men from all
of the tribes volunteered. But Shuʿbah b. Zuhayr scoffed, "Had the
horsemen of Khurāsān been here, they could not have attained
their goal."[534] Among those who volunteered from the Banū
Tamīm were Shuʿbah b. Zuhayr al-Nahshalī; Balʿāʾ b. Mujāhid
al-ʿAnzī; ʿAmīrah b. Rabīʿah, one of the Banū al-ʿUjayf, who is
known as ʿAmīrat al-Tharīd; Ghālib b. al-Muhājir al-Ṭāʾī—the
paternal uncle of[535] Abū al-ʿAbbās al-Ṭūsī; Abū Saʿīd Muʿāwiyah
b. al-Ḥajjāj al-Ṭāʾī; Thābit Quṭnah; Abū al-Muhājir b. Dārah, from
the tribe of Ghaṭafān; Ḥulays[536] al-Shaybānī; al-Ḥajjāj b. ʿAmr al-
Ṭāʾī; Ḥassān b. Maʿdān al-Ṭāʾī; and al-Ashʿath Abū Ḥaṭāmah and
ʿAmr b. Ḥassān, both from the Ṭayyiʾ.

When the forces had assembled, al-Musayyab b. Bishr said,
"You are about to arrive at the arena of the Turks, the arena of the
Khāqān, and others. The reward, if you are steadfast, is Paradise,
and the punishment, if you flee, is Hellfire. Let those of you who
intend to attack and be steadfast come forward." At this point,
thirteen hundred men left him, and he marched forwards with the
rest. After advancing one *farsakh* (6 km.), he addressed the soldiers in terms similar to those in the first speech, and one thou-

[1422]

---

533. Kūrṣul was also known as *Köl-chūr*. See Gibb, *Arab Conquests*, 61.
534. Their goal was to rescue the Muslims from the Turks.
535. The word ʿamm, "paternal uncle," is omitted in the text but supplied in
the Cairo ed.
536. Text: Julays; read Ḥulays, following the Cairo ed.

sand of them withdrew. He advanced another *farsakh* and repeated his speech, and another thousand withdrew.[537] He marched forwards—al-Ashhab b. ʿUbayd al-Ḥanẓalī served as their guide—until he was two *farsakh*s (12 km.) from the enemy, whereupon he set up camp. Then the Turkish Khāqān, the King of Qiyy,[538] approached the Muslims and said, "All of the *dihqān*s have sworn allegiance to the other Turk,[539] but I command three hundred fighters who are at your disposal. According to my information, the inhabitants of the fortress sued the Turks for peace in return for forty thousand (dirhams); they also gave them seventeen men to serve as hostages until the tribute is paid. But when the Turks learned that you were marching towards them, they slew the hostages." Among the hostages were Nahshal b. Yazīd al-Bāhilī, who managed to escape without being slain, and al-Ashhab b. ʿUbaydallāh al-Ḥanẓalī. The (Muslims) had sworn to attack (the Turks) on the morrow or let them conquer the fortress.

[1423]

That night, al-Musayyab sent out two horsemen, one an Arab and the other a non-Arab, instructing them as follows, "When you approach the fortress, tether your animals to a tree and determine the status of the people." The two men set out on a dark night, but the Turks had flooded the area around the fortress in order to prevent anyone from reaching it. When they drew near to the fortress, the sentry called out to them. They responded, "Be quiet and summon ʿAbd al-Malik b. Dithār for us." The sentry complied. The two men said to ʿAbd al-Malik, "We have been sent by al-Musayyab, and deliverance is here." He asked, "Where is he?" He replied, "Two *farsakh*s (12 km.) from here. Can you hold out for the remainder of tonight and tomorrow?" ʿAbd al-Malik said, "We have sworn to protect our women and to send them to their death ahead of us[540] so that we might all die to-

---

537. Thus, of four thousand initial volunteers, seven hundred remained.

538. A town near Samarqand, located on a canal of the Zarafshan River. See Wellhausen, *Arab Kingdom*, 452, n. 2.

539. Text: *al-turk ghayrī*, referring to the "Khāqān of the Turks" mentioned in text above, II/1421.

540. Text: *qad ajmaʿnā ʿalā taslīmi nisāʾinā wa-taqdīmihim* (sic) *li-l-mawti amāmanā*. The translation is conjectural.

gether tomorrow." The two men reported back to al-Musayyab, who then said to his supporters, "I will march against the enemy (immediately). If anyone wants to leave, let him go." Not a single person left him, and they swore to fight to the death.

By the time al-Musayyab set out, additional water had been released around the city in order to render it inaccessible. When he was half a *farsakh* (3 km.) from the Turks, he dismounted and resolved to carry out a surprise attack by night. That evening, he gave the men their orders. They saddled up their horses, and he mounted his. He urged them to be steadfast; he not only incited their interest in the rewards to be received in the next life by those who had accumulated pious deeds and were steadfast but also enticed them with the honor and booty that they would receive in this world, if they were victorious. He instructed them as follows:

[1424]

> Muzzle your horses and lead them forward. When you approach the enemy, mount and attack with earnestness. Exclaim the expression "God is great" and let your battle cry be "O Muhammad." Do not pursue someone who has turned his back and fled. You are responsible for the horses, so make their backs sore,[541] for animals with sore backs will charge them more furiously than you will. A small number of steadfast men is preferable to a large number of cowards. Nor are your numbers insignificant. One cannot strike the enemy with seven hundred swords without weakening him, regardless of his number.

Our source continued: He arranged them in their places, putting Kuthayyir b. al-Dabūsī on the right flank and a man from the tribe of Rabī'ah known as Thābit Quṭnah on the left. They marched forward until they were two bowshots away from them, whereupon they exclaimed, "God is great." This occurred at dawn. The

---

541. The translation is conjectural. The text is *fa-ʿqirūhā*, which literally means "cut their hamstrings." A hobbled camel, however, is presumably immobile. The hobbling of camels was indeed practiced by the Arabs as a military tactic, but as a defensive, not an offensive maneuver. See J. Jandora, "The Battle of the Yarmūk," p. 16. According to Professor Abbas, the text may be amended to read *fa-aʿdhirūhā*, "tighten their reins."

Turks leaped to their feet. The Muslims penetrated to the middle of the camp, having made the backs of their horses sore,[542] but the Turks persevered against them. The Muslims were routed and they withdrew to al-Musayyab, pursued by the Turks, who wounded the back of al-Musayyab's horse. Many Muslims dismounted in order to fight, including al-Bakhtarī Abū ʿAbdallāh al-Murāʾī; Muḥammad b. Qays al-Ghanawī—also known as Muḥammad b. Qays al-ʿAnbarī; Ziyād al-Iṣbahānī; Muʿāwiyah b. al-Ḥajjāj; and Thābit Quṭnah. Al-Bakhtarī fought, and when his right arm was slashed he transferred the sword to his left; it, too, was slashed, and he began to defend himself with his hands until, finally, he was slain as a martyr. Also slain as martyrs were Muḥammad b. Qays al-ʿAnbarī—or al-Ghanawī—and Shabīb b. al-Ḥajjāj al-Ṭāʾī.

[1425]

Then the polytheists were put to flight. Thābit Quṭnah struck one of their best soldiers, slaying him. Al-Musayyab's herald called out, "Do not pursue them, for they do not understand (the meaning of) fear, whether you pursue them or not! Head for the fortress, but do not carry off any goods, except money, and do not carry off anyone who can walk." Al-Musayyab said, "Whoever carries off a woman, a young boy, or a weak person for the sake of God receives his wages from God, and whoever abstains will receive forty dirhams. If there is anyone in the fortress with whom you have a pact, take him with you."

Our source continued: They all headed for the fortress and carried off whoever was in it. A man from the Banū Fuqaym reached a woman who implored him, saying "Help me, may God help you." He halted and said, "Jump onto the back of the horse." She leaped and, behold, there she was on the back of the horse; she was more skillful on a horse than a man. Al-Fuqaymī grabbed her son's hand—he was a young child—and put him between his arms. The Muslims made their way to the Turkish Khāqān, who took them into his fortress and brought them food. He said, "Go to Samarqand and do not retrace your steps." As they were setting out for Samarqand, the Turkish Khāqān asked them, "Is there anyone left in the fortress?" They replied, "Hilāl al-Ḥarīrī." He

---

542. Text: *fa-ʿaqirū-l-dawābba*. See the preceding note.

said, "I will not abandon him." He found him, with over thirty wounds on his body, and carried him away. He recovered, but was slain subsequently together with al-Junayd at the Battle of the Pass.[543] When the Turks returned the next day, they found nothing in the fortress except the corpses of their comrades. They said, "Those who came were not human."

Thābit Quṭnah recited:

My life for the horsemen of Tamīm,   [1426]
    on the morning of the battle in the tight spot.
My life for horsemen who had protected me[544]
    from the enemy amidst the dark dust.
In the fortress of al-Bāhilī. They had seen me
    defending where the defender was reluctant.
With my sword, after the spear had broken, boldly.
    I drove them away with a sharp, well-made sword.
Circling around them with my horse,
    like drinkers passing a jug of wine around.
I charge with it at the time of the adversities until
    the adversities vanish and I no longer feel their tight grip.
Were it not for God—He has no partner—
    and my striking the head of the heroic king.
Then the women of the Banū Dithār would have been driven
    before the Turks with their anklets uncovered.
Who among the Tamīm is conspicuous like al-Musayyab,
    Abū Bishr, like feathers at the wing tips of a pigeon?

Jarīr recited, mentioning al-Musayyab:

Had (the Banū) Yarbūʿ not protected your women,   [1427]
    people other than you would have made use of their days
    of purity.
Al-Musayyab defended (them) when the two armies were in
    trouble,
    since Māzin's neighbor there has no protector.
Since there is no ʿIqāl[545] to defend your sacred things,

---

543. See text below, II/1546–53, sub anno 112; *EI²*, s.v. al-Djunayd.
544. Text: *iktafawnī*; read *aknafūnī*, following the Cairo ed.
545. ʿIqāl b. Shabbah b. ʿIqāl al-Mujāshiʿī.

and no Zurārah[546] to defend them, nor anyone attached to
Zurārah.[547]

Our source continued: That night, Abū Saʿīd Muʿāwiyah b. al-
Ḥajjāj al-Ṭāʾī, who had served as a provincial governor on behalf
of Saʿīd, was blinded in one eye and his hand was crippled. But
when he failed to pay part of what was claimed from him, he was
taken to account. Saʿīd turned him over to Shaddād b. Khulayd al-
Bāhilī so that the latter might settle the account with him and
retrieve (the money). Shaddād treated Abū Saʿīd harshly, causing
the latter to exclaim, "O tribe of Qays, when I went to the fortress
of al-Bāhilī, I was a man of great might and powerful eyesight. But
I was blinded in one eye and my arm was crippled while fighting
with the other warriors in the effort to rescue (the Muslims in the
fortress) who were on the verge of being either slain, captured, or
imprisoned. Now look at the manner in which your comrade is
treating me! Keep him away from me." They released him.

According to ʿAbdallāh b. Muḥammad—a man who was present that night at the fortress of al-Bāhilī: "We were inside the
[1428]   fortress, and when the two armies engaged in battle, we thought
that the Day of Resurrection had arrived on account of what we
heard, namely, the groans emitted by the soldiers, the clashing of
iron, and the neighing of the horses."

In this year, Saʿīd Khudhaynah crossed over the Balkh River and
attacked the Soghdians, who had violated their treaty and aided
the Turks against the Muslims.[548]

Saʿīd Khudhaynah's Military Expedition against the Soghdians

It is reported that Saʿīd carried out this military expedition because, after the Turks returned to al-Sughd, the troops spoke to
him, saying, "The fact that you are no longer carrying out military expeditions has allowed the Turks to take the offensive and
caused the Soghdians to renounce Islam." He therefore crossed
over the river and headed for al-Sughd. He was met by the Turks,

---

546. Zurārah b. ʿUdus.
547. Text: *zurrār*; the Cairo ed. has *wuzzār*. See *Dīwān Jarīr*, I, 326.
548. See Yaʿqūbī, *Taʾrīkh*, III, 55.

together with a detachment of the Soghdian army, but the Muslims put them to flight. Sa'īd said, "Do not pursue them, for al-Sughd is the garden of the Commander of the Faithful, and you have already defeated them. Do you want to annihilate them? O army of Iraq, you have fought against the caliphs several times, but did they destroy you?"

The Muslims advanced until they reached a gorge that stood between them and the meadow.[549] 'Abd al-Raḥmān b. Ṣubḥ declared, "Let no man who is clad in armor nor any foot soldier cross over this gorge; everyone else may cross over." They crossed over. But the Turks saw them and prepared an ambush. The Muslim cavalry appeared before them, and the two armies engaged in battle. The Turks retreated, and the Muslims pursued them until they passed by the ambuscade, where they were attacked (by the Turks) and put to flight, retreating all the way back to the gorge. 'Abd al-Raḥmān b. Ṣubḥ said to them, "Try to defeat them without crossing over, for if you do cross over, they will destroy you." They held off the Turks, who eventually withdrew without being [1429] pursued by the Muslims.

Some authorities say: Shu'bah b. Zuhayr and his forces were killed on that very day. Other authorities say: The Turks withdrew from them on that day, accompanied by a detachment of the Soghdian army, having been defeated. The next day, a Muslim vanguard—the members of the vanguard at that time were from the Banū Tamīm—went out and were surprised by the Turks, who attacked them from behind a thicket. Shu'bah b. Zuhayr, who was in command of the cavalry of the Banū Tamīm, fought against them but was slain when they drove him off his mount. One of the Arab soldiers was slain and his slave girl was brought out carrying some henna. She exclaimed, "How long shall I prepare henna such as this for you when you are dyed with blood?" She spoke for a long time, bringing the inhabitants of the military camp to tears. Approximately fifty soldiers were slain, and the members of the vanguard were put to flight.

When the cry for help reached the troops, 'Abd al-Raḥmān b. al-Muhallab al-'Adawī said, "I was the first one to reach them after we received the news. I was riding a swift horse and, behold, there

---

549. Apparently, a meadow in al-Sughd.

was ʿAbdallāh b. Zuhayr[550] next to a tree. There were so many arrows in his body that he looked like a porcupine. He had been slain."

Al-Khalīl b. Aws al-ʿAbshamī, a young man from the Banū Ẓālim, mounted his horse and cried out, "O Banū Tamīm, I am al-Khalīl. Follow me." A detachment of soldiers joined al-Khalīl, who attacked the enemy with them. They held off the enemy, keeping them far away[551] from the soldiers until the military commander arrived with reinforcements and the enemy was put to flight. Al-Khalīl became the leader of the Banū Tamīm cavalry on that day, a position he held until Naṣr b. Sayyār was appointed governor (of Khurāsān),[552] at which point al-Khalīl's brother, al-Ḥakam b. Aws, became the leader of the Banū Tamīm.

[1430]   According to ʿAlī b. Muḥammad—his shaykhs: Sawrah b. al-Ḥurr said to Ḥayyān, "Leave, O Ḥayyān." He exclaimed, "Shall I abandon God's martyrs and depart?" He said, "O you Nabataean." He said, "May God cause you to become a Nabataean."[553] He said: Ḥayyān al-Nabaṭī's nom de guerre was Abū al-Hayyāj.[554] About him the poet recited:

Verily, Abū al-Hayyāj is generous
    in assistance. The wind makes a sound in his garments.

Our source continued: Saʿīd crossed over the river twice but did not pass beyond Samarqand. On the first occasion, after establishing his camp across from the enemy, he was advised by Ḥayyān, the client of Maṣqalah b. Hubayrah al-Shaybānī, "O commander, attack the Soghdian army." But he replied, "No, these lands belong to the Commander of the Faithful." Later, however, he inquired about some smoke rising into the sky and was told, "The Soghdians have renounced Islam, and some of the Turks are with them." Only then did Saʿīd initiate a skirmish, whereupon the Soghdians were put to flight with the Muslims close on their heels. But Saʿīd's herald called out, "Do not pursue them, for al-Sughd is the garden of the Commander of the Faithful, and you

---

550. ʿAbdallāh b. Zuhayr b. Salīm al-Azdī.

551. Text: *wa-warraʿūhu;* read *wa-wazaʿūhum,* following the Cairo ed.

552. See text below, II/1659ff., sub anno 120.

553. Text: *anbaṭa-llāhu wajhaka.* This was considered an insult. See note 471, above.

554. Abū al-Hayyāj literally means "Father of fury."

have already put them to flight. Do you want to annihilate them?
O army of Iraq, you fought against the Commander of the Faithful
several times; but he forgave you and did not seek to destroy you,
and he withdrew."

The next year, Sa'īd sent some men from the Banū Tamīm on a
mission to Waraghsar.[555] They said, "Would that we might encounter the enemy so that we could attack them." But whenever
a raiding party sent by Sa'īd scored a victory, acquiring booty and
taking prisoners, he would send back the captives' women and
children and punish the raiding party. Al-Hajarī, who was a poet,
recited:

You advanced toward the enemy by night playing with a   [1431]
     concubine,
   with your penis drawn and your sword sheathed.
And you are for your enemies a very courteous wife.[556]
   Against us you are like a sharp sword.
How excellent were the Soghdians when they assembled!
   And how strange your wavering stratagem!

Sawrah b. al-Ḥurr, who had protected Ḥayyān al-Nabaṭī despite
the fact that the latter had insulted him by saying, "May God
cause you to become a Nabataean!," said to Sa'īd, "That slave is
the person most hostile to the Arabs and to the provincial governors. He ruined Khurāsān for Qutaybah b. Muslim and he will fall
upon you, ruining Khurāsān for you. Then he will fortify himself
inside one of those strongholds." Sa'īd replied, "O Sawrah, don't
mention this to anyone." Several days later, Sa'īd asked for sour
milk to be brought to his chamber. Some gold that he had ordered
previously was ground into powder and put in Ḥayyān's cup.
Ḥayyān drank the sour milk that had been laced with gold
powder. Sa'īd and his soldiers then mounted their horses and rode
four *farsakh*s (24 km.) to Bārkath,[557] pretending that they were
pursuing an enemy. Then they returned. Ḥayyān lived for four
days after drinking the milk and died on the fourth day.

---

555. Literally, "the head of the dam"; one of the twelve districts of Samarqand.
See Yāqūt, *Mu'jam*, V, 372; Barthold, *Turkestan*, 83, 92.

556. Text: '*irsu khafiyyatin*, "a hidden wife." This should be amended to read
'*irsun ḥafiyyatun*. I owe this point to Professor Abbas.

557. The chief town in Buzmājan, which was one of the districts of Samarqand,
on the main road to the Syr Darya. See Yāqūt, *Mu'jam*, I, 320; Barthold, *Turkestan*,
94; Le Strange, *Lands*, 466.

Saʿīd placed heavy burdens on the soldiers, who considered him to be weak. There was a man from the Banū Asad by the name of Ismāʿīl who was devoted to Marwān b. Muḥammad.[558] Someone mentioned Ismāʿīl's devotion to Marwān, in the presence of Khudhaynah, causing Saʿīd to exclaim, "Who is this bastard?" In response, Ismāʿīl satirized him, saying:

Khudhaynah alleges that I am a bastard,
   but Khudhaynah has the mirror and the comb.
(Incense) burners and kohl containers have been laid out,
   and musical instruments. On her cheek are spots.
Is this better, or a full coat of mail composed of double rings,
   and a sharp sword fashioned to cut,
In the possession of a trustworthy, powerful male,
   not nourished by effeminacy and effeminate
   embellishments?[559]
Are you angry because your mother's son spent the night
   with them and because your father has no reputation?
Verily, I saw their arrows covered
   with fitting feathers, while your arrows are featherless.[560]
And I saw them reclining on their cushions
   at the assembly place, while you were roaming astray in
   the desert.[561]

In this year, Maslamah b. ʿAbd al-Malik departed for Syria after having been relieved of his duties in Iraq and Khurāsān.[562]

The Dismissal of Maslamah from Iraq and Khurāsān

According to ʿAlī b. Muḥammad, Maslamah was dismissed because, after being put in charge of the provinces of Iraq and

---

558. Marwān b. Muḥammad b. Marwān al-Jaʿdī was an Umayyad general and later Caliph. See *EI*, s.v. Marwān II b. Muḥammad.

559. Text: *wa-l-laqṭu*, "and the (base) status of being a foundling." This should be amended to read *wa-l-luʿṭu*. A *luʿṭah* is a black or yellow line that a woman draws on her cheek. I owe this point to Professor Abbas.

560. Text: *innī raʾaytu nibālahum kusiyat rīsha-l-luʾām wa-nablukum murṭ*. That is to say, their men were positioned in the right places, while yours were not. See Lane, *Lexicon*, pt. 3, p. 1200; *Wörterbuch*, s.v., *luʾām*.

561. Text: *wa-antum khilṭu*, "while you were half-breeds." This should be amended to read *wa-antum ḥulṭu*. I owe this point to Professor Abbas.

562. See Ibn Khayyāṭ, *Taʾrīkh*, I, 335; Dīnawarī, *Akhbār*, 337; Yaʿqūbī, *Taʾrīkh*, III, 55; Azdī, *Taʾrīkh*, 16; *FHA*, 75.

Khurāsān, he did not send the surplus tribute (to Damascus).[563]
Yazīd b. ʿĀtikah[564] wanted to dismiss him, but was ashamed to
do so. He wrote to him, saying, "Appoint a deputy governor and   [1433]
come here."

It is reported that Maslamah consulted with ʿAbd al-ʿAzīz b.
Ḥātim b. al-Nuʿmān regarding his departure to visit Ibn ʿĀtikah.
ʿAbd al-ʿAzīz said to him, "Are you going because you long for
him? Why are you so emotional when you have recently been
with him?" Maslamah said, "I must go." ʿAbd al-ʿAzīz said, "In
that case, no sooner will you leave this province than you will
meet the new governor." Then Maslamah departed. At Dūrayn[565]
he was met by ʿUmar b. Hubayrah, who was traveling with five
post-horses. Ibn Hubayrah came in to greet him, and Maslamah
asked, "Where are you going, Ibn Hubayrah?" He replied, "The
Commander of the Faithful sent me to collect the wealth of the
Muhallabids." When he left, Maslamah sent for ʿAbd al-ʿAzīz,
who came to him. Maslamah said, "Behold, Ibn Hubayrah met us,
as you know." ʿAbd al-ʿAzīz said, "I told you so." He said, "But
Yazīd sent him merely for the purpose of collecting the wealth of
the Muhallabids." He said, "(Do you believe that) Ibn Hubayrah
has been dismissed from al-Jazīrah and sent to collect the wealth
of the Muhallabids? The latter is more astonishing than the former!"[566] Shortly thereafter Maslamah learned that Ibn Hubayrah
had dismissed the governors he had appointed and treated them
roughly. Al-Farazdaq recited:

The horses carried Maslamah away, bidding farewell.[567]
     So graze, Fazārah,[568] (but) may the grazing not fatten you!
Ibn Bishr was dismissed, and Ibn ʿAmr before him,
     and the governor of Herat expects a similar fate.
I know that if the Fazārah are invested with authority,

---

563. Text: *lam yarfaʿ min al-kharāj shayʾan*. See *FHA*, 75, where the text is *lam
yursil ilā Yazīd shayʾan*, "He did not send anything to Yazīd."
564. That is, his brother, the Caliph, Yazīd b. ʿAbd al-Malik. See note 153,
above.
565. There is no entry for Durayn in Yāqūt's geographical dictionary. Dūr and
Dūrān were common place names in Iraq.
566. ʿAbd al-ʿAzīz means that Maslamah's naiveté with regard to the real purpose of Ibn Hubayrah's mission is more astonishing than his naiveté with regard
to his recall by the Caliph.
567. Text: *muwaddaʿan*; read *muwaddiʿan*, following the Cairo ed.
568. ʿUmar b. Hubayrah was from the tribe of Fazārah.

the Ashjaʿ will soon covet the emirate.
What is their situation vis-à-vis your Lord's creatures? The
    likes of them
    do covet something similar to what the Fazārah
    attained.[569]

[1434]   "Ibn Bishr" refers to ʿAbd al-Malik b. Bishr b. Marwān; "Ibn ʿAmr" refers to Muḥammad Dhū al-Shāmah b. ʿAmr b. al-Walīd; and "the governor of Herat" refers to Saʿīd Khudhaynah b. ʿAbd al-ʿAzīz, who served as governor of Khurāsān on behalf of Maslamah.

In this year, ʿUmar b. Hubayrah attacked the Byzantines in Armenia, putting them to flight and capturing large numbers of prisoners. According to some sources, he took seven hundred prisoners.

It is reported that in this year, Maysarah sent his messengers from Iraq to Khurāsān, where the (ʿAbbāsid) propaganda began to circulate.[570] A man from the Banū Tamīm by the name of ʿAmr b. Baḥīr b. Warqāʾ al-Saʿdī came to Saʿīd Khudhaynah and said, "There are people here who are saying ugly things." Saʿīd sent for them, and when they were brought to him, he asked, "Who are you?" They replied, "We are merchants." He asked, "What is the meaning of the things that are being said about you?" They replied, "We don't know." He asked, "Have you come to disseminate propaganda?" They replied, "We are too busy with our personal affairs and with our business to be able to do that." He asked, "Who knows these people?" Some soldiers from the army of Khurāsān, the majority of whom were from the tribes of Rabīʿah and Yaman, came and said, "We know them and will assume responsibility for them should they do anything that you find displeasing." Then he released them.[571]

[1435]   In this year, that is, the year 102/720–21, Yazīd b. Abī Muslim was slain in Ifrīqiyah,[572] where he had been serving as governor.[573]

---

569. See *Dīwān al-Farazdaq*, I, 408.
570. See text above, II/1358, sub anno 100, note 310.
571. Many of the clients who served as leaders of the ʿAbbāsid propaganda movement posed as members of the merchant and artisan class in order to provide camouflage for their clandestine activities. See Dīnawarī, *Akhbār*, 335; Sharon, *Black Banners*, 144.
572. The eastern part of the Maghrib. See *EI*², s.v. Ifrīkiya.
573. See Ibn Khayyāṭ, *Taʾrīkh*, I, 333; Yaʿqūbī, *Taʾrīkh*, III, 56–57.

The Slaying of Yazīd b. Abī Muslim

It is reported that the circumstances of Yazīd's death were as follows: He had determined to apply to (the inhabitants of Ifrīqiyah) the policy that al-Ḥajjāj b. Yūsuf had applied to those Muslims living in the garrison towns who were originally protected peoples (ahl al-dhimmah) from the rural districts; although they converted to Islam in Iraq, al-Ḥajjāj sent them back to their villages and lands, where they were made to pay the poll tax,[574] just as they had been prior to their conversion. When Yazīd determined to carry out such a policy, they plotted against him, reportedly resolving to murder him. They slew him and appointed as their leader the person who had served as their governor prior to Yazīd b. Abī Muslim, that is, Muḥammad b. Yazīd, a client of the Helpers, who was a soldier in Yazīd b. Abī Muslim's army. They wrote to Yazīd b. ʿAbd al-Malik as follows: "We have not renounced our allegiance to you. However, Yazīd b. Abī Muslim imposed on us things that were displeasing to God and to the Muslims, so we slew him and reappointed your governor." Yazīd b. ʿAbd al-Malik wrote back to them, saying, "Indeed, I was not pleased with the policies of Yazīd b. Abī Muslim and I hereby confirm Muḥammad b. Yazīd as governor of Ifrīqiyah."[575]

In this year, ʿUmar b. Hubayrah b. Muʿayyah b. Sukayn b. Khudhayj b. Mālik b. Saʿd b. ʿAdī b. Fazārah was appointed governor of Iraq and Khurāsān. [1436]

In this year, the pilgrimage was led by ʿAbd al-Raḥmān b. al-Ḍaḥḥāk, as reported by Abū Maʿshar and al-Wāqidī.

ʿAbd al-Raḥmān b. al-Ḍaḥḥāk was governor of Medina; ʿAbd al-ʿAzīz b. ʿAbdallāh b. Khālid b. Asīd was governor of Mecca; Muḥammad b. ʿAmr Dhū al-Shāmah was governor of al-Kūfah; al-Qāsim b. ʿAbd al-Raḥmān b. ʿAbdallāh b. Masʿūd was in charge of the judiciary in al-Kūfah; ʿAbd al-Malik b. Bishr b. Marwān was governor of al-Baṣrah; Saʿīd Khudhaynah was governor of Khurāsān; and Usāmah b. Zayd was governor of Egypt.

---

574. Literally, "The jizyah was sealed on their necks."
575. But see Yaʿqūbī, Taʾrīkh, III, 57, where it is reported that Yazīd appointed Bishr b. Ṣafwān al-Kalbī as the new governor.

The
Events of the Year

103
(JULY 1, 721—JUNE 20, 722)

The Dismissal of Saʿīd Khudhaynah as Governor of Khurāsān

Among the events of this year was ʿUmar b. Hubayrah's dismissal of Saʿīd Khudhaynah as governor of Khurāsān.[576] The circumstances of his dismissal, as reported by ʿAlī b. Muḥammad on the authority of his shaykhs, were as follows: Al-Mujashshir b. Muzāhim al-Sulamī and ʿAbdallāh b. ʿUmayr al-Laythī approached ʿUmar b. Hubayrah and complained to him about Saʿīd. As a result, ʿUmar dismissed Saʿīd and appointed as governor of Khurāsān Saʿīd b. ʿAmr b. al-Aswad b. Mālik b. Kaʿb b. Waqdān b. al-Ḥarīsh b. Kaʿb b. Rabīʿah b. ʿĀmir b. Ṣaʿṣaʿah. Khudhaynah, at the time, was on a military expedition near the Gate of Samarqand. The soldiers learned of his dismissal, and Khudhaynah turned back, leaving a thousand horsemen in Samarqand. Nahār b. Tawsiʿah recited:

[1437]   Who will inform the youths of my tribe
       that the arrows are completely covered with feathers?[577]

---

576. See Balādhurī, *Futūḥ* (Cairo), III, 525; Ibn Kathīr, *Bidāyah*, IX, 223.
577. Text: *rīshat kulla raysh.* See note 560, above.

And that God replaced one Saʿīd
with another—not the effeminate one from the Quraysh?

Our source continued: Saʿīd al-Ḥarashī did not interfere with
any of Khudhaynah's governors. When the man who read out his
document of appointment made a grammatical mistake, Saʿīd exclaimed, "Be quiet. Whatever you people heard is the responsibility of the scribe, and the governor (that is, ʿUmar b. Hubayrah) is
free from any guilt." In connection with this statement, the poet
recited the following verse in which he attributed weakness to al-
Ḥarashī:

We were given one Saʿīd for another—
bad fortune and the ordained fate.

Al-Ṭabarī reported: In this year, al-ʿAbbās b. al-Walīd attacked
the Byzantines and conquered a city known as Raslah.[578]
In this year, the Turks invaded Alān.[579]
In this year, Mecca was added to the jurisdiction of ʿAbd al-
Raḥmān b. al-Ḍaḥḥāk al-Fihrī and combined with his jurisdiction
over Medina.
In this year, ʿAbd al-Wāḥid b. ʿAbdallāh al-Naḍrī was appointed
governor of al-Ṭāʾif, and ʿAbd al-ʿAzīz b. ʿAbdallāh b. Khālid b.
Asīd was dismissed from Mecca.
In this year, ʿAbd al-Raḥmān b. al-Ḍaḥḥāk was ordered to effect
a reconciliation between Abū Bakr b. Muḥammad b. ʿAmr b.
Ḥazm and ʿUthmān b. Ḥayyān al-Murrī. The relations between
ʿAbd al-Raḥmān and the other two men in previous years has
already been mentioned.[580]
In this year, the pilgrimage was led by ʿAbd al-Raḥmān b. al-
Ḍaḥḥāk b. Qays al-Fihrī—as reported by Abū Maʿshar and al-
Wāqidī.
In this year, ʿAbd al-Raḥmān b. al-Ḍaḥḥāk was governor of Mec-
ca and Medina on behalf of Yazīd b. ʿĀtikah; ʿAbd al-Wāḥid b.
ʿAbdallāh al-Naḍrī was governor of al-Ṭāʾif; ʿUmar b. Hubayrah
was governor of Iraq and Khurāsān; Saʿīd b. ʿAmr al-Ḥarashī was

[1438]

---

578. Raslah may be the Byzantine city of Larissa. See Cheira, *Arabes et Byzantines*, 222, n. 1, and the sources cited there. Azdī, *Taʾrīkh*, 17, gives the name of
the city as Awāsā.
579. A region in the northern Caucasus near Bāb al-Abwāb inhabited by the
Alans, an Iranian people. See *EI²*, s.v. Alān; Yāqūt, *Muʿjam*, V, 8.
580. See text above, II/1281–82, sub anno 96; and II/1372–75, sub anno 101.

governor of Khurāsān on behalf of ʿUmar b. Hubayrah; al-Qāsim b. ʿAbd al-Raḥmān b. ʿAbdallāh b. Masʿūd was in charge of the judiciary in al-Kūfah; and ʿAbd al-Malik b. Yaʿlā was in charge of the judiciary in al-Baṣrah.

In this year, ʿUmar b. Hubayrah appointed Saʿīd b. ʿAmr al-Ḥarashī as governor of Khurāsān.[581]

ʿUmar b. Hubayrah's Appointment of Saʿīd al-Ḥarashī as Governor of Khurāsān

According to ʿAlī b. Muḥammad—his authorities: When Ibn Hubayrah was appointed governor of Iraq, he sent Yazīd b. ʿAbd al-Malik the names of those men who had demonstrated their bravery at the battle of al-ʿAqr.[582] Al-Ḥarashī's name did not appear on the list, causing Yazīd b. ʿAbd al-Malik to exclaim, "Why didn't he mention al-Ḥarashī?" Yazīd then wrote to Ibn Hubayrah, ordering him to appoint al-Ḥarashī as governor of Khurāsān, which he did. Al-Ḥarashī dispatched al-Mujashshir b. Muzāḥim al-Sulamī to take command of his vanguard in the year 103/721–22. Then al-Ḥarashī traveled to Khurāsān, where he found the army face to face with the enemy, having already suffered a disastrous defeat. In a speech to the soldiers, he urged them to engage in holy war, saying, "The struggle against the enemy of Islam is not undertaken on the basis of numbers, but on the basis of the support of God and the might of Islam. Say, 'There is no power and no strength except in God.'" Then he recited the following lines:

I don't belong to the ʿĀmir if you do not see me
    in front of the horsemen stabbing with the spearheads.
[1439] For I will strike the head of their greatest warrior
    with the edge of a well-polished, sharp sword.
I am not one who submits in battles,
    nor do I fear the combat of the soldiers.
My father protected me from every censure,

---

581. See Balādhurī, *Futūḥ* (Cairo), III, 525; Kūfī, *Futūḥ*, VIII, 26; Ibn Kathīr, *Bidāyah*, IX, 223; Wellhausen, *Arab Kingdom*, 452.
582. See text above, II/1395ff., sub anno 102.

and my maternal uncle is the best maternal uncle during
    times of misfortune.
When the tribe of Ka'b paraded haughtily before me,
    and the Banū Hilāl strutted like mountains.

In this year, at the time of Sa'īd b. 'Amr al-Ḥarashī's arrival, the
Soghdian army left their lands and traveled to Farghānah, where
they asked the king for assistance against the Muslims.[583]

The Soghdians Leave Their Country for Farghānah

According to 'Alī b. Muḥammad—his authorities: The Soghdians
had aided the Turks during the administration of Khudhaynah.
Therefore, when al-Ḥarashī was appointed as their governor, they
feared for their lives, and their leaders resolved to leave their
lands. Their king, however, advised them as follows: "Don't do
this. Stay where you are; pay him whatever tribute you owe and
guarantee him all future tribute; promise him that you will maintain your lands in a good state of cultivation and that you will
accompany him on raids should he desire that; apologize for your
past behavior, and give him hostages to hold." They said, "We
fear that he will not be satisfied and that he will not accept these
terms from us. Therefore, we are going to Khujandah,[584] where
we will ask the king for protection. Then we will send a message
to the governor (that is, al-Ḥarashī), asking him to forgive us for
our past behavior and assuring him that henceforth we will not
commit any repugnant acts." Their king said, "I am one of you,
and my advice to you is in your best interests." But they rejected   [1440]
his advice and set out for Khujandah.

Kārzanj, Kishshīn, Bayārkath, and Thābit took the army of
Ishtīkhan,[585] and they sent a message to al-Ṭār, the King of Farghānah, asking him to protect them and to allow them to settle in

---

583. See Ibn Khayyāṭ, Ta'rīkh, I, 335–36; Balādhurī, Futūḥ (Cairo), III, 525;
Wellhausen, Arab Kingdom, 452–54.
    584. A town and district in Transoxiana; the town was strung out along the left
bank of the middle Sir Darya at the entrance to the Farghānah valley. See EI², s.v.
Khudjand(a); Yāqūt, Mu'jam, II, 347–48.
    585. A city five farsakhs (30 km.) from Samarqand that was administered inde-
pendently of the latter. See Yāqūt, Mu'jam, I, 196.

his city. He was on the verge of agreeing when his mother said to him, "Don't let those satans enter your city. Rather, clear out some rural district for them to reside in." He sent to them, saying, "Name a rural district so that I might clear it out for you. Give me a delay of forty days"—according to some sources—twenty days. "If you wish, I will clear out for you the pass occupied by ʿIṣām b. ʿAbdallāh al-Bāhilī, who had been left behind by Qutaybah to serve as their governor. They agreed to accept ʿIṣām's Pass and sent to al-Ṭār, saying, "Clear it out for us." He said, "I will, but you have no agreement and no covenant of protection with me until you enter it. If the Arabs should overtake you before you enter it, I will not protect you." They accepted his terms, and he cleared out the pass for them.

Some authorities say: Ibn Hubayrah appealed to them before they left their lands, asking them to remain and offering to appoint a governor of their choice. But they rejected his offer and set out for Khujandah.

ʿIṣām's Pass is in the rural district controlled by Asfarah, who at that time was the heir apparent to the King of Farghānah, Bilā-dhā.[586] Bilādhā,[587] Abū Anūjūr, was the King.

It is said that Kārzanj said to them, "I will give you three options from which to choose. Failure to choose at least one will result in your destruction. Saʿīd, who is known as "the horseman of the Arabs," has sent ʿAbd al-Raḥmān b. ʿAbdallāh al-Qushayrī with his vanguard, leading a detachment of his men. Carry out a surprise attack against him at night and kill him. Thus, when al-Ḥarashī learns of this, he will not attack you." But they rejected this suggestion. He said, "Cross over the Shāsh River[588] and ask them, 'What do you want from us?' If they respond then you are saved; if not, then go to Sūyāb."[589] This, too, they rejected. He said, "Then pay them (the tribute)."

[1441]

---

586. But see text above, II/1440, where the King of Farghānah is identified as al-Ṭār.

587. The discrepancy in the spelling of the King's name is in the text. De Goeje suggests that Bilādhā and Bīlādhā should both be read Naylān as at text below, II/1442 sub anno 104 and II/1554, sub anno 112.

588. The Shāsh River is in Transoxiana. See *EI*, s.v. Tashkent; Yāqūt, *Muʿjam*, III, 308–09.

589. The Turgesh capital, destroyed by the Chinese in A.D. 748. See Barthold, *Turkestan*, 195, 201.

Our source continued: Kārzanj and Jalnaj set out with the army of Qiyy, while Abār b. Mākhnūn and Thābit set out with the army of Ishtīkhan. The army of Bayārkath[590] and the army of Sabaskath[591] set out with a thousand men wearing gold belts, accompanied by the *dihqān*s of Buzmājan.[592] Al-Dīwāshinī set out with the army of Bunjīkath[593] for the fortress of Abghar. Kārzanj and the Soghdian army reached Khujandah.

---

590. There is no entry for Bayārkath in Yāqūt's geographical dictionary. Bayār-kath may be identical with the place name Bārkath mentioned at text above, II/1431, sub anno 102, or with the personal name mentioned at text above, II/1440. *Kath* is the usual ending of town names.

591. Yāqūt mentions a town by the name of Isbaskath, two *farsakh*s (12 km.) from Samarqand. See *Muʿjam*, I, 172.

592. One of the twelve districts of Samarqand; its chief town was Bārkath. See Barthold, *Turkestan*, 92, 94; Le Strange, *Lands*, 466.

593. A town near Samarqand; it is not to be confused with the town of the same name in Ushrūsanah (see n. 598, below). See Wellhausen, *Arab Kingdom*, 452, n. 2; Yāqūt, *Muʿjam*, I, 499.

The
Events of the Year

104
(JUNE 21, 722—JUNE 9, 723)

In this year, the battle took place between al-Ḥarashī and the Soghdian army in which he slew many *dihqāns*.[594]

The Battle between al-Ḥarashī and the Soghdian Army

According to ʿAlī—his authorities: Al-Ḥarashī undertook a military expedition in the year 104/722–23. He crossed over the river and reviewed the soldiers. Then he traveled to Qaṣr al-Rīḥ ("The Castle of the Winds"),[595] two *farsakhs* (12 km.) from al-Dabū-siyah,[596] where he set up camp. But his army did not join him. Therefore, al-Ḥarashī ordered the soldiers to pack up and leave. But Hilāl b. ʿUlaym al-Ḥanẓalī rebuked him, saying, "I say! You

[1442]

---

594. See Balādhurī, *Futūḥ* (Cairo), III, 525; Kūfī, *Futūḥ*, VIII, 26–27.
595. A village in the area of Nīshāpūr. See Yāqūt, *Muʿjam*, IV, 357; Le Strange, *Lands*, 388, 430.
596. A town in Transoxiana located in the administrative district of al-Sughd. See Yāqūt, *Muʿjam*, II, 437–38; Le Strange, *Lands*, 468, 471.

are a better political leader than you are a military commander.
The land has no one to defend it. Yet, when your army failed to
join you, you gave the order to pack up and leave." Al-Ḥarashī
asked, "What should I do?" Hilāl replied, "Order them to establish camp." Al-Ḥarashī accepted his advice.

Al-Naylān, the paternal cousin of the King of Farghānah, came
to al-Ḥarashī, who had set up camp near Mughūn,[597] and said,
"The Soghdian army is in Khujandah." Al-Naylān apprised al-
Ḥarashī of their actions and said, "Try to overtake them before
they reach ʿIṣām's Pass, for their protection agreement with us
does not take effect until the expiration of the (forty day) time
period." Al-Ḥarashī put ʿAbd al-Raḥmān al-Qushayrī and Ziyād b.
ʿAbd al-Raḥmān al-Qushayrī in command of a division of soldiers
and sent them off, accompanied by al-Naylān. Subsequently,
however, he regretted what he had done, saying, "I have endangered the lives of a division of Muslims on the strength of
what I was told by an infidel. But I don't know if he was telling
the truth or lying." Al-Ḥarashī set off in pursuit of them, reaching
Ushrūsanah,[598] where he made peace with (the inhabitants of
that district) in return for a trifling sum. Then, while he was
eating his dinner, one of his men interrupted him, saying, "ʿAṭā'
al-Dabūsī is here." He was one of the men whom al-Ḥarashī had
sent with al-Qushayrī. Startled, al-Ḥarashī dropped the morsel of
food that was in his hand and summoned ʿAṭā'. When he entered,
al-Ḥarashī asked, "Woe is you! Have you engaged anyone in battle?" He replied, "No." He said, "Praise be to God." Al-Ḥarashī
resumed his meal and informed ʿAṭā' of his regrets regarding the
mission.[599]

Al-Ḥarashī set out at an extremely quick pace and managed to
catch up with al-Qushayrī after three days. He advanced and,   [1443]
upon reaching Khujandah, he asked al-Faḍl b. Bassām, "What do
you think we should do?" He replied, "I think we should attack

---

597. One of the villages of Busht, in the administrative district of Nīshāpūr. See
Yāqūt, *Muʿjam*, V, 162.

598. The mountainous district between Samarqand and Khujandah, including
the upper course of the Zarafshan River. See Yāqūt, *Muʿjam*, I, 197; *EI²*, s.v.
Afshīn; Le Strange, *Lands*, 474–76.

599. Text: *mā qadama lahu ʿalayhi*. The translation is conjectural.

them immediately." He said, "I disagree. Where can a soldier go if he is wounded, and where can we take the body of someone who is slain? I think that we should establish camp here, proceed deliberately, and make preparations for battle." He established camp, erecting some buildings and busying himself with preparations. But when the enemy did not come forward, the soldiers accused al-Ḥarashī of cowardice, saying, "That one is renowned for his valor and good judgment in Iraq, but when he comes to Khurāsān, he acts like a fool."

One of the Arab soldiers attacked, striking the Khujandah gate with a pole, whereupon the gate was opened. Earlier, the Soghdians had dug a defensive trench on the outskirts of the city, beyond the outer gate. They covered the trench with reeds and placed dirt on top of it, as a trick. They reasoned that if they were forced to retreat after the two armies met in battle, they would know the way, while the Muslims, who would not, would fall into the trench. When the Soghdians emerged, they fought the Muslims and were put to flight, but they took the wrong path and fell into the trench. The Muslims removed forty soldiers from the trench, each one wearing a double coat of mail. Al-Ḥarashī surrounded the city, setting up mangonels. The Soghdians sent a message to the King of Farghānah, claiming that he had deceived them and asking for assistance. In his reply, he said to them, "I did not deceive you, nor will I help you. Take care of yourselves, for the Arabs reached you before the deadline expired. Thus, you are not under my protection." When the Soghdians had despaired of receiving his assistance, they sued for peace and asked for safe-conduct so that they might return to al-Sughd. Al-Ḥarashī im-

[1444]   posed the following stipulations on them: they were to return the Arab women and children who were in their possession, pay all arrears in tribute, not murder anyone, and not leave anyone behind in Khujandah. Furthermore, if they caused any mischief, their blood would become lawful.

The man who negotiated the agreement between the two sides was Mūsā b. Mishkān, a client of the Bassām family. Kārzanj approached al-Ḥarashī and said, "I have a favor to ask of you." He asked, "What is it?" He said, "If one of my men commits a crime after the peace treaty has taken effect, I want you to absolve me of responsibility for his action." Al-Ḥarashī said, "I have a favor to

ask of you." He asked, "What is it?" He said, "Don't attach anything repugnant to my stipulations!"

He removed the nobles[600] and merchants from the eastern side
of the town, but left the people of Khujandah, who were the
inhabitants of the town, as they were. Kārzanj asked al-Ḥarashī,
"What are you doing?" He replied, "I fear that the army will
attack you without permission."[601]

The Soghdian leaders who were with al-Ḥarashī in the military
camp stayed as guests with the soldiers who were known to
them. Kārzanj stayed with Ayyūb b. Abī Ḥassān. When al-Ḥarashī
was told that the Soghdians had slain one of the women who had
been in their possession, he said to them, "I have learned that
Thābit al-Ishtīkhanī slew a woman and buried her under a walled
garden." But they denied the allegation. Al-Ḥarashī sent for the
judge of Khujandah and upon investigation it was determined
that the woman had, indeed, been slain.

Our source continued: Al-Ḥarashī summoned Thābit. Meanwhile, Kārzanj sent his servant to the Surādiq Gate to gather
information. Al-Ḥarashī asked Thābit and others about the woman, but Thābit denied the charge. Convinced that Thābit had slain
her, al-Ḥarashī put him to death. The servant then returned to
Kārzanj and informed him that Thābit had been slain, whereupon
Kārzanj grabbed his beard and began to bite it off with his teeth.
Fearing that al-Ḥarashī would slay the Soghdians indiscrimi-
nately, Kārzanj said to Ayyūb b. Abī Ḥassān, "I am your guest and   [1445]
your friend. How will it look if your friend is slain wearing old,
worn-out trousers?" Ayyūb said, "Take my trousers." Kārzanj
replied, "How will it look if I am slain wearing your trousers?
Send one of your servants to my nephew, Jalnaj, so that he might
bring me new trousers." Earlier, Kārzanj had explained to his
nephew, "If I send to you asking for trousers, you will know that
they intend to slay me." When his nephew received the request
for trousers, he took out some green cloth, cut it into strips, and
tied the strips around the heads of his armed retinue. Then he
went out, accompanied by his armed retinue, and advanced

---

600. Text: *al-mulūk*, literally "kings."
601. Text: *akhāfu ʿalaykum maʿarrata-l-jund.* This may also mean, "I want to
spare you the disgrace that may be brought upon you by the soldiers."

against the soldiers, killing many men. He passed by Yaḥyā b. Ḥuḍayn and wounded him slightly on his leg, leaving him with a permanent limp. The inhabitants of the military camp submitted, and the soldiers suffered greatly from Jalnaj, until he encountered Thābit b. ʿUthmān b. Masʿūd on a narrow road. Thābit slew him using ʿUthmān b. Masʿūd's sword.

The Soghdians slew one hundred and fifty Muslim prisoners who were in their possession. Some say: they slew forty of them. A young boy escaped and informed al-Ḥarashī of the slaughter. Some say: A man came to him and reported what was happening. He asked the Soghdians about the Muslim prisoners but, when they denied the allegation, he sent someone to them in order to determine what was happening. Upon discovering that the report was true, al-Ḥarashī ordered that the Soghdians be put to death. First, however, he separated the merchants from the rest of them—there were four hundred merchants who possessed large quantities of merchandise; they had brought the wares from China.

Our source continued: Although they did not have any weapons the Soghdian soldiers tried to defend themselves. They fought with wooden clubs and were slain to the last man. The next day, al-Ḥarashī summoned the farmers, who were unaware of what their comrades had done. He put a seal on every man's neck and sent him from one field to the next, whereupon the man would be slain. There were three thousand of them. Some say: There were seven thousand. Al-Ḥarashī sent Jarīr b. Himyān, al-Ḥasan b. Abī al-ʿAmarraṭah, and Yazīd b. Abī Zaynab to assess the value of the property belonging to the merchants who had been separated from the others. The merchants said, "We shall not participate in the fighting." He made a selection from the property of the Soghdians and from their women and children, taking whatever he wanted. Then he summoned Muslim b. Budayl al-ʿAdawī, from the tribe of ʿAdī of al-Ribāb and said, "I am putting you in charge of dividing up the spoils." Muslim said, "After what your agents did during the night, you can give the job to someone else!" Al-Ḥarashī then assigned this task to ʿUbaydallāh b. Zuhayr b. Hay-yān al-ʿAdawī, who put aside the fifth and then divided up the wealth. Al-Ḥarashī wrote a letter to Yazīd b. ʿAbd al-Malik, but he did not write to ʿUmar b. Hubayrah. This is one reason why ʿUmar

[1446]

b. Hubayrah was angry with him. Thābit Quṭnah recited, recalling the leaders that they had slain:

There is consolation in the slaughter of Kārzanj
    and Kishshīn and the fate of Bayār,
And Dīwāshinī, and the fate of Jalnaj,
    in the fortress of Khujandah, when they perished and were
    annihilated.

According to another transmission, the first line cited reads: "There is consolation in the slaughter of Kārzanj and Kishkīsh." It is said that Dīwāshinī was a Samarqandian *dihqān* whose name, Dīwā-shanj, was arabicized as Dīwāshinī.

It is reported that 'Ilbā' b. Aḥmar al-Yashkurī, who was in charge of the spoils in Khujandah, sold a small basket to a man for two dirhams. When the man found gold ingots in the basket, he returned clutching his beard; his eyes bulged out of his head.[602] He returned the basket and took back his two dirhams. They looked for him, but did not find him.

Our source said: Al-Ḥarashī sent Sulaymān b. Abī al-Sarī, a client of the Banū 'Uwāfah, to a fortress that was surrounded by the wādī of al-Sughd[603] on all sides except one. He was accompanied by Shawkar b. Ḥamīk, by the Khwārazm Shāh,[604] and by 'Awram, the ruler of Akhrūn[605] and Shūmān.[606] Sulaymān b. Abī al-Sariyy put al-Mussayab b. Bishr al-Riyāḥī in command of his vanguard and dispatched him. The Soghdians met him one *farsakh* (6 km.) from the fortress in a village known as Kūm,[607] where al-Musayyab defeated them, forcing them back into the fortress. Sulaymān then besieged them. The *dihqān* of the fortress was known as "Dīwāshinī."

Al-Ḥarashī wrote to Sulaymān offering to send reinforcements.

[1447]

---

602. Text: *ka-annahu ramada*. Literally: "as if he were suffering from ophthalmia."

603. Text: *lā yuṭīfu bihā wādī al-sughd*. In the translation, I ignore the negative particle *lā*, following Ibn al-Athīr, *Kāmil*, V, 109.

604. On the use of this title, see *EI²*, s.v. Khʷārazm-Shāhs.

605. A province in Transoxiana west of Shūmān. See Barthold, *Turkestan*, 74, 185.

606. A small, independent principality in Transoxiana bounded by the Zarafshan and Qizil-Ṣu Rivers. See *EI²*, s.v. Ḥiṣār; Le Strange, *Lands*, 440.

607. There is no entry for Kūm in Yāqūt's geographical dictionary.

But the latter wrote back, saying, "The spot where we would rendezvous is very narrow, so march towards Kiss.[608] We are under the protection of God, if God wills." Al-Dīwāshinī asked Sulaymān to place him under the authority of al-Harashī and to send him to the latter, accompanied by al-Musayyab b. Bishr. Sulaymān kept his promise and sent him to Saʿīd al-Harashī, who treated him with kindness and generosity, but only as a ploy. The inhabitants of the fortress sued for peace after al-Dīwāshinī's departure on the condition that Sulaymān agree not to harm one hundred families who were living there. In return, they agreed to deliver the fortress to him. Sulaymān wrote to al-Harashī requesting that he send trustworthy agents to collect the contents of the fortress.

[1448]   Al-Harashī dispatched Muḥammad b. ʿAzīz al-Kindī and ʿIlbāʾ b. Aḥmar al-Yashkurī, who auctioned off the contents of the fortress to the highest bidders. He took the fifth and divided the rest among them. Al-Harashī set out for Kiss, the inhabitants of which sued him for peace, agreeing to pay ten thousand sheep.[609] It was stated that al-Harashī made peace with the *dihqān* of Kiss, whose name is Wayk, in return for six thousand sheep to be delivered in forty days, on the condition that he would not attack him. When he was done in Kiss, al-Harashī set out for Rabinjan,[610] where he slew al-Dīwāshinī, crucifying him on a (Christian) burial place. He imposed upon the people of Rabinjan the obligation to pay one hundred (dīnārs) if the body were removed from its place. He put Naṣr b. Sayyār[611] in charge of collecting the settlement agreed upon in Kiss. Then he dismissed Sawrah b. al-Hurr, replacing him with Naṣr b. Sayyār, and put Sulaymān b. Abī al-Sarī in charge of military and fiscal affairs in Kiss and Nasaf. He sent al-Dīwāshinī's head to Iraq and his left hand to Sulaymān b. Abī al-Sarī in Ṭukhāristān.

---

608. A fortified town on the Kushkah Daryā River, known in Persian as Shahr-i-Sabz ("The Green City"). See Le Strange, *Lands*, 469.

609. Text: *ra's*; literally, "heads."

610. A town between Bukhārā and Samarqand, on the south side of the Sughd River. See Le Strange, *Lands*, 468, 471.

611. Naṣr b. Sayyār al-Laythī, d. 131/748 at the age of 85. See *EI*, s.v. Naṣr b. Saiyār.

Our source continued: When Khuzar[612] proved to be impregnable, al-Mujashshir b. Muzāḥim asked Saʿīd b. ʿAmr al-Ḥarashī, "May I recommend to you someone who will conquer it on your behalf without a fight?" Saʿīd replied, "Of course." Mujashshir said, "Al-Musarbal b. al-Khirrīt b. Rāshid al-Nājī." Al-Ḥarashī sent him to that province. Now, al-Musarbal was a friend of Subuqrī,[613] the King of Khuzār, whose people held al-Musarbal in high esteem. He frightened the King by telling him what al-Ḥarashī had done to the people of Khujandah, whereupon the king asked him, "What do you think I should do?" He replied, "I think that you should accept his protection." The King replied, "But what shall I do with all of my retainers?" He said, "Include them with you in the protection agreement." He sued them for peace, and they granted protection to him and his lands.   [1449]

Al-Ḥarashī returned to Marw, taking Subuqrī with him. He encamped at Usnān[614] and, after dispatching Muhājir b. Yazīd al-Ḥarashī with an order to deliver Bardhūn b. Kushānīshāh, he slew Subuqrī and crucified him, although he had a guarantee of protection. It is said: That was a *dihqān* from Buzmājan[615] who approached Ibn Hubayrah and received a guarantee of safe-conduct for the Soghdian army. But al-Ḥarashī imprisoned him in the Marw citadel. When al-Ḥarashī reached Marw, he summoned him. Then he slew him, crucifying him in the public square. The poet recited, in the *rajaz* meter:

Behold, Saʿīd marched off with the tribal divisions,
    in dust that takes the breath away.
The bitterest cup turned against the Turks,
    who fled on the backs of their camels.
They turned in flight, with no strings on their bows.

In this year, Yazīd b. ʿAbd al-Malik dismissed ʿAbd al-Raḥmān b. al-Ḍaḥḥāk b. Qays al-Fihrī from Medina and Mecca. This oc-

---

612. A site near Wakhsh, in the district of Balkh, south of Nasaf. See Yāqūt, *Muʿjam*, II, 364. Note: Ibn al-Athīr, *Kāmil*, V, 110, has *khazāʾin*, "treasure houses," instead of Khuzar.
613. Vocalization follows Gibb, *Arab Conquests*, 64.
614. One of the villages of Herat. See Yāqūt *Muʿjam*, I, 189.
615. The text is *dihqān Ibn Mājir*. See Ṭabarī, *Addenda et Emendanda*, DCCII, where the reading *dihqān Buzmājan* is given.

curred in the middle of the month of Rabīʿ I (early September, 704), after he had served as governor of Medina for three years.

In this year, Yazīd b. ʿAbd al-Malik appointed ʿAbd al-Wāhid (b. ʿAbdallāh b. Bishr) al-Naḍrī as governor of Medina.

Yazīd b. ʿAbd al-Malik's Dismissal of ʿAbd al-Raḥmān b. al-Ḍaḥḥāk from Medina

The circumstances of his dismissal,[616] as reported by Muḥammad b. ʿUmar—ʿAbdallāh b. Muḥammad b. Abī Yaḥyā: ʿAbd al-Raḥmān b. al-Ḍaḥḥāk b. Qays al-Fihrī proposed to Fāṭimah bt. al-Ḥusayn,[617] but she replied, "By God, I do not want to marry, for I already have these children to raise." She tried to hold him off without antagonizing him, for she was afraid of him. But he pressed her, saying, "By God, if you don't marry me, I will flog your oldest son"—that is, ʿAbdallāh b. al-Ḥasan—"for drinking wine." Now, at that time, the military register in Medina was headed by Ibn Hurmuz, a soldier in the Syrian army. Yazīd wrote to Ibn Hurmuz, asking him to prepare his reckoning and deliver the register. The latter went to see Fāṭimah bt. al-Ḥusayn in order to say good-bye to her. He asked, "Is there anything I can do for you?" She replied, "Inform the Commander of the Faithful of the manner in which Ibn al-Ḍaḥḥāk is treating me and how he imposes himself on me."

Fāṭimah sent a messenger to Yazīd, carrying a letter in which she informed him of what had transpired; she reminded Yazīd of the blood ties that connected her to him, and mentioned Ibn al-Ḍaḥḥāk's threat and his behavior toward her. Ibn Hurmuz and Fāṭimah's messenger arrived together. Ibn Hurmuz went in to see Yazīd, who inquired about the situation in Medina. When asked if there was any news to relate, Ibn Hurmuz said nothing about Bint al-Ḥusayn. Then the chamberlain announced, "May God cause the Commander to prosper! A messenger sent by Fāṭimah bt. al-Ḥusayn is at the gate." Then Ibn Hurmuz said, "May God cause the Commander to prosper! On the day I set out, Fāṭimah bt. al-

---

616. See Yaʿqūbī, *Taʾrīkh*, III, 56; Azdī, *Taʾrīkh*, 17; Ibn Kathīr, *Bidāyah*, IX, 229.
617. Fāṭimah bt. al-Ḥusayn b. ʿAlī b. Abī Ṭālib, d. 111/729–30. See Dhahabī, *Kāshif*, III, 478.

Ḥusayn gave me a message for you." Only then did he tell him [1451] the story.

Our source continued: Yazīd came down from on top of his cushions and said, "You bastard![618] Why didn't you tell me about the message you were carrying when I asked you if there was any news to report?" Ibn Hurmuz claimed that he forgot. Then the messenger was granted permission to enter. Yazīd took the letter, read it, and began to strike the ground with a rod that was in his hand,[619] exclaiming, "How dare Ibn al-Ḍaḥḥāk! What man will give me the pleasure of hearing him scream in pain while I am reclining on my cushions?" Someone said to him, "ʿAbd al-Wāḥid b. ʿAbdallāh b. Bishr al-Naḍrī." Then he called for some papyrus and wrote the following letter in his own hand to ʿAbd al-Wāḥid, who was in al-Ṭāʾif: "Greetings. Now to the matter at hand. I have appointed you to serve as governor of Medina. When you receive my letter, go there and remove Ibn al-Ḍaḥḥāk from office. Fine him forty thousand dīnārs and torture him so that I can hear him screaming while I am reclining on my cushions."

Our source continued: The postal messenger took the letter and brought it to Medina, where Ibn al-Ḍaḥḥāk became apprehensive when the courier did not come to see him; he summoned the courier and showed him a thousand dīnārs that were hidden under a blanket, saying, "These thousand dīnārs are for you. You have my solemn promise that if you tell me why you were sent here, I will give you the money." The messenger told him. Ibn al-Ḍaḥḥāk asked the courier to wait three days before leaving for al-Ṭāʾif, and he complied with this request. Then Ibn al-Ḍaḥḥāk set [1452] out at a quick pace and, when he had reached Maslamah b. ʿAbd al-Malik,[620] he said, "I am under your protection." The next day, Maslamah went to visit Yazīd, to whom he addressed some carefully chosen words regarding a certain need on account of which he had come. Yazīd said, "I am willing to grant you any request so long as it does not involve Ibn al-Ḍaḥḥāk." He said, "By God, it is

---

618. Text: *lā umma laka*, literally, "You have no mother," said in anger and reviling. See Lane, *Lexicon*, pt. 1, p. 89.

619. Text: *fī yadayhi*, "in his hands." Ibn al-Athīr, *Kāmil*, V, 114, reads *fī yadi-hi*, "in his hand."

620. Maslamah was reportedly in Damascus at the time. See Ibn Kathīr, *Bidāyah*, IX, 229.

about Ibn al-Daḥḥāk!" He said, "By God, I will never forgive him after what he has done." So Maslamah sent Ibn al-Daḥḥāk back to Medina, to al-Naḍrī.

'Abdallāh b. Muḥammad said: I saw Ibn al-Daḥḥāk in Medina, wearing a wool garment, begging from the people, after having been tortured and ill-treated. Al-Naḍrī arrived in Medina on a Saturday in the middle of Shawwāl in the year 104 (March 27, 723).

According to Muḥammad b. 'Umar—Ibrāhīm b. 'Abdallāh b. Abī Farwah—al-Zuhrī: I advised 'Abd al-Raḥmān b. al-Daḥḥāk as follows: "You are putting (yourself) ahead of your kinsmen, but they reject everything that is contrary to their customs.[621] Therefore, adhere to whatever they have resolved upon and consult with al-Qāsim b. Muḥammad[622] and Sālim b. 'Abdallāh,[623] for they will spare no effort in guiding you." Al-Zuhrī said, "But he rejected my advice, acted in a hostile manner towards all of the Helpers, and unjustly and wrongfully flogged Abū Bakr b. Ḥazm on the basis of a false accusation. The poets all mock him in verse, and righteous men reproach him and say ugly things about him. When Hishām became Caliph,[624] I saw Ibn al-Daḥḥāk in a state of abasement."

'Abd al-Wāḥid b. 'Abdallāh b. Bishr became governor of Medina and established his residence in that city. The Medinese were never fonder of a man who came to them as governor, for he pursued excellent policies and always consulted with al-Qāsim and Sālim before deciding on a matter.

[1453]   In this year, al-Jarrāḥ b. 'Abdallāh al-Ḥakamī, the governor of Armenia and Ādharbayjān, carried out an expedition in the land of the Turks.[625] He commanded the conquest of Balanjar[626] and

---

621. Text: *innaka tuqdimu 'alā qawmika wa-hum yunkirūna kulla shay'in khālafa fi'lahum*. The translation is conjectural.

622. Abū Muḥammad al-Qāsim b. Muḥammad b. Abī Bakr, d. 107/725–26. See Dhahabī, *Kāshif*, II, 393; Juynboll, *Muslim Tradition*, 42.

623. Sālim b. 'Abdallāh b. 'Umar, d. 106/724–25. See Dhahabī, *Kāshif*, I, 344; Juynboll, *Muslim Tradition*, 42.

624. See text below, II/1466, sub anno 105.

625. See Ibn Khayyāṭ, *Ta'rīkh*, I, 337; Ya'qūbī, *Ta'rīkh*, III, 56; Kūfī, *Futūḥ*, VIII, 29–34; Ibn al-Athīr, *Kāmil*, V, 111–13.

626. An important Khazar town lying on the river of the same name, north of Bāb al-Abwāb at the eastern extremity of the Caucasus. See *EI²*, s.v. Balanjar.

defeated the Turks, slaying them, together with most of their women and children, by drowning them in water.[627] The Muslims took as many prisoners as they desired. Al-Jarrāḥ also conquered the strongholds adjacent to Balanjar, forcing most of their inhabitants into exile.

It is reported that in this year, Abū al-'Abbās 'Abdallāh b. Muḥammad b. 'Alī[628] was born in the month of Rabī' II (September 18—October 16, 722).

In this year, Abū Muḥammad al-Ṣādiq went to visit Muḥammad b. 'Alī, accompanied by a number of his Khurāsānī supporters.[629] The visit took place fifteen days after the birth of Abū al-'Abbās. Muḥammad b. 'Alī brought out the infant, wrapped in diapers, and said to them, "By God, this cause will be fulfilled so that you might take revenge upon your enemy."

In this year, 'Umar b. Hubayrah dismissed Sa'īd b. 'Amr al-Ḥarashī as governor of Khurāsān, replacing him with Muslim b. Sa'īd b. Aslam b. Zur'ah al-Kilābī.[630]

'Umar b. Hubayrah's Dismissal of Sa'īd b. 'Amr al-Ḥarashī as Governor of Khurāsān

It is reported that 'Umar dismissed al-Ḥarashī because the latter had angered him in connection with al-Dīwāshinī.[631] This is because al-Ḥarashī had slain al-Dīwāshinī, despite the fact that 'Umar had written to him ordering him to release the Turk. Al-Ḥarashī regularly treated Ibn Hubayrah's orders with contempt: Whenever a courier or messenger arrived from Iraq, al-Ḥarashī would ask him, "How is Abū al-Muthannā?" Then he would say to his scribe, "Write to Abū al-Muthannā"—without saying 'the governor.' He would often say, "Abū al-Muthannā said" and "Abū al-Muthannā did." When Ibn Hubayrah learned about this, he summoned Jumayl b. 'Imrān and said to him, "I have heard certain

[1454]

---

627. Azdī, *Ta'rīkh*, 17, specifies that al-Jarrāḥ drowned the Turks in a river.
628. The first 'Abbāsid caliph, d. 136/754. See *EI²*, s.v. Abū 'l-'Abbās al-Ṣaffāḥ.
629. See text above, II/1358, sub anno 100; Balādhurī, *Ansāb*, III, 82; Azdī, *Ta'rīkh*, 18; Maqdisī, *Bad'*, VI, 59; Sharon, *Black Banners*, 143, n. 162.
630. See Balādhurī, *Futūḥ* (Cairo), III, 525; Ibn Kathīr, *Bidāyah*, IX, 229–30; Wellhausen, *Arab Kingdom*, 453–54.
631. See text above, II/1448.

things about al-Ḥarashī. Go to Khurāsān and pretend that you are there for the purpose of inspecting the military registers, but let me know what you find out about him." Jumayl arrived, and al-Ḥarashī asked him, "How is Abū al-Muthannā?" Then he began to inspect the military registers. Someone said to al-Ḥarashī, "Jumayl has come here to spy on you, not to inspect the military registers." Ibn Hubayrah therefore laced a watermelon with poison and sent it to Jumayl, who ate it and became sick, losing all of his hair. Jumayl returned to Ibn Hubayrah where, after receiving medical treatment, he recovered and regained his health. He said to Ibn Hubayrah, "Things are even worse than you thought. Saʿīd thinks that you are merely one of his agents." Enraged, Ibn Hubayrah dismissed Saʿīd and tortured him until his stomach was covered with small pustules. At the time of his dismissal, Saʿīd made the following statement, "Were ʿUmar to ask me for a dirham so that he might buy some kohl with it,[632] I would not give it to him." But when he was tortured, he paid. Someone mocked him, saying, "Didn't you claim that you wouldn't give him a single dirham?" To which Saʿīd replied, "Don't chide me, for I broke down when the iron struck me." Udhaynah b. Kulayb, or Kulayb b. Udhaynah, recited:

Be steadfast, Abū Yaḥyā, for according to our knowledge you
    used to be
    patient, rising up under the weight of debts.

[1455] According to ʿAlī b. Muḥammad: Ibn Hubayrah's anger with Saʿīd is related to the following incident: Ibn Hubayrah sent Maʿqil b. ʿUrwah to Herat to serve either as his governor there or in some other capacity. Maʿqil went down to Herat without stopping to see al-Ḥarashī. Maʿqil arrived in Herat, but al-Ḥarashī wouldn't allow him to assume his new position. Maʿqil wrote to al-Ḥarashī, who wrote to his governor as follows, "Send Maʿqil to me." When he was brought to him, al-Ḥarashī asked, "Why didn't you come to me before you went to Herat?" He replied, "I am one of Ibn Hubayrah's governors, having been appointed by him in the same manner as you were." Saʿīd administered two hundred lashes to Maʿqil and shaved off his hair. This was why Ibn Hubayrah dis-

---

632. Text: *yaḍaʿuhu fī ʿaynihi,* literally, "so that he might put it in his eye."

missed Sa'īd and appointed Muslim b. Sa'īd b. Aslam b. Zur'ah as governor of Khurāsān.

Ibn Hubayrah wrote a letter to al-Ḥarashī in which he called him the son of a foul-smelling woman. After reading the letter, Sa'īd exclaimed, "He is the son of a foul-smelling woman." Then Ibn Hubayrah wrote to Muslim saying, "Send al-Ḥarashī to me, together with Ma'qil b. 'Urwah." He sent al-Ḥarashī to Ibn Hubayrah, who treated him with great severity. Then, one day he gave an order to torture al-Ḥarashī, saying, "Torture him until he dies." That evening, while Ibn Hubayrah was engaged in conversation with his companions, he asked, "Who is the most eminent man among the Qays?" They replied, "You are." He said, "What! The most eminent man among the Qays is al-Kawthar b. Zufar.[633] He has only to sound the bugle at night and twenty thousand men show up; furthermore, they do not ask, 'Why have you summoned us?' nor do they question his orders. But that ass lying in prison whom I have ordered to be slain is their bravest man. Am I not the man who seeks the best interests of the Qays? Indeed, whenever some matter comes to my attention and I think that I will be able to derive some benefit or advantage from it (for the Qays), I pursue it." To which a bedouin from the tribe of Banū Fazārah replied, "You are not what you claim to be, for if you really had the best interests of the Qays in mind, you would not have ordered that their bravest man be slain." He then sent a message to Ma'qil, saying, "Ignore my previous order."

According to 'Alī—Muslim b. al-Mughīrah: When Ibn Hubay-   [1456] rah fled, Khālid[634] sent Sa'īd b. 'Amr al-Ḥarashī to apprehend him. He overtook him at a point on the Euphrates as he was crossing over to the other side of the river in a boat. Inside the boat was a servant of Ibn Hubayrah by the name of Qubayḍ. Al-Ḥarashī recognized him and asked, "Are you Qubayḍ?" The servant replied,

---

633. Zufar b. al-Ḥārith, whose family was considered to be the very incarnation of Qaysiyyah, is invariably described as a man of great nobility who was above political considerations. His sons, Hudhayl and Kawthar, inherited the respect accorded to him. They too were held in high esteem by the caliphs. See text above, II/1300, sub anno 96 and II/1360, sub anno 101; Wellhausen, *Arab Kingdom*, 211, 321; Crone, *Slaves*, 100, no. 19.

634. Khālid b. 'Abdallāh al-Qasrī replaced Ibn Hubayrah as governor of Iraq and Khurāsān in Shawwāl of the year 105 (March, 724). See text below, II/1467–71, sub anno 105.

"Yes." He asked, "Is Abū al-Muthannā in the boat?" Again, the servant said, "Yes." Then Ibn Hubayrah emerged, and al-Harashī asked him, "Abū al-Muthannā, what do you imagine that I am going to do with you?" He said, "I think that you are a man who would not hand over a fellow tribesman to a Qurashī.[635] He said, "You are right." Ibn Hubayra said, "Then I am saved."

According to ʿAlī—Abū Isḥāq b. Rabīʿah: When Ibn Hubayrah imprisoned al-Harashī, Maʿqil b. ʿUrwah al-Qushayrī approached the former, saying "May God cause the governor to prosper! You have put the bravest man of the Qays in chains and disgraced him. Now, although I don't like him, I wouldn't want you to torture him to the extent that I was tortured." He said, "Serve as an arbiter between us. When I came to Iraq, I appointed him governor of al-Baṣrah; subsequently, I appointed him governor of Khurāsān. But I dismissed him because he sent me a diseased horse, treated my orders with contempt, and betrayed me. I referred to him as Ibn Nasʿah, and he referred to me as Ibn Busrah."[636] Maʿqil said, "Did he act like that, the son of the prostitute?"

Maʿqil went to visit al-Harashī in the prison. "O Ibn Nasʿah," he said, "your mother entered and was sold for eighty mangy she-goats. She was with the shepherds, who came to her one after the other as if she were the riding animal of someone who is constantly coming and going.[637] Do you consider her the equal of Bint al-Hārith b. ʿAmr b. Harajah?"[638] And he uttered other calumnies against him.

[1457]

When Ibn Hubayrah was removed from office and Khālid[639] arrived in Iraq, al-Harashī asked for permission to take vengeance on Maʿqil b. ʿUrwah. Al-Harashī brought proof that Maʿqil had

---

635. ʿUmar and Saʿīd were both Qaysīs. See Wellhausen, *Arab Kingdom*, 319–21.

636. Nasʿah and Busrah were the mothers of al-Harashī and ʿUmar b. Hubayrah, respectively. It was considered an insult to refer to someone by his matronymic rather than his patronymic.

637. Text: *tarādafahā al-riʿāʾ maṭiyyat al-ṣādir wa-l-wārid.* The translation is conjectural.

638. Al-Hārith was a military commander who fought against the Turks in Adharbayjan. See text below, II/1526, sub anno 111, and II/1532, sub anno 116; Caskel, *Ǧamharah*, I, 130.

639. Khālid al-Qasrī. See note 634, above.

made false accusations against him, whereupon Khālid said to al-Ḥarashī, "Flog him." As al-Ḥarashī was administering the *ḥadd* punishment to him, he said, "Were it not for the fact that Ibn Hubayrah sapped my strength, I would have pierced you through the heart." A tribesman from the Banū Kilāb said to Maʿqil, "You mistreated your paternal cousin and slandered him; therefore God has allowed him to prevail over you, and you are no longer a credible witness among the Muslims." As the *ḥadd* punishment was being administered to Maʿqil, he slandered al-Ḥarashī again, causing Khālid to order that the punishment be administered a second time. But the qāḍī said, "He is not to be flogged again."

He said: ʿUmar b. Hubayrah's mother is Busrah bt. Ḥassān, of the tribe of ʿAdī, from ʿAdī of al-Ribāb.

In this year, ʿUmar b. Hubayrah appointed Muslim b. Saʿīd b. Aslam b. Zurʿah b. ʿAmr b. Khuwaylid al-Ṣāʿiq as governor of Khurāsān, after having dismissed Saʿīd b. ʿAmr al-Ḥarashī from that office.[640]

The Appointment of Muslim b. Saʿīd as Governor of Khurāsān

According to ʿAlī b. Muḥammad—Abū al-Dhayyāl, ʿAlī b. Mujāhid, and others: When Saʿīd b. Aslam was killed, al-Ḥajjāj took his son, Muslim b. Saʿīd, and raised him together with his own children, providing him with an excellent education. When ʿAdī b. Arṭāt arrived,[641] he wanted to confer an appointment upon Muslim, so he consulted with his scribe, who said, "(First) give him a minor appointment and then promote him." ʿAdī put him in charge of a certain province, where he established himself, doing a fine job of managing its affairs. At the time of Yazīd b. al-Muhallab's revolt,[642] (Muslim) took the revenues (of that province) to Syria. Subsequently, when ʿUmar b. Hubayrah arrived,[643] he summoned Muslim, having resolved to appoint him to a gover-

[1458]

---

640. See Balādhurī, *Futūḥ* (Cairo), III, 525; Kūfī, *Futūḥ*, VIII, 28.
641. That is, arrived in al-Baṣrah, to serve as governor. See text above, II/1346, sub anno 99.
642. See text above, II/1379ff., sub anno 101.
643. That is, arrived in Khurāsān, to serve as governor. See text above, II/1433, sub anno 102.

norship. ʿUmar looked at Muslim, who until then had no grey hair, and saw white hair in his beard. "God is great," he exclaimed.

ʿUmar stayed up late one night talking, and Muslim, who was one of his companions, stayed behind after the other men had left. Ibn Hubayrah threw a quince that he was holding in his hand at Muslim, saying, "Would it please you if I were to appoint you as governor of Khurāsān?" He said, "Yes." He said, "Tomorrow, if God wills." The next morning ʿUmar held an audience and when the people came to see him, he appointed Muslim as governor of Khurāsān. He wrote out the document of appointment and ordered him to depart. He also wrote to his fiscal agents, ordering them to correspond with Muslim b. Saʿīd. Then he summoned Jabalah b. ʿAbd al-Raḥmān, a client of the Bāhilah, and appointed him governor of Kirmān. Jabalah said, "What has my clientage done to me? It was Muslim's hope[644] that I would become governor of a great province and then put him in charge of a district. Now he has been appointed governor of Khurāsān, while I have been appointed governor of Kirmān!"

Muslim set out, reaching Khurāsān at the end of the year 104/722–23 or 103/721–22. He arrived in the middle of the day, but found the gate of the royal residence locked. He went to the royal stable, but it, too, was locked. Finally, he entered the mosque, where the gate to the ruler's enclosure (al-maqṣūrah) was locked. As Muslim was performing his prayers, a servant emerged from the enclosure, and someone said to him, "The governor is here." The servant led him to the governor's audience room in the royal residence. Al-Ḥarashī was told that Muslim b. Saʿīd b. Aslam had arrived, and he sent him the following message: "Have you come as a governor, as a minister, or as a visitor?" Muslim replied, "A man of my stature would not come to Khurāsān as either a visitor or as a minister." Al-Ḥarashī approached Muslim, who swore at him and ordered that he be thrown into prison. Someone said to him, "If you send him out in broad daylight, someone may slay him." Muslim therefore ordered that al-Ḥarashī be kept near him until evening. Then, during the night, he sent him to the prison, where he was tied up in

[1459]

---

644. Text: *yanbaghī yaṭmaʿ*; read *yanbaghī*, following the Cairo ed.

shackles. Some time later he ordered the jailor to put on additional shackles. The latter approached al-Ḥarashī with a sad look on his face. "What is the matter with you?" al-Ḥarashī asked. "I have been ordered to put on more shackles," he replied. Al-Ḥarashī then said to his scribe, "Write to Muslim as follows: "Your jailor tells me that you ordered him to put additional shackles on me. If this order issued from a higher authority, we hear and obey; but if this was your idea, you will pay for this."[645] He recited:

> If they manage to find me, they will slay me;
>   but whomever I overtake will not last.

But some relate it thus:

> If you find me, then slay me;
>   but whomever I overtake will not last.
> They are the enemies, whether present or absent,
>   full of hatred, with black livers.
> Do pursue me in your own manner, for verily I,
>   with (my horse) Ḥadhfah,[646] am like the bone sticking fast
>   in the throat beneath the carotid artery.

And some relate it thus:

> Do seek me in your own manner.

Our source continued: Muslim dispatched a man to his districts to serve as his agent in charge of military affairs there.

Previously, Ibn Hubayrah, in his zeal, had arrested and imprisoned a man who had worked as a steward for Yazīd b. al-Muhallab and who was knowledgable about Khurāsān and its leading men. The steward accused all the leading men of the province (of misappropriating revenues). Ibn Hubayrah dispatched Abū ʿUbaydah al-ʿAnbarī, together with a man known as Khālid, and he wrote to al-Ḥarashī ordering him to hand over those men who had been named by the steward so that he might demand the money from them. But al-Ḥarashī refused and he sent back Ibn Hubayrah's messenger. Now, when Ibn Hubayrah appointed Muslim b. Saʿīd

[1460]

---

645. Text: *fa-sayruka al-ḥaqḥaqah*, literally, "You will be driven to exhaustion."
646. The text is Ḥidhqah. See Lane, *Lexicon*, pt. 3, p. 1189, s.v. *r-w-gh*.

as governor, he ordered him to collect those revenues. Muslim arrived and wanted to hold the people accountable for the revenues that had been distributed among them,[647] but he was advised as follows:

> If you do that to those men, you will not have any peace and quiet in Khurāsān. If, on the other hand, you are dismissed because of your failure to accomplish this,[648] Khurāsān will be ruined, both for you and for them. The men whom you want to hold accountable for those revenues—the chiefs of the country—have been falsely accused: Mihzam b. Jābir owed only three hundred thousand (dirhams), but they added a hundred thousand, raising the debt to four hundred thousand. But most of those whose names have been given to you are among those whose debts have been greatly exaggerated.

Muslim wrote to Ibn Hubayrah informing him of the situation, and sent him a delegation that included Mihzam b. Jābir among its members. Mihzam said to Ibn Hubayrah, "O Commander, the accusation that has been brought before you is false and unjust. If the truth were told, we are accountable for only a small portion of that sum, which we would pay—if we were asked to do so." Then Ibn Hubayrah recited, "God commands you to deliver trusts back to their owners." But Mihzam said, "Recite the remainder of the verse: 'And when you judge between the people, that you judge with justice.'"[649] Ibn Hubayrah said: "We must have that money." Mihzam declared:

> By God, if you take it, you will be taking it from men who are capable of inflicting great havoc upon your enemies. Furthermore, that would harm the army of Khurāsān with respect to its military equipment, horses, and weapons. We live on a frontier where we fight against an enemy that is constantly at war. We wear iron so often that the rust sticks to our skin; indeed, the smell of iron causes a female servant to turn her face away from her

[1461]

---

647. Text: *qurifat ʿalayhim*; read *furriqat ʿalayhim*, following the Cairo ed.
648. Text: *taʿmal fī hādhā ḥattā tūḍaʿa ʿanhum*. The translation is conjectural.
649. Qurʾān 4:58.

master and from other men that she serves. You, on the
other hand, stay at home, adorning yourselves in fine
clothes dyed with saffron. Now, the men who have been
accused of appropriating those revenues—the leaders of
the army of Khurāsān and the army of the provinces—
undertake enormous expenses in order to carry out military expeditions. There are men here who have come to
us riding on donkeys from the deepest ravines. Having
been appointed as governors of the provinces, they collected the revenues which are heaped up in abundance.[650]

Ibn Hubayrah wrote to Muslim b. Saʿīd informing him of the
delegation's statement and ordering him to seize the revenues
from the men who, according to the delegation, possessed them.
When Muslim received Ibn Hubayrah's letter, he arrested the
tributaries in connection with those revenues and ordered Ḥājib
b. ʿAmr al-Ḥārithī to torture them. After they had been tortured,
he seized the revenues that had been distributed among them.[651]

In this year, the pilgrimage was led by ʿAbd al-Wāḥid b. ʿAbdallāh
al-Naḍrī, as was related to me by Aḥmad b. Thābit—his authority—Isḥāq b. ʿĪsā—Abū Maʿshar. Al-Wāqidī reported the same.

The governor of Mecca, Medina, and al-Ṭāʾif in this year was
ʿAbd al-Wāḥid b. ʿAbdallāh al-Naḍrī. ʿUmar b. Hubayrah was governor of Iraq and the East.[652] Ḥusayn b. al-Ḥasan al-Kindī was in
charge of the judiciary in al-Kūfah. ʿAbd al-Malik b. Yaʿlā was in
charge of the judiciary in al-Baṣrah.

---

650. Text: *muwaffarah*; the Cairo ed. reads *mawqarah*, "a tree overladen with
fruit."
651. Text: *qurifa ʿalayhim*; read *furriqa ʿalayhim*, following the Cairo ed.
652. 'The East' refers to Khurāsān.

The Events of the Year

105

(June 10, 723—May 28, 724)

[1462]

The events of this year included a military expedition against
Alān that was carried out by al-Jarrāḥ b. ʿAbdallāh al-Ḥakamī,
who passed through that country to the towns and strongholds
beyond Balanjar.[653] He conquered some of that region, expelling
many of its inhabitants and collecting considerable quantities of
booty.

In this year, Saʿīd b. ʿAbd al-Malik raided Byzantium. He dispatched a military detachment that included approximately one
thousand fighters, all of whom reportedly perished.

In this year, Muslim b. Saʿīd carried out a military expedition
against the Turks, but when he did not conquer any lands, he
returned to Khurāsān. Later in the year, he carried out a raid
against Afshīnah,[654] one of the towns in al-Sughd, where he concluded a peace agreement with its king and inhabitants.[655]

---

653. See Ibn Khayyāṭ, *Taʾrīkh*, I, 339; Azdī, *Taʾrīkh*, 20.
654. Afshīnah was located in the district of Samarqand. See Wellhausen, *Arab
Kingdom*, 454, n. 1.
655. See Balādhurī, *Futūḥ* (Cairo), III, 525.

Muslim b. Sa'īd's Expedition against the Turks

According to 'Alī b. Muḥammad—his authorities: Muslim b. Sa'īd appointed Bahrām Sīs as a provincial governor.[656] Late in the summer of the year 105/723–24, Muslim undertook a military expedition, but when he did not make any conquests, he turned back. The Turks pursued him, overtaking him as the soldiers were crossing over the Balkh River. The cavalry of Tamīm, led by 'Ubaydallāh b. Zuhayr b. Ḥayyān, was in command of his rear-guard and they protected the other soldiers until they had crossed over the river. (This was when) Yazīd b. 'Abd al-Malik died, and Hishām became Caliph. Then Muslim raided Afshīn[657] and concluded a peace agreement with its King whereby he was to receive six thousand head (of sheep). He left at the end of the year 105/723–24, after the King had delivered the fortress to him.

[1463]

The Death of Yazīd b. 'Abd al-Malik

In this year, the Caliph, Yazīd b. 'Abd al-Malik b. Marwān, died on the twenty-sixth of Sha'bān (January 28, 724).[658] This was related to me by Aḥmad b. Thābit—his authority—Isḥāq b. 'Īsā—Abū Ma'shar. Al-Wāqidī transmitted the same report.

According to al-Wāqidī: He died in Balqā',[659] which is in the district of Damascus, at the age of thirty-eight. Some authorities say that he died at the age of forty, while others maintain that he was thirty-six.

According to Abū Ma'shar, Hishām b. Muḥammad, and 'Alī b. Muḥammad, he served as Caliph for four years and one month. According to al-Wāqidī, he was Caliph for four years. Yazīd b. 'Abd al-Malik's patronymic was Abū Khālid. This was related by Abū Ma'shar, Hishām b. Muḥammad, al-Wāqidī, and others.

---

656. Text: *al-marzubān*. On this term, see note 97 above.

657. Note the discrepancy between the spelling of the name here and in the previous paragraph. On the distinction between Afshīn, a personal name, and Afshīnah, the name of a town, see Wellhausen, *Arab Kingdom*, 432, 454; Balā-dhurī, *Futūḥ* (Cairo), III, 525.

658. See Ibn Khayyāṭ, *Ta'rīkh*, I, 339–40; Dīnawarī, *Akhbār*, 336; Ya'qūbī, *Ta'rīkh*, III, 58; Kūfī, *Futūḥ*, VIII, 35; Azdī, *Ta'rīkh*, 18; Mas'ūdī, *Murūj* (Beirut), III, 195; FHA, 80–81; Ibn Kathīr, *Bidāyah*, IX, 231.

659. The administrative district of Transjordan, dependent on the *jund* of Damascus. See *EI²*, s.v. Balqā'.

According to ʿAlī b. Muḥammad: Yazīd b. ʿAbd al-Malik died at the age of thirty-five or thirty-four, on Friday the twenty-sixth of Shaʿbān in the year 105 (January 28, 724). He died in Arbad,[660] in the district of Balqāʾ. His son, al-Walīd, who was fifteen years old, prayed over him.[661] On that day, Hishām b. ʿAbd al-Malik was in Ḥimṣ. This was related to me by ʿUmar b. Shabbah, on the authority of ʿAlī.

According to Hishām b. Muḥammad: Yazīd b. ʿAbd al-Malik died at the age of thirty-three.

[1464]   According to ʿAlī: Abū Māwiyah or some other Jew said to Yazīd b. ʿAbd al-Malik, "You will reign for forty years." One of the Jews said, "He lied, may God curse him. He predicted that he would reign for forty *qaṣabah*s." A *qaṣabah* is equivalent to one month. But he turned a month into a year.

Aspects of His Character[662]

According to ʿUmar b. Shabbah—ʿAlī: Yazīd b. ʿĀtikah was one of their (that is, the Marwānids') youths.[663] One day, when he was in a good mood, he said, in the presence of Ḥabābah[664] and Sallāmah,[665] "Let me fly." Ḥabābah said, "To whom will you entrust the Muslim community?"[666] When he died, Sallāmah of al-Qass[667] recited:

---

660. A village in Jordan, near Tiberias. See Yāqūt, *Muʿjam*, I, 136ff.

661. It is also reported that Yazīd's brother, Hishām, prayed over his body. See Ibn Khayyāṭ, *Taʾrīkh*, I, 340; Ibn Kathīr, *Bidāyah*, IX, 233.

662. See Azdī, *Taʾrīkh*, 18–21; Maqdisī, *Badʾ*, VI, 48–49; Ibn Kathīr, *Bidāyah*, IX, 232–33.

663. Text: *min fityānihim*. According to Azdī, *Taʾrīkh*, 5, Yazīd's nickname was *al-fatā*, "the youth."

664. Ḥabābah was a singing slave girl of Medina who exerted complete control over the Caliph Yazīd b. ʿAbd al-Malik due to his infatuation with her. See *EI²*, s.v. Ḥabāba.

665. Sallāmah was a Medinese slave girl, purchased by the Caliph Yazīd, who performed as a singer. See *EI²*, s.v. Ḥabāba; *Aghānī* (Beirut), VIII, 336–53.

666. Yazīd reportedly answered, "To you." See Masʿūdī, *Murūj* (Beirut), III, 199; Ibn al-Athīr, *Kāmil*, V, 121.

667. An allusion to her love affair with the Meccan jurist and Qurʾān reciter, ʿAbd al-Raḥmān b. ʿAbdallāh b. Abī ʿAmmār al-Jushamī, who was known as al-Qass ("the priest"), because of his great piety. See *Aghānī* (Beirut), VIII, 336ff.; Ibn al-Athīr, *Kāmil*, V, 122–23.

Do not criticize us if we submit
    or are on the point of submitting.
By my life, I stayed up all night,
    as if afflicted by a painful disease.
Anxiety slept closer to me
    than did my bedfellow.[668]
Because of what happened to us to-
    day, namely, the difficult affair.[669]
Every time that I saw a home
    that was empty, my eyes began to tear.
It is empty of a lord who
    never neglected us.[670]

Then she cried out, "O Commander of the Faithful!"[671] The poetry was composed by one of the Helpers.[672]

According to ʿAlī: Yazīd b. ʿAbd al-Malik performed the pilgrimage during the caliphate of Sulaymān b. ʿAbd al-Malik, and it was on this occasion that he purchased Ḥabābah, whose (original) name was al-ʿĀliyah, for four thousand dīnārs from ʿUthmān b. Sahl b. Ḥunayf. Sulaymān said, "I want to prohibit Yazīd from squandering his money." As a result, Yazīd returned Ḥabābah, who was then purchased by an inhabitant of Egypt. Subsequently, Suʿdah asked Yazīd, "O Commander of the Faithful, is there anything in the world that you still desire?" He said, "Yes there is: [1465] Ḥabābah." Suʿdah therefore sent a man who purchased Ḥabābah for four thousand dīnārs. Suʿdah made her up and adorned her so that she would not look travel weary, and then she brought her to Yazīd and placed her behind a curtain. She asked, "O Commander of the Faithful, is there anything in the world that you still desire?" He replied, "Yes. Didn't I tell you when you asked me this question previously?" Then she lifted up the curtain and said, "Behold! Ḥabābah." Suʿdah stood up, leaving Ḥabābah alone with

---

668. Text: *thumma bāta-l-hammu minnī dūna man lī min ḍajīʿ*. Literally, "Then anxiety slept with respect to me not as close as (my) bedfellow."

669. Text: *al-faḍīʿ*; read *al-faẓīʿ*, following the Cairo ed.

670. See al-Aḥwaṣ, *Shiʿr*, no. 103, p. 152; *FHA*, 80.

671. Her cry signaled the Caliph's death. See *Aghānī* (Beirut), VIII, 348.

672. It is reported that al-Aḥwaṣ composed the poem for Sallāmah, who recited it as a lamentation. See *Aghānī* (Beirut), VIII, 350; Masʿūdī, *Murūj* (Beirut), III, 196.

the Caliph. This act endeared Suʿdah to Yazīd, who was generous with her and gave her many presents. Suʿdah, who was from the family of ʿUthmān b. ʿAffān, was Yazīd's wife.

According to ʿAlī—Yūnis b. Ḥabīb: One day, Ḥabābah, a slave girl belonging to Yazīd b. ʿAbd al-Malik, sang the following song:

Between the collarbones and the uvula is a burning heat
    that does not subside and is not easy to swallow, and thus
    cool down.[673]

Yazīd extended his arms to fly, but she said, "O Commander of the Faithful, we need you." When she became very ill,[674] he asked, "How are you, Ḥabābah?" But she did not answer. He cried and recited:

If the soul forgets you, or desire abandons you,
    the heart forgets out of despair, not out of hardness.

Yazīd heard one of her servants recite the following line:

It is sufficient mourning for the love-sick, bewildered one to
    see
    the abodes of the one he desired left untended and
    deserted.

Yazīd also recited this.

[1466]   According to ʿUmar—ʿAlī: Yazīd b. ʿAbd al-Malik refused to see anyone for seven days after Ḥabābah died, on the recommendation of Maslamah, who feared that Yazīd would appear foolish in the eyes of the people.[675]

---

673. See *FHA*, 77.

674. Yazīd, who wanted to be alone with Ḥabābah, ordered his servants not to disturb him under *any* circumstances. While the two of them were sitting together in a garden, Ḥabābah began to choke on a pomegranate seed (according to some versions: a grape seed that the Caliph threw at her). Ḥabābah died after Yazīd's pleas for assistance were dutifully ignored by his servants. See *FHA*, 77–78; Maqdisī, *Bad'*, VI, 48–49; Ibn al-Athīr, *Kāmil*, V, 121.

675. That is, because of his grief over Ḥabābah. See *FHA*, 77.

Bibliography of Cited Works

al-Aḥwaṣ al-Anṣārī, *Shiʿr*. Edited by ʿĀdil Sulaymān Jamāl. Cairo: al-Hayʾah al-Miṣriyya al-ʿĀmma li-l-Taʾlīf, 1970.

Akhbār al-Dawla al-ʿAbbāsiyya. Edited by ʿAbd al-ʿAzīz al-Dūrī. Beirut: Dār al-Ṭalīʿah li-l-Ṭibāʿah wa-l-Nashr, 1971.

al-Aʿshā, Maimūn b. Kais. *Dīwān*. Edited by R. E. Geyer. London: Luzac & Co., 1928.

al-Azdī, Yazīd b. Muḥammad. *Taʾrīkh al-Mawṣil*. Edited by ʿAlī Ḥabībah. Cairo: Dār al-Taḥrīr li-l-Ṭabʿ wa-l-Nashr, 1967.

al-Azraqī, Abū al-Ḥasan Muḥammad. *Akhbār Makkah al-Musharrafah*. Vol. II. Edited by F. Wüstenfeld in *Chroniken der Stadt Mekka*. Leipzig: F.A. Brockhaus, 1857–61. Reprinted Beirut: Khayats, 1964.

al-Balādhurī, Aḥmad b. Yaḥyā. *Ansāb al-Ashrāf*. Vol. III. Edited by ʿAbd al-ʿAzīz al-Dūrī. Beirut: Dār al-Taʿāruf li-l-Maṭbūʿāt, 1978.

————. *Futūḥ al-Buldān*. Edited by Ṣalaḥ al-Dīn al Munajjid. 3 vols. Cairo: Maṭbaʿat Lajnat al-Bayān al-ʿArabī, 1956. Translated by P.K. Hitti and F.C. Murgotten as *Origins of the Islamic State*. 2 vols. New York: Columbia University, 1916–24.

Barthold, W. "The Caliph ʿUmar II and the Conflicting Reports about His Personality," *Islamic Quarterly* 15 (1971):69–95.

————. *Istoriko-geograficheskii obzor Irana*. Translated by S. Soucek as *An Historical Geography of Iran*. Princeton: Princeton University Press, 1984.

————. *Turkestan down to the Mongol invasion*. 2nd ed. London: Luzac & Co., 1928.

Bosworth, C. E. "Rajāʾ ibn Ḥaywa al-Kindī and the Umayyad Caliphs," *Islamic Quarterly* 16 (1972):36–80. Reprinted in idem, *Medieval Arabic Culture and Administration*. London: Variorum Reprints, 1982.

Brooks, E. W. "The Arabs in Asia Minor (641–750), from Arabic Sources," *Journal of Hellenic Studies* 18 (1898):182–208.

Cahen, C. "Points de vue sur la 'Révolution 'abbāside.'" *Revue Historique* 230 (1963):295–338.

Caskel, W. *Ǧamharat an-nasab: Das genealogische Werk des Hišām Ibn Muḥammad al-Kalbī.* 2 vols. Leiden: E. J. Brill, 1966.

Cheira, M. A. *La lutte entre Arabes et Byzantines.* Alexandria: Société de Publications Egyptiennes, 1947.

Crone, P. *Slaves on Horses.* Cambridge: Cambridge University Press, 1980.

Crone, P., and M. Hinds. *God's Caliph: Religious Authority in the First Centuries of Islam.* Cambridge: Cambridge University Press, 1986.

al-Dhahabī, Muḥammad b. Aḥmad. *Al-Kāshif fī Maʿrifat man lahu Riwāyah fi-l-Kutub al-Sitta.* Edited by ʿIzzat ʿAlī ʿĪd ʿAṭiyyah and Mūsā Muḥammad ʿAlī al-Muwashshī. 3 vols. Cairo: Dār al-Naṣr li-l-Ṭibāʿa, 1972.

Dictionary of the Middle Ages. New York: Charles Scribner's Sons, 1982–.

al-Dīnawarī, Aḥmad b. Dāwūd. *Kitāb al-Akhbār al-Ṭiwāl.* Edited by V. Guirgass. Leiden: E. J. Brill, 1888.

Dixon, A. A. A. *The Umayyad Caliphate: 65-86/684–705.* London: Luzac & Co., 1971.

The Dīwāns of aṭ-Ṭufail and aṭ-Ṭirimmāḥ. Edited and translated by F. Krenkow. London: Luzac & Co., 1927.

Dozy, R. *Supplément aux dictionnaires arabes.* 2 vols. Leiden: E. J. Brill, 1881. 2nd ed. Paris: Maisonneuve Frères, 1927.

Encyclopaedia of Islam, 1st ed. Leiden: E. J. Brill, 1913–34. 2nd ed. Leiden: E. J. Brill, 1954–.

al-Farazdaq. *Dīwān.* 2 vols. Beirut: Dār Ṣādir, 1966.

Fragmenta Historicorum Arabicorum. Edited by M. J. De Goeje. Leiden: E. J. Brill, 1869–71. Reprinted Baghdad: Maktabat al-Muthannā, 1964.

Gibb, H. A. R. *The Arab Conquests in Central Asia.* London: The Royal Asiatic Society, 1923.

———. "The Fiscal Rescript of ʿUmar II." *Arabica* 2 (1955):1–16.

Gilliot, C. "Traduire ou trahir aṭ-Ṭabarī?" *Arabica* 39 (1987):366–70.

Hinz, W. *Islamische Masse und Gewichte.* Leiden: E. J. Brill, 1955.

Hopkins, S. *Studies in the Grammar of Early Arabic.* Oxford: Oxford University Press, 1984.

Ibn ʿAbd al-Ḥakam, Abū Muḥammad ʿAbdallāh. *Sīrat ʿUmar b. ʿAbd al-ʿAzīz.* Edited by Aḥmad ʿUbayd. Damascus: Dār al-Fikr, 1964.

Ibn al-Athīr, ʿIzz al-Dīn. *Al-Kāmil fi-l-Taʾrīkh.* 12 vols. Beirut: Dār Ṣādir, 1965.

Ibn Ḥajar al-ʿAsqalānī, Aḥmad b. ʿAlī. *Tahdhīb al-Tahdhīb.* 12 vols. Hyderabad: Maṭbaʿat Majlis Dāʾirat al-Maʿārif al-ʿUthmāniyya, 1907–09. Reprinted Beirut: Dār Ṣādir, 1968.

Ibn Kathīr, Ismāʿīl b. ʿUmar. *Al-Bidāyah wa-l-Nihāyah.* 14 vols. Cairo: Maṭbaʿat Kurdistān al-ʿIlmiyya, 1929–32.

Ibn Khallikān, *Wafayāt al-Aʿyān.* 8 vols. Edited by Iḥsān ʿAbbās. Beirut: Dār Ṣādir, 1968–72.

Ibn Khayyāṭ, Khalīfah al-ʿUṣfurī. *Taʾrīkh.* 2 vols. Edited by Akram Ḍiyyā al-ʿUmarī. Najaf: Maṭbaʿat al-Ādāb, 1967.

Ibn Qutaybah, ʿAbdallāh b. Muslim. *Al-Imāmah wa-l-Siyāsah.* 2 vols. Edited by Ṭāha Muḥammad al-Zaynī. Cairo: Muʾassasat al-Ḥalabī wa-Shurakāhu, 1967.

———. *Al-Maʿārif.* Edited by Tharwat Okāsha. Cairo: Dār al-Maʿārif, 1969.

———. *Al-Shiʿr wa-l-Shuʿarāʾ.* Edited by Aḥmad Muḥammad Shākir. 2nd ed. 2 vols. Cairo: Dār al-Maʿārif, 1967.

al-Iṣfahānī, ʿAlī b. al-Ḥusayn. *Kitāb al-Aghānī.* 23 vols. Beirut: Dār al-Thaqāfah, 1955–61.

al-Jāḥiẓ, ʿAmr b. Baḥr. *Al-Bayān wa-l-Tabyīn.* Edited by ʿAbd al-Salām Muḥammad Hārūn. 4 vols. Cairo: Maktabat al-Khānijī, 1968.

Jandora, J. W. "The Battle of the Yarmūk: A Reconsideration," *Journal of Asian History* 19 (1985):8–21.

———. "Developments in Islamic Warfare: The Early Conquests," *Studia Islamica* 64 (1986):101–114.

Jarīr. *Dīwān.* Edited by Nuʿmān Muḥammad Amīn Ṭāha. 2 vols. Cairo: Dār al-Maʿārif, 1969.

Jeffery, A. "Ghevond's Text of the Correspondence between ʿUmar II and Leo III," *The Harvard Theological Review* 37 (1944):269–332.

Juynboll, G. H. A. *Muslim Tradition: Studies in Chronology, Provenance and Authorship of Early Hadith.* Cambridge: Cambridge University Press, 1983.

———. "The Qurrāʾ in Early Islamic History," *Journal of the Economic and Social History of the Orient* 16 (1973):113–29.

al-Kūfī, Abū Muḥammad Aḥmad b. Aʿtham. *Kitāb al-Futūḥ.* 8 vols. Hyderabad: Maṭbaʿat Majlis Dāʾirat al-Maʿārif al-ʿUthmāniyya, 1968–75.

Lane, E. W. *An Arabic-English Lexicon.* 8 parts. London and Edinburgh: Williams and Norgate, 1863–93.

Lassner, Jacob. *Islamic Revolution and Historical Memory.* New Haven: American Oriental Society, 1986.

Le Strange, G. *Lands of the Eastern Caliphate.* Cambridge: Cambridge University Press, 1905.

al-Maqdisī, Muṭahhar b. Ṭāhir. *Kitāb al-Badʾ wa-l-Taʾrīkh.* Edited by

Clément Huart. 6 vols. Paris: Ecole des langues orientales vivantes, 1899–1918. Reprinted Baghdad: Maktabat al-Muthannā, 1960.

al-Mas'ūdī, 'Alī b. al-Ḥusayn. *Murūj al-Dhahab*. Edited by Yūsuf As'ad Dāghir. 4 vols. Beirut: Dār al-Andalus, 1385/1965.

Morony, M. *Iraq after the Muslim Conquest*. Princeton: Princeton University Press, 1984.

The Naḳā'iḍ of Jarīr and al-Farazdaq. Edited by A. A. Bevan. 3 vols. Leiden: E. J. Brill, 1905–12. Reprinted Baghdad: Maktabat al-Muthannā, 1964.

Omar, F. *The 'Abbāsid Caliphate, 132–70/750–86*. Baghdad: National Print and Publishing Co., 1969.

———. *'Abbāsiyyāt: Studies in the History of the Early 'Abbasids*. Baghdad: 1976.

Sezgin, F. *Geschichte des arabischen Schrifttums*. Leiden: E. J. Brill, 1967–.

Shaban, M. A. *The 'Abbāsid Revolution*. Cambridge: Cambridge University Press, 1970.

———. *Islamic History: A.D. 600–750 (A.H. 132)*. Cambridge: Cambridge University Press, 1971.

———. "Khurāsān at the Time of the Arab Conquest," in *Islam and Iran: In memory of the late Vladimir Minorsky*. Edinburgh: Edinburgh University Press, 1971.

Sharon, Moshe. *Black Banners from the East*. Jerusalem: The Magnes Press, 1983.

al-Ṭabarī, Muḥammad b. Jarīr. *Ta'rīkh al-Rusul wa-l-Mulūk*. Edited by M. Abū al-Faḍl Ibrāhīm. 11 vols. Cairo: Dār al-Ma'ārif, 1960–77.

———. *Chronique*. Translated by W. H. Zotenberg. 4 vols. Paris: Maisonneuve, 1867–74.

Ta'rīkh al-Khulafā' li-Mu'allif Majhūl min al-Qarn al-Ḥādiyy 'Ashar. Edited by P. A. Gryaznevich. Moscow: Akademia Nauk SSSR, 1967.

Theophanes the Confessor. *Anni mundi 6095–6305*. Translated by Harry Turtledove as *The Chronicle of Theophanes*. Philadelphia: University of Pennsylvania Press, 1982.

al-Ṭirimmāḥ b. Ḥakīm al-Ṭā'ī. *Dīwān*. Edited by Izzat Ḥasan. Damascus: Wizārat al-Thaqāfah, 1968.

Wellhausen, J. *The Arab Kingdom and its Fall*. Calcutta: University of Calcutta, 1927. Reprinted Beirut: Khayats, 1963.

Wörterbuch der klassischen arabischen Sprache. Edited by M. Ullmann. Wiesbaden: Harrassowitz, 1970–.

al-Ya'qūbī, Aḥmad b. Abī Ya'qūb. *Ta'rīkh*. Edited by Muḥammad Ṣādiq. 3 vols. Najaf: al-Maktaba al-Ḥaydariyy, 1964.

Yāqūt, Abū 'Abdallāh al-Ḥamawī. *Mu'jam al-Buldān*. 5 vols. Beirut: Dār Ṣādir, 1955.

Index

This index contains all names of places, persons, and tribal and other groups that occur in the introduction, the text, and the footnotes, except that only names belonging to the medieval or earlier periods have been included from the footnotes. An asterisk after a name indicates that it occurs only in the chains of transmitters.

The definite article al *and the abbreviations* b. *(for ibn, "son") and* bt. *(bint, "daughter") have been disregarded for purposes of alphabetization.*